Praise for *All M*

'It will pull at every heartstri
written and wisely laid out memoir'
Donna Ashworth, author of *Wild Hope*

'A stunning meditation on the joy of nurturing . . . a haven in a cynical world – exactly the book we all need to read right now'
Catherine Simpson, author of *When I Had a Little Sister*

'Spellbinding . . . the most moving portrait of a mother and child I've ever read'   Tanya Shadrick, author of *The Cure for Sleep*

'Asks what we might be willing to sacrifice for an artistic life, and what we lose of our selves when we attend to the needs of others before our own'
Cal Flyn, author of *Islands of Abandonment*

'Written with tremendous care for the reader too'
Jini Reddy, author of *Wanderland*

'A fascinating, tangled read on gardening as resistance and using ancient ways to heal in the modern world'
Amy Liptrot, author of *The Outrun*

'A beautiful bruise of a book. Full of technicolour pain and joy . . . a compelling story that grabs at your heart'
Rebecca Schiller, author of *Earthed*

'Prismatically beautiful . . . a radical act of quiet rebellion. Celebrating the strength, wisdom and resolve of women that carry the cradle of care, wounds and joy'
Nicola Chester, author of *On Gallows Down*

'Utterly beautiful'
>Kathryn Mannix, author of *With the End in Mind*

'Tender and moving' Samantha Clark, author of *The Clearing*

'A beautiful, raw, meditative book on grief, mothering, and the wild both within and without'
>Kerri ní Dochartaigh, author of *Thin Places*

'Intimate and immense, it's wrapping tendrils around my heart'
>Amy-Jane Beer, author of *The Flow*

'Warm, questing and beautifully written'
>Dan Richards, author of *Outpost*

'What a brave, and graceful, honest and wild piece of writing. Such an important and beautiful book'
>Amaia Dadachanji, author of *Wild Apothecary*

'The honesty, bravery and openness of Victoria's writing was a privilege to read' Greg Wise, author of *Not That Kind of Love*

'A unique memoir and more than a memoir: the whole book is an apothecary'   Fr Murray Bodo, OFM

'A spellbinding, richly written work . . . captivating'
>*Emma Bridgewater's Best April Reads 2023*

'One of the most achingly precious books that I have encountered in recent times'   *On Magazine*

'Beautiful and subtle, it offers a perspective much needed in today's world'   The Nan Shepherd Prize

All My Wild Mothers

All My Wild Mothers

Motherhood, loss and an apothecary garden

VICTORIA BENNETT

First published in Great Britain in 2023 by Two Roads
An imprint of John Murray Press

This paperback edition published in 2024

1

Copyright © Victoria Bennett 2023

The right of Victoria Bennett to be identified as the
Author of the Work has been asserted by her in accordance with
the Copyright, Designs and Patents Act 1988.

The author would like to acknowledge the financial support of a Northern
Writers' Award from New Writing North, supported by Northumbria University
and Arts Council England, and an Authors' Foundation grant
from the Society of Authors.

The quote from *In Search of Our Mothers' Gardens* by Alice Walker on page ix has
been reprinted by permission of The Joy Harris Literary Agency, Inc.

Internal illustrations © Adam Clarke

All rights reserved. No part of this publication may be reproduced,
stored in a retrieval system, or transmitted, in any form or by any means
without the prior written permission of the publisher, nor be otherwise
circulated in any form of binding or cover other than that in which
it is published and without a similar condition being imposed
on the subsequent purchaser.

A CIP catalogue record for this title is available from the British Library

Paperback ISBN 978 1 529 39865 6
ebook ISBN 978 1 529 39863 2

Typeset in Hoefler Text by Palimpsest Book Production Limited,
Falkirk, Stirlingshire

Printed and bound in Great Britain by Clays Ltd, Elcograf S.p.A.

John Murray policy is to use papers that are natural,
renewable and recyclable products and made from wood grown
in sustainable forests. The logging and manufacturing processes are expected
to conform to the environmental regulations of the country of origin.

Carmelite House
50 Victoria Embankment
London EC4Y 0DZ

www.tworoadsbooks.com

John Murray Press, part of Hodder & Stoughton Limited
An Hachette UK company

*For my mother, who gave me the gift of life,
my sisters, for teaching me how to fight for it,
my husband, for helping me live in it,
and my son, for showing me how to love it.*

*. . . In search of my mother's garden,
I found my own . . .*

ALICE WALKER,
IN SEARCH OF OUR MOTHERS' GARDENS

Author's Note

When I started writing these words, I did not know they would become a book, just as I did not know that the weeds we planted would one day be a wild apothecary garden. In the broken ground of grief, I wanted to see what could grow.

We try so hard to cut out the things that do not fit the idealised garden of this life – the loneliness, the loss, the struggle of it all – that sometimes we forget to see the beauty it holds. And it is so beautiful.

So, plant the seed. Find the small thing worth the gift of your hope. Whatever else comes, trust that it will grow, even if you do not see it flower.

Note on Safety

All My Wild Mothers is for entertainment purposes only. It is not intended as a guide to self-diagnosis or treatment. Do not take a plant at a medicinal level if you are pregnant, are taking medication or have any medical condition, or give a plant medicine to a child without professional consultation. Always consult an affiliated medical herbalist before taking any plant at a medicinal level or to treat a long-term condition. Neither the author nor the publisher assume any liability for any injury and/or damage to persons or property for any use or operation of any methods, products, instructions or ideas contained in this book. If you are foraging, remember to be sure of the identity of your plant, and always make sure you pick with respect for the wild.

Contents

SEED ONE
Rosebay Willowherb — 3
Daisy — 7
Cleavers — 10
Common Houseleek — 15
Blackthorn — 21
Laburnum — 26
Hairy Bittercress — 29
Horse Chestnut — 33
Rosemary — 41
Foxglove — 48
Mugwort — 52
Elder — 54

SEED TWO
Methuselah's Beard Lichen — 59
Red Campion — 63
Broad-Leaved Dock — 69
Great Mullein — 75
Selfheal — 78
Field Poppy — 81
Sow Thistle — 84
Lady's Mantle — 87
Creeping Cinquefoil — 93

Spearmint	99
Common Nettle	102
Oxeye Daisy	105
Wild Thyme	111
Common Fumitory	116
Meadowsweet	118
Lungwort	121
Comfrey	126

SEED THREE

Creeping Buttercup	131
Feverfew	136
Sweet Woodruff	142
Field Scabious	145
Ivy-Leaved Toadflax	149
Wild Columbine	153
German Chamomile	158
Borage	161
Enchanter's Nightshade	165
Alkanet	168
Herb Robert	172
Hedge Woundwort	179
Dog Rose	183
Fox and Cubs	187
Wild Cherry	191
Garlic Mustard	195

SEED FOUR

Lemon Balm	201
Agrimony	204

Field Horsetail	206
Lesser Celandine	210
Cow Parsley	214
Good King Henry	217
Dandelion	226
Wood Cranesbill	232
Wild Marjoram	235
Honeysuckle	239
Goldenrod	249
Greater Plantain	253
Lesser Periwinkle	257
Motherwort	261

SEED FIVE

Pellitory-of-the-wall	267
Burdock	271
Forsythia	274
Blackcurrant	278
Wild Daffodil	281
Wild Pansy	286
Nasturtium	289
Bugleweed	292
Calendula	295
Blackberry	299

SEED SIX

Germander Speedwell	307
Honesty	311
Bluebell	315
Common Mallow	318

Hedge Bindweed	321
Woodland Sunflower	325
Yarrow	330
Wood Avens	332
Hawthorn	336
Pineapple Weed	340
Red Clover	344
Lavender	348
Cowslip	354
Tufted Vetch	358

SEED SEVEN
St John's Wort	365
Viper's Bugloss	368
Grape Hyacinth	371
Dog Violet	375
Common Tansy	379
Mountain Cornflower	382

SEED EIGHT
Gorse	387

Suggestions for an Apothecary Bookcase	393
Acknowledgements	395
About the Author	398

'Might I,' quavered Mary, 'might I have a bit of earth?'

In her eagerness she did not realise how queer the words would sound and that they were not the ones she had meant to say. Mr Craven looked quite startled.

'Earth!' he repeated. 'What do you mean?'

'To plant seeds in – to make things grow – to see them come alive,' Mary faltered . . .

FRANCES HODGSON BURNETT,
THE SECRET GARDEN

SEED ONE

Rosebay Willowherb

CHAMERION ANGUSTIFOLIUM
Passion fire, fireweed, bombweed, bloodvine

Use to release stuck energy

Rosebay willowherb gained its common name of bombweed
after its prolific growth on urban bomb sites during the Blitz.
A pioneer species, it is one of the first plants to grow in areas
devastated by fire. It is antispasmodic, antimicrobial, antiviral
and astringent, and can be used as a tea or wash
to treat urinary and gastric complaints, asthma, whooping
cough, burns, ulcers and other skin irritations. The stem
can be used topically on infected wounds and boils
to draw out poison.

Rosebay willowherb grows virulently
in disturbed and scorched ground.

The woman under the stairs is not me. I need her to leave. Excavating levels of personal archaeology, I unearth faded love letters tied up with string, a green velvet smoking jacket from pre-parenthood days, a bag of baby outfits saved for the future children I never had, an old leather suitcase filled with family photographs, and thirty-four years' worth of journals, stained with the ink of six million words. I keep digging, until this stranger expands herself into the room, filling the floor. I am suffocated by her lives. She has to go.

Today is that day. I call on a friend for help. She arrives with chocolate cake, cardboard boxes and heavy-duty refuse sacks. A member of the Wild Women group, we have been friends for thirteen years. When I need help, she is ready with wild wisdom and practical support.

'Where do we start?' she asks, perching herself on the arm of an overcrowded sofa. I look around, unsure where to begin. She picks out a magenta feather boa from a box, dust scattering into the air.

'Let's start with this,' she says.

'It's for poetry readings. I might need it,' I tell her.

'Yes, but do you need it now?' she asks, cutting me short.

'No,' I say. It is a relic of another life. Truth is, I do not need any of this now. Why hold on to things, when I cannot keep hold of the people I love?

We divide the artefacts of my life into four piles: keep, recycle, throw away, burn. As I sort, my son watches from the corner of the room. He is four and delights at these new discoveries, salvaging toys and trinkets from the growing mounds. For him, this unveiling offers excitement and the possibility of treasure. For me, it feels like the flaying away of skin, layer after layer, leaving me raw.

I rip out the pages from my journals, deleting memories that betray me with their blind hope. I tear up the fading snapshots, four sisters smiling back at me from saturated Kodak frames. When I look at them, I see what is to come. I wish I could say something to change the course of what is already written, but I am Cassandra, cursed by the knowledge of a future that they would not believe. My eldest sister, so alive in these photographs, is dead. I file the photographs and the notebooks under 'Burn'.

Once we are done, we build a pyre in the garden.

'It is as big as a tractor!' my son declares. He measures most things by tractor-scale. He is puzzled by what is happening, and asks why I am throwing all our things on the fire. I tell him that we can't take everything with us to the new home; that sometimes, we have to let things go.

'Even this?' he asks, reluctantly handing over the one-armed, one-eyed teddy bear I treasured as a child. I hesitate, seeing his small hand wrapped around its paw, an echo of my own. The past tugs at me, asking to be saved. No. I will not listen. I take the bear from his hands, stretch up and put it on the top, an effigy to a person that no longer exists. It tilts its misshapen head in a question, a single eye unblinking.

'Even this,' I say.

My friend leads my son back to the house. She knows this is something I must do alone. I light a match to the memory-tinder, and watch it burn. The heat stings but I do not turn away. I will be witness to this furious end.

In the morning, my son wakes early. He wants to see the big fire. We leave my husband sleeping, and go out into the garden. The night-cloud still clings to the valley, a pale sun cresting the Pennines to the east. There is a lingering trace of smoke, but no fire.

'All gone now, Mummy. All gone,' my son tells me, part wistful and part impressed. The early-September breeze blows the ghost pages away, leaving only shadows behind. Only a dark ring remains where I have burned my life. I kneel on the damp ground and touch the ash, feel the echo of flame. In this time of death, so much has been lost. It is time to move on, to see what might live again.

I pull my son close, and kiss his cheek. He is uncertain of this change, which takes away his future, and his past.

'Come on, let's see what seeds we can find for the new house. We can plant a garden there,' I say. He smiles and takes my hand, and together we walk, gathering calendula, corncockle, columbine and willowherb into our palms. There will be flowers again.

Daisy

BELLIS PERENNIS
Day's eye, bairnwort, bruisewort, poor man's arnica

To ensure your child is not replaced with a changeling, tie a daisy chain around their neck

The daisy symbolises childbirth, motherhood and new beginnings, and is the sacred flower of the Norse goddess Freya. Linked to the spring equinox, it is a sign of brighter times to come. Used in the Middle Ages to treat battle wounds, it is now a common remedy for bruising, joint pain, bronchitis and inflammation, as well as used to support childbirth. The plant is high in saponins, and can be applied as a skin tonic to improve collagen.

Daisy is a sign of resilience, due to its ability to survive in disturbed wastelands.

When I imagined our future, it held no grief. In that wished-for life, my husband and I live in a remote farmhouse, with chickens in the doorway, fresh bread rising in the Rayburn and our many children playing barefoot among the cottage flowers. During the day, I write in my whitewashed studio, and my husband paints at his easel, and at night we share food and conversation with our friends.

The reality is not this. What was meant to be our happy-ever-after has turned out to be our barely-hanging-on. It has been four years since my sister died, and my son was born. Since then, I have walked like a ghost-mother, broken by grief that wraps itself around me and will not let go. I am worn down and tired of failing to be the lover, the mother, the woman I thought I was meant to be.

What little energy is left over from loss is exhausted by the constant pressure of debt. We are offered austerity as the cure, but it is harsh-lipped and cruel, cutting the safety nets from those who need them most. As the politicians talk of tightening our national belt, my husband worries about being a good father, about providing for his family. He is frightened that he will not be able to support us. He says that he should get a *real job*. I tell him that being an artist is a real job, that what we do matters, that we will survive as we always have; but we don't live in a culture that values what we can give, and it gets harder to do. The work gets less, the pay lower, the distance to travel further. He spends longer away, trading in the days of our son's early years for the hope of security later on; an echo of my own childhood.

Meanwhile, I spend my days as a carer for my son. I am

frightened for his future, for the lifetime of medical care his body demands. When I see news reports of parents in America, unable to pay for the insulin their children need, I fear what would happen to him if the NHS was privatised. At night, when he sleeps, I fill out forms for Carer's Allowance and disability support, laying bare our worst days, page after page, just to get the help we need. I try to ignore the headlines that shout about *scroungers* and *benefit cheats*.

Mostly we make ends meet, though sometimes the stretch is too far and we fall through. Some months, the bills aren't met. Some months, we have to rely on the kindness of others to feed ourselves. We fall behind on our rent. As oil prices increase, we can't afford to pay for fuel. At night, I cook two-pot meals on a camping stove and put sticks onto the fire. The pretty railway cottage, with its sandstone floors and Rayburn stove, grows damp and cold. When I lose the last twenty pounds from my pocket, and cannot pay for the food in our basket, my son offers me his pennies from his purse.

'Don't be sad, Mummy. I can help,' he says. I try to hide my tears.

This is the future where we live. It is not what I imagined, but then again, none of this is.

Cleavers

GALIUM APARINE
Sticky-willows, clivers, goose-grass, Robin-run-the-hedge

Use cleavers to help increase tenacity and bind commitment

Cleavers were traditionally used to treat venomous bites.
All parts of the plant except the root are edible. Astringent,
tonic, diuretic and anti-inflammatory, it is commonly used
as a tincture or infusion to cleanse the lymphatic system
and boost immunity, or as a tonic to improve
skin radiance and reduce signs of ageing.

Cleavers grow abundantly in hedges and on waste ground.

Cleavers

Where do we call home when home is always shifting? All my life, it has felt as though I am only passing through, even though for ten years I stayed still. For my five older siblings, this changing landscape was true.

When my two brothers and eldest sister were six, four and nearly two, my father was relocated for the first time, from England to Kuala Lumpur, to set up a new factory. After that, his work as an engineer took him around the world, and where he went, the family followed. Soon after they moved to Malaysia, a second daughter was born. A year after this, they transferred to Australia and then New Zealand, where a third arrived. On they went, to Mexico and Canada. By 1971, the year I was born, my mother had given birth to her sixth child and moved to her seventh country. We packed and left for Switzerland when I was one week old.

Though they had swapped their peripatetic life for a settled home by the time I turned five, my father did not stay still. He continued to work his way around the world and we remained, watching for his return. While he was gone, my mother took me to visit empty houses, picking them out from the estate agent's window for us to view. Together, we roamed the overgrown gardens and wandered through the vacant rooms, imagining ourselves into this other life, until I could almost smell the sweet lilac growing by the door, or feel the heat of the fire in the empty grate. Each house would be *'the place'*, promising a future happiness just out of reach, but by morning fault would be found and a familiar sadness would fold itself around her again. The brochures would be rendered rubbish in the bin, and her good mood stoppered up like the pickle jars in the cupboard. I knew better than to ask if we would be moving, but at school I told stories about our new homes.

Whatever it was that my mother hoped to find, she never found it there.

When I have been lost, I have anchored myself the same way; browsing brochures of rambling houses, imagining myself into the duck-egg-blue kitchens, cooking home-cooked meals and drinking wine with friends beside the fire. In these houses, there is no grief, no sadness to wade through. *One day*, I have promised myself, *one day*. When my son nursed and the world slept on, I plotted ways to make this future happen because there – *there* – we would be happy. I went as far as making arrangements to view, reassuring the owners that *of course* we were in a position to buy, even though we could not afford to pay our rent. I kept my plans secret. I didn't want my husband to ask me how, or why, or tell me *the trouble with that is . . .* I wanted to hang on to the version of me that lived in those rooms. I wanted to believe that it could be my life. In doing so, I came to understand something of what was going on, all those years ago, when my mother and I travelled the country looking at empty houses, yet never moved.

Now, as I reach the same age she was then, I sense the passing days. Even though I try to taste each one, like the summer plums, autumn comes too soon. I watch my son leave behind his baby years, marking off the little griefs that go unnoticed in the forward-push and backward-glance of days. So much has been lost to sorrow. Sometimes, it feels as though I am just catching up. I want to pull him back, press rewind, start again.

It is time to stop hiding in a future I cannot have. This

moment is where I need to live, before that too is lost. We need a place to heal but it won't be the lime-washed cottage with its rambling rose, nor the smallholding with its orchard and perfect view. Those imaginary futures, cut out and collaged from the magazines, are not part of our world. Instead, we put our names down for a house on the new-build social housing estate, near to where my mother and father live. It is affordable, and safe, and the closest we can get to a secure home of our own. We tick the boxes on the form: carer, disabled, elderly parents, low income, school-aged child. These ticks are translated into points, and we move.

I am thankful for the chance this house gives us to rebuild. It does not have a past. I like this about it. I do not want ghosts. I have enough of those to carry, and their voices are too loud. This house is a silence. It lets me breathe. Built over a brownfield site, each property is identical: grey-render walls, blank magnolia rooms and an empty, scrub-grass patch of lawn. It is different from where I expected to be, but it is what I need.

As I unpack the boxes of our previous life into our new home, I watch my son playing diggers outside the back door, our old cat sleeping by his side.

'What are you building?' I call out to him from the kitchen.

'The new house. Come look, Mummy,' he says, grumbling construction sounds. I stop what I am doing, and join in his game. Picking up a yellow excavator, I take a scoop of small stones.

'Where do you want these, boss?' I ask, in my best yellow-digger voice. As I scoop and shovel, I wonder if I will ever tell him about the years that I worked with a road crew, and the man I once married before his daddy came along. The stories that we hand down are chosen with care. Some do not make it through. Which woman will he grow to know?

He stops mid-dig, and turns to me, tears rising in his eyes.

'What is it, darling?' I ask, putting the digger down to hold his hand.

'I didn't know it would be like this. I thought moving would be like going to the shops. I really miss the dirty, little house, and I am sad, Mummy, all the way through,' he pours out, overwhelmed with the sudden awareness that nothing will be the same again. I pull him into my arms and we sit there, in the mud and rubble, both of us crying. His hot tears soak through my dress as I stroke his hair, murmuring the mother-mantra of 'there, there', over and over.

This change is meaningful, not just for him but for me as well. Since his birth, I have been trying to take us forward into a happy-ever-before that did not exist: an amalgamation of memory, my own wished-for days and my mother's quiet longing. My son is four and I am forty-one, and together we cry for the same loss, the same awakening that hits our hearts like a fist to the stomach, forcing the tears from us: *I didn't know it would be like this.*

He stands up, wipes his cheeks with his sleeve and picks up his digger again.

'I think it will be okay now, Mummy,' he says.

I hope he is right.

Common Houseleek

SEMPERVIVUM TECTORUM
Healing blade, homewort, imbroke, thunderplant

Grow houseleek on your rooftop to protect against storms

Common houseleek was traditionally grown in the walls
of the home to protect against thunderstorms, fire and
witchcraft. Its botanical name *Sempervivum* translates as
'always alive'. The young shoots and leaves are edible and
taste similar to cucumber. With anti-inflammatory properties,
it was widely used in herbal medicine as a
poultice to treat burns, scalds, ulcers, shingles,
conjunctivitis and other skin and eye conditions.

Common houseleek grows well on rocky ground,
walls, rooftops and broken buildings.

The estate is a strange enclave of suburban planning in the middle of agricultural land; a cul de sac of matching houses, facing inwards around a communal green. Half the site is given over to social housing, built to provide homes for those who cannot afford to live anywhere else. The other half is earmarked for those who can buy into the dream of building their own home. Set up by the local community trust, it is heralded as a successful example of 'Big Society' ideology; David Cameron's photo hanging proudly above the bar in the local, community-owned pub. It is a curious, and uncomfortable, juxtaposition of aspiration and lack.

Yet, for all its newness, there is a history hidden under its ground. Once an industrial stoneworks, for over a hundred and fifty years it produced the stone for hearths and homes. When it closed in 2004, it left behind the debris of its life: weathered buildings, deep slurry holes, mangled metal, asbestos and rock. This is what lies buried below our home.

It is here that my son and I decide to create our magical garden.

I am not a gardener; at least, not in the sense of what I think a gardener should be. I do not plant at the right time, or dig where I am meant to dig. I do not know what should or should not be planted. My gardening is haphazard, born from curiosity and chance, but here, in this disturbed and broken ground, I need to believe that new life can grow.

The idylls of my mother's magazines are beyond our means. The Bloomsbury Group gardens of Sackville-West, Woolf and Bell remain in the books on my shelf. This will be no Sissinghurst, Monk's House or Charleston, though I love them all. This garden will be wild, but it must also be cheap, and thrive in poor and rocky soil.

From our old house, we have carried seeds, a blackcurrant bush and a potted horse chestnut, given to me by the Wild Women when I was pregnant and afraid of losing another child. They told me to plant the conker and, like the chestnut tree, my child would grow strong. Since that day, I have tended it, taking it with us through each move, planning to plant it out when we have a place of our own. Meanwhile, the tree still grows. Now the sapling is two foot tall and sits outside the door of our new home, swaddled in a large terracotta pot.

For the rest of the garden, we look to the ruderal weeds that grow beneath our feet. Their name coming from the Latin word *rudus*, meaning 'rubble', these are the pioneer plants that take root where all else is waste. The overlooked weed that grows feral at the edge of things, between the pavement cracks and borderlines of otherwise respectable lands; it will not be contained.

The dictionary defines a weed as a '*wild plant growing where it is not wanted*', and yet, who decides its fate? Unlike other wildflowers, the common weed has a codependent history of human interference, cultivated and cast out in equal measure over the years. This history is hinted at in the names, whispering of magic and medicine, food and folklore, the botanist's herbarium and the wise woman's spells. These tenacious seeds were once prized and harvested for their ability to feed, heal, clothe and colour.

From the earliest documented medicinal garden at the Abbey of St Gall in Switzerland, established during the reign of

Emperor Charlemagne, to the world-renowned Chelsea Physic Garden, founded in 1673 by the Worshipful Society of Apothecaries, the power of weeds and wildflowers has been a part of medicine, sanctioned by physicians of both state and church. At the same time, those who practised herbal medicine outside the confines of these sanctioned walls were deemed witches, and were tortured, hanged or burned. Nearly two hundred thousand people were murdered this way during the witch hunts in Western Europe, the majority women. I can't help but wonder what medicine might have been had the wise women been respected, instead of persecuted, burned and drowned.

For each thing, a rise and fall. The apothecary garden put what was known behind walls, but it could not be contained, and the monasteries would come to ruin. When they did, the plants that once were prized pushed beyond the boundary line and found their way back to the wild. Its value forgotten, the weed, like the wise woman, became something to be eradicated and reviled.

Now, as nature is homogenised, the garden becomes a tidy lawn, becomes a parking space, becomes plastic grass, and the fields that once held a pharmacy are claimed by industrial agriculture and the privatisation of land. Over the last century, we have lost ninety-seven per cent of our native wildflower meadows to the machinery of supply and demand. The little weed moves ever outwards, rooting itself into spaces nobody wants to claim.

I think about this unloved plant; how furious its will to hold on, how resolute the life it seeds. Yet, the weed is only a weed if it is unwanted. Like the monks, my son and I will seek them out, and grow an apothecary in our garden. Maybe, in time, its medicine will heal.

My mother-in-law gives us her yellowing copy of the Collins *Wild Flowers of Britain and Northern Europe*. With it to hand, my son and I head out onto the building site to see what we can find. Between the rubble, we discover plantago, dandelion, speedwell, mullein. I find an old copy of Culpeper's *Complete Herbal* in a second-hand bookshop, and begin to teach my son about the signature of plants; that if we look closely, they will show us what we need.

Together, we learn about permaculture techniques and the principles of sustainable gardening. We research Hügelkultur beds and find out that, by using common biomass – from fallen wood to kitchen compost – we can make a self-sustaining, nutrient-rich bed that will hold moisture and heat and build fertile soil for a decade to come. We decide to use this method for our vegetable beds.

As we learn about weeds, we find out about the importance of backyard biodiversity. The RSPB *State of Nature Report* (2012) tells us that the UK has lost seventy-two per cent of butterfly species over the last ten years, and forty-four million breeding birds. My son worries about this. I tell him we can be the change we want to see. We add in plans for ponds and bog gardens to provide a habitat for amphibians and thirsty bats; woodpiles, bug hotels and dead hedges for insects and hedgehogs to hide in; wildflowers and long grasses for the butterflies and bees; berry bushes and wild strawberry patches for hungry birds and boys. Each day, my son draws these treasure maps through wondrous lands, conjuring our garden into being, while I rip up old gardening magazines, adding hollyhocks and lavender to his dreams.

All My Wild Mothers

When I tell the Wild Women of our plans, they gift us books on tree medicine, flower wisdom and hedge-witchery; their knowledge, deeply sown, now passed on to me. Over the years, these friends have become kin, quietly nurturing the small seeds of my life. I have seen their children grow, and they have helped mark the losing, and birthing, of mine. It is right that they should be part of this garden we grow.

As the year turns its final quarter, our imagined garden begins to take shape. But first, we must dig out what lies beneath.

Blackthorn

PRUNUS SPINOSA
*Dark-mother-of-the-woods, draighean,
wishing thorn, spiny plum, sloe-berry*

Bring a flower from the blackthorn
into the home and death will follow

Blackthorn is associated with dark witchcraft, warfare,
wounding and death. Associated with the crone, it is
known as 'the keeper of dark secrets' and represents
the cycle of life and death. Astringent, diuretic and
high in vitamin C, the flowers, leaves, berries and bark can
all be used as a tonic or infusion to treat skin complaints,
urinary issues, throat infections, rheumatism and insomnia,
and the ripe fruit is commonly used to make syrup,
wine or sloe gin.

Blackthorn is a native hedging tree, and grows widely
in woodland and scrub.

It is three in the morning . . .

I write the words over and over, just to see the ink take shape, but still it does not fit. Twelve hours. That is all it takes to change a life.

Here I am, before: sitting beside my husband as we drive the slow road home, a low light flickering through the October trees. We have just celebrated our wedding anniversary. Blue sky gives way to the bruising of clouds. Rain falls against the window. We are singing. What are we singing? Does it matter now?

Forward on the day to late afternoon, and we are sharing home-cooked stew with a good friend in front of the fire. It is dark outside, and the room smells of dumplings, coal smoke and rosemary. In this moment, we are falling in love; with life, with each other, with our baby that kicks and rolls inside my womb. It has taken a long time to reach here. We have been cautious of trust, not daring to window-shop the future again, afraid to hope *this time, this time*. And then, the blue line, the expectant hush, the fragile hope that this pregnancy will last. We have celebrated each moment, each growing ball of nerves, each small increment of life: this day our baby is growing fingernails; this day, our baby is six centimetres small; this day our baby can recognise our sounds. It has taken seven months, but recently, we have started to believe. We have been making plans.

The telephone rings.

'Leave it. If it's important, they can call back,' I say, not wanting to disturb our meal. October pivots on its axis. Like winter hovering, I sense some shadows, but this day gives itself to light. These are the moments we almost miss; the purity of joy. We think we can hold it forever, that we have arrived at some state of being but, as all things, this too shall pass.

The third time the telephone rings, my husband answers it. Something in his voice is strange. He hangs up and turns to me, and I can see he is trying to find the words to speak what comes next.

My eldest sister has been in a canoeing accident. She has been airlifted to the hospital. They are trying to revive her. My mouth is full of powdery potato. I retch, unable to swallow it down. No one mentions drowning. No one explains. I want to go to the hospital, but my husband tells me to wait. I hold on to his hand, chanting the same prayer over and over.

She will be okay.
She will be okay.
She will be okay.

The telephone rings again. My husband answers. There is a pause.

She is not okay.

A scream leaves my belly, rips out whatever was there before, and hurls it across the room. I rock, back and forth, back and forth, repeating the only word I can say.

No.

Hands try to comfort. I am told not to cry. I must think about the baby. I must think about the baby.

And that is that. She is gone, and will never come home.

*

The night slips away and I must rest, but I cannot. The sight of my husband's sleeping face makes me furious. How can he find that peace? I get up and go to another room, sit in bed and try to write.

It is three in the morning, and my sister is dead . . .

I write the words on the page, but still they will not make sense. Exhaustion takes hold. I sleep, but only briefly. When I wake again, for a moment the world is reset, and my sister is not dead. Then, it hurts even more. The baby is agitated. It kicks against my ribs. I want to escape this body, knock myself out until the light comes but I don't, because I am carrying life inside of me and I must think about the baby. This baby, who will be born into loss and will never know that, once upon a time, life was different to this.

They will never know my big sister, the one who took me swimming at midnight under a city moon; who sang the 'Reefer Blues' as we rowed out across a lake in France, her firstborn baby sleeping on a blanket by her side; who taught me 'not-to-let-the-bastards-get-you-down' and stuck my life together with hope and love and lentils more than once; whose hair was the colour of honey and fairy tales; who danced barefoot in long grass and played the penny whistle around the fire; who arrived late to my wedding in a rainbow of ribbons, her three children singing by her side, apologising her way into my day; who painted the ceiling with stars and grew wildflowers by her door; who placed her hand on my growing belly, and chattered to my unborn child. My sister, whom I loved, is gone. It makes no sense. It will never make sense.

BLACKTHORN

Against the hugeness of this incomprehensible loss, it is suddenly very important to anchor myself with the smallness of facts. Was she alone? Was the water cold? What made her canoe capsize? Where exactly did she drown? To know the how she died seems urgent when knowing the why is impossible and yet, it is not important at all, because she is dead. My sister, always late for everything, is early for death, and her death leaves behind a shape I do not know.

I touch my pregnant belly in the dark. I am scared. How much can I bend in the storm? My body vibrates in pain. Everything aches, throbs, stings. Sleep runs faster away. The future disappears, and so does the past. I do not know how to breathe in this new world.

A swift kick to the ribs tells me that life continues, even in the fog of this pain. I must rest, eat, nest, prepare, be strong, give birth, release. How am I supposed to do this? The words are too small, the loss too big. The poets and the mystics tell me life is transient, that as one life ends another waits to be born, but right now, the metaphor brings no comfort.

The monster under the bed turns out to be real, after all. It has come out from the dark and eaten my sister, and what do I do with that?

Laburnum

CYTISUS LABURNUM
Anagyris, bean trefoil, golden chain

To dream of laburnum is to foresee
that your heart will be broken

Laburnum was once a popular substitute for rosewood and used in cabinet-making, musical instruments and archery bows. Traditionally used to treat hypotension and asthma, laburnum contains cytisine, found in modern smoking-cessation and antidepressant drugs. However, the plant is not commonly used in modern herbal medicine. All parts of the laburnum are potentially fatal if ingested, and improper consumption can result in vomiting, diarrhoea, convulsions, coma and death.

Laburnum is an important food source during the larval stage for many species of butterfly and moth.

Laburnum

The sudden rupture of my sister's death rips the past apart. Like a film out of synch, it unspools, each scene surfacing without warning, demanding witness, dragging me through time.

Here I am, at six years old, sitting under the laburnum tree. It is yellow and in flower. I want to pick the pea-pod seeds that hang down so deliciously, but I know that it is poison.

'Whatever you do, don't eat the laburnum seeds, they will kill you,' my mother tells me, but I like to play here, underneath the laburnum with its pretty flowers and deadly seed.

I am looking at the yellow leaves, and the blue sky, and somewhere I can smell plums but no, that can't be right. The fruit and the flower don't meet.

I am looking at my hands, whittling a piece of ash. Or is it sycamore? Does it make a difference? My hands are sharpening the end to a point, the way my father has shown.

'This is how you do it,' he tells me. My hands are smaller than his. His are rough like steel wool, and his fingernails are broken. Or is that just how I see them now?

I am looking at the laburnum and my hands, and the green bark curling away onto the dark soil, rolling under my chubby, childish knuckles, white against the knife.

I am thinking about knives, and the shape of my mother's shoulders as she peels potatoes, the skin falling away onto the blue carpet tiles beneath the pine butcher's table.

I am thinking about the table, and the smell of beeswax and garlic. What else can I smell? Lamb fat, and rosemary, and the sting of bitter lemon.

I am thinking about lemons, and the taste of yellow sweets as they roll around my mouth, all sugar and sour.

I am thinking about sweets, and the colour of yellow, and my father going away to work.

'Look after Mummy for me,' he says, and my eyes are going tingly but I must not cry, because I must be a big girl now.

I am thinking about lemons and leaving, and how I was always watching the window, counting cars and crossing fingers, expecting him not to return.

I am thinking about waiting, and all the things that are said and never spoken, and how these memories hold no sound.

I am thinking about silence, and the Mr Magoo cartoons we watched on the Bell and Howell projector, all scratchy-jumpy-jumpy; the words in my head but not in their mouths.

I am thinking about the words that are silent, and how I had this house and garden, and brothers and sisters and then, the film runs out.

Don't go.

Hairy Bittercress

CARDAMINE HIRSUTA
Jumping Jesus, lamb's cress, touch-me-not

Use to treat spasms of the womb

Hairy bittercress is a commonly foraged plant. It has a milder heat than watercress and can be eaten raw in salads or cooked as a vegetable. Rich in vitamins A and C, calcium, phosphorus and magnesium, it is a gentle diuretic and can be used to cleanse the lymphatic system. When touched, the seed pods pop and scatter like confetti.

Hairy bittercress grows abundantly on disturbed ground.

For thirty-six hours after my sister's death, I slip in and out of wakeful sleep, unable to get a fix on time. As I lie in bed, my husband holds my hand, trying to coax me to eat and drink.

'You need to keep up your strength,' he says. When he has to go to work, he recruits a friend to sit in his place and keep me safe. I cannot stop myself from crying, heaving wretched sobs until I am sore with grief. I cannot move. My body seems to splinter and fall, its already weakened state shattered by shock.

On the third day, my husband begs me to get up.

'You have to try,' he says, and I know he is right. Taking his hand, I try to stand, but the pain forces me down again, as contractions start in sharp, short bursts. Something is wrong. I am at twenty-eight weeks, and this is not meant to be happening.

'Do something!' I shout, curling myself around my pregnant belly like a shell. My husband runs to the phone and, through the wall, I hear him explain to the midwife about the accident. Shock. Sister. Drowned. There is a pause, and he comes back to the room.

'We have to go to the hospital now,' he says. He looks afraid.

'I haven't packed a bag,' I reply, remembering the checklist in the birthing book about making sure your birth bag is ready when the time comes.

'Now. We have to go now,' he repeats, already coaxing my feet into a pair of shoes. I let him guide me, leaning my body into his.

When we get to the maternity ward, the midwife requests

Hairy Bittercress

an ambulance. As we speed along the motorway, the siren wails into life and the blue light pulses above our heads. My husband grins with excitement. He has never been in an ambulance before and, for a brief moment, he is a little boy playing make-believe. Then he remembers why we are here. Our child, too early to be born. I reach for his hand. He holds on, and doesn't let go.

At the hospital, I am wheeled past a young woman who smokes a cigarette by the entrance door. Her body is partially covered by a blue, furry dressing gown, loosely tied over a large, rounded pregnancy bump. Just inside, a man in low-slung jeans and a red football shirt taps his feet to silent beats as he watches the clock on the wall. I am trolleyed past them both, counting the strips of light that slip by above my head. I hear double doors swoosh open, and close.

This is not a ward. This is an operating room. My husband is still holding my hand. I am given a sedative that makes the world blob and squish like marshmallow and I am told, once again, not to cry. More machines are attached. They blip and wheeze around my bed. A Hollywood-handsome man and woman enter the room. They are dressed in medical scrubs. The man tells me he needs to do an internal examination. I pull my husband closer.

'Is this real?' I ask. I am worried this is a film studio and not a hospital, that I am in a Brazilian soap opera. I am not sure what is real right now.

Time slides. The handsome doctor tells me that there is a bed in Bristol. We live in Cumbria. Why would I want to go to sleep in Bristol? That is nearly three hundred miles away. I am trying to understand what this means, not realising that he is talking about an emergency birth. He tells me that the helicopter is on standby, and asks if I have anyone he can call to bring an overnight bag. I think of my family, the way their own lives are taut with shock. They cannot stretch any further without snapping. I tell the doctor to call a friend instead.

We wait. The nurse administers drugs through an IV drip to slow the contractions and boost the baby's lungs. My breasts become full and painful, leaking milk that has nowhere to go. I want to cry out but each time I do, the contractions increase. I am told to focus on my breathing. In, two-three; out, two-three. As I try to hold on to this tiny life inside of me, my sister's body lies in the morgue. I must hold on to my baby, and let go of her. I try not to fall apart, try not to comprehend how small and human I am. For this baby, I am all.

The machines start to calm down. Spaces stretch out between the pain. Another doctor comes into the room. The baby is out of immediate danger, but my blood pressure is too high. They stand down the transfer to the neonatal ICU bed in Bristol, and move me up to the maternity ward.

All around me, life begins. The birdlike shrill of newborn babies breaks through the muted hum of the ward. Partners hover, awkward and invasive, under the stare of the elderly matron. She keeps a tight watch, ushering out unwanted visitors when the hour is done. When she reads my notes, she tells my husband he can stay.

As the night shift starts, he falls asleep in the upright vinyl chair. A small moon hangs in the sky outside my window. I rest my hand on the shape of this little being within me. I am all it has. Light falls to night, and all is still; the sharp dawn call of memory waiting to return.

Horse Chestnut

AESCULUS HIPPOCASTANUM
Conker, buckeye, bongay

Carve a wand or staff made from
chestnut wood to ground energy

Horse chestnut is astringent and anti-inflammatory. Both the bark and fruit have been widely used as a remedy for vascular problems such as varicose veins, phlebitis, haemorrhoids and other circulatory problems, and its derivatives are frequently used in topical sport and beauty creams. The seeds are high in saponins and can be soaked overnight and safely used to make a detergent soap. However, the leaves, bark and fruit can be highly toxic and should not be ingested without professional guidance.

Horse chestnut is a common urban tree and is adaptable to most soils.

The housing association sends a man to plant a tree on the communal green outside our new house. My son watches from the window, nose close to the glass, trying to get a better view. He is excited to see what will grow.

'It is not a very big tree,' he says. A silver birch sapling, it looks too weak to hold itself against the wind, but birch is a pioneer species, quick to claim its space on exposed land. The wide roots can stretch far to find the nutrients it needs, and its leaves will feed back to the soil below. This little tree might survive, even in this unyielding ground, if it can last its first winter.

As a sapling, a tree has large cells and supple bark to help it absorb water and grow. When winter comes, the heartwood shrinks and its skin thickens. Called the hardening, it is something the little tree must go through if it is to reach maturity. Each year, a new ring will form around its tender heart. In warm years, the ring will grow wide and fast. In years of stress, it will hardly grow at all. Catastrophic events will leave a scar. Dendrochronology, or the reading of tree-ring data, can help us gain insight into climate history and our impact upon it, going back more than a thousand years, and forward into the story yet to come.

My son watches the man as he digs down and hits rock. He digs again. And again, and again. We smile. We know how far the rock goes down, how deep you must go to cast it out. After a few more attempts, he looks at the birch, and the resistant ground, and decides the hole is big enough as it is. His job is to plant the tree, not nurture its growth.

*

Horse Chestnut

When I was a child, a horse chestnut grew outside my window. Tall and wide, and nearly three hundred years old, it reached forty metres in height. Sat in my hand-me-down bedroom, with its floral wallpaper and shiny mahogany furniture, I watched that tree change through its seasons. In spring, I saw the sticky buds unfurling. In midsummer, white blossom candles lit each branch. In autumn, I prised the conkers from prickly shells, soaking them in vinegar to harden for the fight. When winter came, I gathered snow from below its wide branches, rolling it into figures with stick noses and blind, pebble eyes. All the while, the house moved around me. Siblings came and went, rooms and territories shifted, pinned posters of ponies and pop stars gave way to revolution and punk; the sounds of play made way for slamming doors, and late-night creaking floors. Nothing ever stayed still, but that tree kept coming back.

My brothers and sisters can claim more exotic trees to mark their childhoods. The scarlet leaves of the sugar maple, shining against the white Toronto snow. The slow-growing, evergreen Petaling tree that gave its name to the colonial township outside Kuala Lumpur, where my middle sister was born. Or the kōwhai, its yellow blooms the unofficial flower of New Zealand, where my mother gave birth to her fifth child. These were the trees that watched over their lives, but not mine.

The first home I remember has no tree, and no memories but one: I am in my own high seat, a tray in front, on which sits a bowl. My mother sits beside me. She is crying. I watch her face. I watch my sisters' faces, which stare at me from around a long wooden table; three little silent moons. Far away, at the other end of the table, my father's face is twisty, and his mouth is full of noise. His fist is closed, and when it hits the wood, the plates go jumpy. My eldest brother is standing too. Their faces are very close. A chair scrapes along the floor, and clatters to the ground. There is food in my bowl. It is soft and squishy under my fingers. The little moons don't make a sound.

The second house has shiny marble floors, and a staircase that goes up-up-up, all the way to a glass ceiling that lets in the sky. I have inherited hand-me-down memories from this time, stories of sadness, and silence, and rage. My body whispers pain, but what my mind remembers is a sky lit with fireworks, hot soup in a stoneware cup, and a cherry tree, with its confetti flowers that ripened into bloody fruit. Built next door to the birthplace of Frankenstein's monster, this house was the borrowed show home of ambition; a place of opulence and tears, in which we did not fit.

And so, a rupture then, within this ring of life. In 1975, our family split in two: three children kept, three sent away. They were there, and then they weren't, and no one thought to explain to the little girl, who looked and looked but could not find. It took until I was twenty-eight to find out what happened, and why they went away.

'There are things you don't understand,' my sister said, as she pulled the car into the lay-by at the top of the track, and switched off the engine. Rain pelted down the windowpanes, blurring the fields outside. She looked ahead. I sat in the passenger seat, my feet jammed in between the toys and climbing gear, and I listened to her story, of things that were hidden and things that broke, and so much buried. It was a story, and it was hers to tell.

But it was not mine. My story is this: into this house, I was born. I was loved, and I was scared. Like the ash tree near the beck that grows around the wire, I grew myself a crooked shape but could not see the wounds. My mother, isolated and lonely in a land she did not fit, was struggling to cope. My father, reaching for success, was often absent; a vague warning of *'wait until your father gets home'*. My eldest brother, driven by a worsening addiction to drugs and alcohol, coupled with undiagnosed mental health problems, ricocheted between violence and threats of suicide. Like the Cytospora canker that finds its way into the wood, his illness spread deep into our lives. It hit the oldest siblings worst, though they often hid the damage that it did. When that damage grew too deep, my parents made a decision. Our family tree was under threat. To keep it intact, my parents set to cut the canker out but, like the canker, what had been touched was also to be removed.

My eldest sister and second brother were sent away to boarding school in England. It was an absence easy to explain in the world my parents lived in at this time, but strange in a family where my mother had always insisted on keeping her children close. When I look now, I can question the choices that they made, but that is from the privilege of my current view. Wrong or right, whatever thought lay behind the choice, it would turn out to be the beat of a butterfly wing in my sister's life, and mine. Cause, and effect, unfolding over time.

My eldest brother was dealt a different fate. Where my parents could not fix their son, nature might prevail to cure the demons that he hid. They gave him a ticket, a tent and a copy of the Suttons' *Escape to the Wilderness,* and sent him off to trek the Pacific Crest Trail. Stretching just short of three thousand miles, from the border of Canada to the border of

Mexico, it traverses mountains, deserts, forests and snows. Most hikers take the trail in segments, to avoid the harshest extremes of heat and cold. My brother would do it unaccompanied, and in one go. He was nineteen. Like any true quest, there was no certainty that he would survive to return.

But the diseased spores only enter through an already damaged spot. Not knowing how to treat the deeper wounds, all their actions did was trap the canker inside until it spread and girdled each branch. Soon it would be change, and change again.

In the long, dry summer of 1976, when drought made the ladybirds bite, and riots ignited on the city streets, what was left of my family moved back to England. After seventeen years of living out of packed bags and borrowed houses, it was time to have a home of our own.

At first, we moved to a little red-brick cottage in Oxfordshire, with a garden filled with roses, but no trees. Though the shadows still held sadness, my mother tried to make it work. She picked the flowers and, once a week, baked biscuits which I ate hot from the stove, and on Saturdays we got ten pence to fill our paper bag with pink shrimps, rhubarb-and-custards, blackjacks and sherbets for our treat. This was a house of butterflies, summers, red wellingtons, sugar and change, but still it was not my childhood home. The following spring we moved again, to a house of sandstone and mullion windows, and the old chestnut tree.

In all the noise and chaos, it was easy not to notice that certain voices had gone. Though the second son returned from school, my eldest sister did not come home. At sixteen, she ran away. Groomed by an older man into the Divine Light

Horse Chestnut

Mission cult, she renounced all former ties, and disappeared. The weekends were spent driving around in our old green Peugeot, following last-known sightings and fading scents. Too young to be left home with my other siblings, I sat alone in the back, my bare legs sticking to the vinyl bench seat, as my parents knocked on strangers' doors. Sometimes, it would be a blind trail. Often, the doors just slammed. Once, I heard a woman tell my mother she was '*not her mother now*'. I didn't understand what she meant but my mother cried all the way home, and my father drove in silence, his knuckles gripped tight around the steering wheel.

My sister did not want to be found, at least not then, but every so often she would come back, appearing in a haze of sandalwood and chants. When she did, I wished on my wishbone pinkies for her to stay, but it wouldn't be long before the shouting would start and she would leave again. Afterwards, there would be raised voices behind closed doors, and a sadness that swallowed my mother and made me scared.

As for my eldest brother, he tried to come home, but some things stay broken, and cannot be fixed. It was many years before that sealed wound was opened, and many more before what was wounded could begin to heal.

Yes, this was the house of my childhood. A sandstone cottage with an old butcher's wheel, wildflowers, white chickens roaming on the lawn, and a horse chestnut growing outside my bedroom. I watched it change through all its seasons. It grew through winters, and through droughts, the years marked within its rings; the bounties and the wounds. When I left home at sixteen, I was sad to let it go.

*

Now, a tree grows outside my son's window: a silver birch, the symbol of renewal. Like me, he will see its seasons passing, each turn to mark a memory of his own. How many of his years will this tree witness? How many times will it survive the cold?

I watch him as he wraps his arms around the sapling, kisses it and welcomes it with a soft 'hello'. How I want to shelter him, to shield his tender heart, but he is five and his life has already had its winters. There is nothing I can do to keep him hidden from the weather-change but, like the tree, I can show him that our lives are ringed by the years, and their seasons. To survive them, there must be a little hardening. Keep watch, though, and you will see there will also be the return of spring.

Rosemary

ROSMARINUS OFFICINALIS
Polar plant, compass-weed, incensier

Place a twig over the crib to prevent
faeries from stealing your child

Rosemary and juniper berries were traditionally burned together as a 'reeking bundle' to aid recovery after a long illness, and remove negative energy from the home. Placing rosemary under the pillow is said to help you remember your dreams and keep away nightmares, and scientific studies suggest that rosemary stimulates the memory centres of the brain. Antiseptic and astringent, it can be used as an infusion to condition the scalp and stimulate hair growth, and as a massage oil to aid circulation and relieve muscle pain. A good companion plant, it helps to keep away moths, bean beetles and carrot flies.

Rosemary thrives in areas with dry, poor, rocky and sandy soils.

The day of my sister's funeral reveals itself clear blue, swathed in postcard mist. Bright October sun warms our faces. Autumn beech leaves sing with firecracker reds. A white Picasso bull snorts out steam against a black river edge. Within me, my baby turns, digs a row of tiny toes between my ribs, stretches one lazy limb to imprint a fist against my skin. I stroke the whale-back lump of its shape. It has been eleven days since my sister died, and it is time to say goodbye.

Mourners flock, black carrion birds, seeking one last look. They smile with strained sympathy, break line to shake a hand. I sit in a red wheelchair, unable to walk, broken by pregnancy and shock. No one sees me down here. I am like a child, invisible to their adult eye. My body cocoons itself around me, swelling, stretching, softening. We keep a stoic face on our grief. It is our duty to hold the line.

'It looks like our old wicker washbasket,' I whisper, pointing at the eco-friendly casket where my sister lies. We giggle behind our hands, like schoolchildren hoping not to get caught.

'Behave yourselves!' my father reprimands. My mother stretches out her arms around us, sheltering us under her wings.

'Don't make a scene,' she tells him, making sure he lip-reads her words. He pulls himself up straight, and looks ahead.

The pallbearers have advised us to use a trolley to transport the coffin, but my father refuses. 'It is undignified,' he says. He is insistent. When it is time, my sister's two sons lift their mother onto their shoulders. The youngest is just sixteen, the oldest twenty-one. Their legs wobble under the strain, but they manage to keep walking, determined not to fail. The weight of death is much heavier than we expect.

Rosemary

She used to say that no one would notice if she died, but she was wrong. Cars flank the road, stretching past the houses and up the hill. There are too many mourners to fit into the little village church. They spill out into the churchyard, gathering on colourful picnic blankets between the graves. The scene is not appropriate for this terrible end and yet, entirely fitting for her. These are the people whose lives my sister changed. Those whose first connection with nature was guided under her care as children, now returning with children of their own. Old friends, who knew her in those early, post-cult days, as she found her way back to the world. Homeless strangers who became family, after she gave them a place to stay. Police officers, teachers, politicians, activists, hippies and punks; each here because of her. My sister campaigned all her adult life to protect this Earth, to be its voice, to stand with the disenfranchised and dispossessed. She was once featured as a 'Rural Champion' in *Country Living*; now the local papers write about the loss of a 'true hero', and she was, but to us, she is a sister, a mother, a wife.

'She was my daughter,' is all my mother says, when the journalist calls.

Faces turn to stare as we enter the dark of the church. How like an uncomfortable wedding this funeral is; all the guests lined up, waiting for the corpse bride. My sister is walked down the aisle by her husband and sons, her teenage daughter following behind, a bunch of sweet-scented freesias in her hands. We step quietly, moving slowly through this sticky grief to take our seats.

The vicar begins. She is kind, and tries to make the service personal, but this is not a funeral we expected to have. The religious service is my father's choice. It is his way to grieve, but the language exiles us from our grief, and does not reflect who my sister is. When the vicar speaks of the goodness of God and the burden of sin, I want to scream. How can a merciful God let my sister drown? What right has that God to judge her sins?

My mother raised us atheist. It wasn't that she didn't want to believe, she just couldn't find a way to trust what she couldn't see. For her, death meant the end. When my father tells her he can speak to their daughter, my mother cries. When she closes her eyes, all she sees is her daughter's terrified face, fighting against the water and the cold. Where my father finds peace, my mother feels the crush of her daughter's ribs, and cannot breathe.

'Why doesn't she speak to me?' she questions, confused that her daughter would choose him in the end.

The organ wheezes out 'Morning Has Broken', its notes stuttered out over the dwindling Eden light. It takes me back to another time, when I was a child, laid out on the scratchy, woollen rug, listening to Cat Stevens sing, my body baked with late-summer heat. The sweet, blue smoke of my father's pipe drifts between dust motes, leaving the scent of cedarwood and vanilla in the air. Everything moves in slow motion. Smoke curls around the morning light. I watch it all unfold again, hear the hiss and jump of vinyl, and the sound of the static as the record turns.

The organist stops. The memory ends. Sun slices through the stained-glass window, sending dust angels dancing above my sister's head. It is my turn to speak. My husband pushes the wheelchair to the steps of the altar, and helps me up the four steps to the lectern. I cling on to the edge to keep myself standing. Rows of faces stare back, waiting for me to make some sense of this loss.

I begin to tell them about my big sister, about how she turned every difficult experience into something good for others, how she worked to protect this planet for the generations to come. I talk about the way she fought for the wild spaces that she loved, and all the young lives she inspired over the years. These are the things they know, these are the ways she touched their worlds.

I want to tell them about the hobby horse she made me as a child, how she stitched patches of leather around a broken broom to make its face, using buttons for its eyes and scraps of wool for a mane. I want to tell them that I have carried it through all the moves in life, even though its patches are worn and shabby, and the buttons no longer remain. I want to tell them how she used to smell of sandalwood and incense, about midnight swimming, and moon-shadows, and what milk tastes like stolen at dawn. I want to tell them about the gardens she grew, about the names of plants, the dirt under her fingernails, and the stars she painted across her walls.

I want to tell them so much, but we have run out of time. Debussy's 'The Girl with the Flaxen Hair' plays across the silent church. It is too quiet. I want the volume to be louder, loud enough to give us the privacy of tears in this silent space. Instead, we choke our horror into our sleeves, ashamed of our need to keen.

Then it is over. We are expelled into the sharp October light. My sister is to be cremated but my father has asked the vicar to perform the committal before we leave, even though she will not be buried in this consecrated ground.

'In sure and certain hope of the resurrection to eternal life through our Lord Jesus Christ, we commend to Almighty God our sister . . .' she begins. We look on, and wait. This last act of Christian ritual is a gift to my father, that he will never even realise we gave.

After this, the wicker washbasket coffin is placed in the hearse to carry my sister on her final journey, sixty miles north, to the crematorium and the second service of the day. It is hard to let it end. As the hearse pulls away, an old friend of my sister approaches.

'You are very good at it,' he says.

'At what?' I ask, not quite following what he is talking about.

'Funerals,' he replies. I don't know how to respond to this. I am not sure what it means to be *good* at funerals. Beached by my body, I mumble thanks, and try to recollect his name.

The crematorium is large and cold, with plastic seats instead of pews. There are even more people here, and instead of hymns, there is Irish folk music, and reggae, and people who get up to read poems. I watch it all from the front line, holding on to my husband's hand. As the curtain closes around her coffin, the creaking cogs of the electric pulley echoing in the municipal hall, I finally allow myself tears. They are hot and angry. I still don't understand how she can be dead. I stroke the rounded, pregnant shape of my belly, holding on to this hidden life like a buoy against a storm.

'Stop crying, or the baby will cry for a year and a day,' my father whispers over my shoulder.

'Please, stop crying, or you'll end up back in hospital,' my husband begs.

'You've got to think about the baby now,' my mother says.

Rosemary

I sob myself into submission. I want to run far away, tear at my clothes, beat my chest and weep until this sharp sorrow is spent, but that day will not be today. Today, I must stop crying. Today, I must keep on living so this baby, this longed-for child, can grow and be born: one measure love, two measures loss.

Foxglove

DIGITALIS
Witches' gloves, dead men's bells, bloody fingers, fairy thimble

Plant foxgloves to grant your house protection

Foxglove was traditionally used in folk medicine to treat complaints of the heart. It contains digitoxin, which has been used as a treatment for congestive heart disease in mainstream medicine since 1775 and is widely used in modern prescription cardiac drugs. Highly poisonous and potentially fatal if consumed, it should only be used with guidance from a qualified herbalist.

Foxglove grows well on broken walls, roadsides and disturbed ground.

FOXGLOVE

My sister wafted in and out of my childhood as if a ghost, but to me she will always belong to a world of music and dancing, and summer flowers. It is an old memory, wrapped in the tissue of time. June 1980, the year I turned nine, and a day so hot it coated everything in the soft hum of summer. My sister is twirling in circles on the lawn, arms raised, eyes closed, singing along to Kate Bush, 'Babooshka' drifting through the open window from the radio indoors. Her long blonde hair hangs loose down to her tie-dye skirt, and her feet are bare, daisies poking up through her toes.

She had left the Divine Light by this time, and was working as a gardener at a private boys' school in south London, but she still belonged somewhere outside of the world that I knew; an exotic apparition that appeared in an aura of sandalwood and flowers. I longed to live in her intoxicating orbit, so when she suggested I go and stay with her, I begged my mother to let me go. Somewhat surprisingly, she agreed. I was put on a coach in Banbury, with a packed lunch and instructions not to get off until I had reached Victoria station. I had never been away on my own before and, all the way, I pressed my face to the glass, opening myself wide to each new thing.

My sister's garret bedsit was at the top of a narrow flight of stairs. It had pigeons nesting in the eaves above. They rustled and warbled as we slept, head to foot, in her single bed. The ceiling was painted with golden suns, and silver stars, and smiling crescent moons. A worn Indian cotton bedspread was pinned to the wall, the scent of prayer-incense, burnt toast and Barleycup lingering in its thread. It was magical to me.

For a whole week, I got to be a part of her world. Each

morning she took me to work, our heads bent close as she showed me how to handle seedlings, nurture and cut away. In the greenhouse, she grew plants with names that sounded like ingredients for spells: bloody butcher, calf's snout, wolf's-foot. She showed me what could kill, and what could cure, and what should never be picked. It seemed these were things she had always known, and I listened closely, eager to learn.

When the sun fell, she showed me a world that hid in the milky-orange dark of city nights, staying late at all-night parties, where smoke hung heavy as my sister talked of protest, and long-haired men sang about redemption, and suicide, and the swords of time. She took me skinny-dipping in the school pool, trespassing after dark to dive naked into the uninterrupted expanse of blue, then on to the top of Addington Hills, where we feasted on Hula Hoops and sweet orange Kia-Ora, watching the night's lights flicker under a starless sky. When dawn came, we walked back through the early-waking streets, my small, sleepy hand wrapped into hers, drinking milk stolen from the float, singing Bob Marley songs as the city woke.

For that week, I felt more love than I had words to explain, but when my sister put me on the coach to return home I refused to look back as it pulled away. Even though I knew it would hurt, I pretended not to see her waving. She was sending me away, and my need for her hurt in ways I could not explain.

What I remember now is her face as the bus pulled away, and the yellow and brown seats that prickled my naked legs like an angry shame. It was an anger that would return throughout our relationship, fuelled by a sense of being guilty for something I had done but could not name. When she didn't turn up to a lunch we had planned for my thirty-sixth birthday,

I tried not to feel like I was somehow to blame. She was often late and always seemed to be running against time, but I was heavily pregnant and felt rejected by her lack of care. I did not wait. Instead, I left the café angry, and we did not speak again.

There is always time to be angry, it seems.

Within two weeks, she would drown and the world would fold into a scream, my mouth repeating over and over – *no-no-no* – willing her to survive. When the call came to say she had died, I felt anger because I could not save her. Underneath this, there was another feeling that made me feel ashamed: I was angry that she could not save herself and that, in drowning, she had stolen my chance at happiness away.

Mugwort

ARTEMISIA VULGARIS
Cronewort, felon weed, mugweed

Drink cronewort tea to aid communication
between the topside and other realms

Mugwort is associated with witchcraft, moon-magic and feminine shamanic practice. It can be inhaled or consumed to induce deep and lucid dreaming. Mildly hallucinogenic, it was traditionally considered a 'woman's herb', used to promote menstruation and induce childbirth. It improves overall immune function, and is excellent for supporting the stomach, pancreas and liver. It can be used to treat general aches and pains, insect bites, burns, irritated skin, colds, coughs and sore throats.

Mugwort grows well on wastelands, gravel pits, quarries, waysides, hedge-banks and other rough ground.

Mugwort

I am not what I was. I do not know what I am to become. I am at the hinterland, the space of fog and clearing, beyond the cliff edge but a long way before the horizon.

Life offers so many different ways to arrive at the end. We like to imagine we know the way. Mostly, we do not. Mostly, we are lost. We only see it when we get beyond where we thought we were going. And then, maybe, we begin again.

Seventy-eight days after my sister drowns, my son is born. The meaning of his name: *I awake*.

Elder

SAMBUCUS NIGRA
Pipe tree, bore tree

A child placed in an elder crib will be stolen by the faeries

Elder has long been considered one of the most powerful trees, both magically and medicinally. Said to be the manifestation of the Elder Mother, or Mother of Earth, it was traditionally used in cremations and placed in the grave to protect against evil spirits, and was associated with sorrow and grief. Regenerative and healing, and rich in tannins, potassium, folic acid, flavonoids and vitamins A and C, the root, bark, leaves, flowers and berries can be used to treat a wide range of ailments, from food poisoning, warts, toothache and inflammation, to fever, sore throats, wounds, skin complaints, headaches and flu. The flowers and berries are edible and can be made into wine, soups, cordials, puddings and chutneys. An infusion from the leaves and flowers can be used as a spray to repel insects and protect roses against mildew or aphid attack.
In large doses, or in its raw state, elder can be poisonous.

Elder grows abundantly on wastelands, eroded riverbanks and chalk pits.

Elder

Last week, a man with a chainsaw came and chopped down all the elders that grew in the village, including the one that I had marked for harvest, growing on the roadside near our house. Sacred to the goddess Holda, and guarded by the Elder Mother, the elderberry tree is said to have the power to protect, and to bestow long life. Folklore warns that to cut the elder will bring about a death within three days. It is also said to harbour witches in its wood. Now, all that is left is the wounded stump, but elders are resourceful, and he did not find them all.

We decide to try along the back lane, between the estate and the beck. My son runs ahead, scouting, his bird-binoculars in hand.

'Found one!' he shouts, waving to me. It is full with berries, ripe and black. Together, we gently bow the branches, and snip off heavy stems that drop softly into the basket below.

'Leave some for the birds, Mummy. They will get hungry soon,' he reminds me. The berries are an important food source for birds before the approaching winter, and we must be careful to leave the higher ones for their share.

When our basket is full we carry it home, our hands sticky and stained violet. As we rinse our harvest under the tap, I watch the inky water fall in spirals down the drain.

'Can I try one, please?' my son asks, his hand reaching into the colander.

'We have to cook them first, or they will make your tummy sick,' I tell him. Elderberry, prized for its medicinal use, is not kind to humans when raw. We put the berries into our largest pan, and add water, lemon slices, root ginger, sticks of cinnamon and cloves. It is a potent brew, and fills the kitchen with scents of citrus and spice as it cooks. This Elder Mother will keep us safe when times are dark.

When all the juice is drawn, I pull the bag from the pan and cool it in a bowl, before squeezing it like an udder to drain the liquid out.

'Can I do the next bit?' my son asks. I hand him the honey from the cupboard and he pours it in, watching it gather and melt into the heat. As we stir, I whisper a wish over the pot. It is always the same one: *let him stay*.

These are our slow, healing days. The pot bubbles on the stove. Wine-deep, sticky and sweet, this potion is nearly complete. When it is ready, we pour it into glass bottles, stopper it, and store. We will use it through the coming winter to keep us well. Sometimes, the line between magic and medicine is finely drawn.

SEED TWO

Methuselah's Beard Lichen

USNEA LONGISSIMA
Woman's long hair, old man's beard, tree's dandruff, lungs of the earth

Carry beard lichen to remind you to slow down

Beard lichen is associated with regeneration, growth and strength. Well known for its antibiotic, antiseptic and antibacterial properties, it has been used medicinally to treat wounds, gangrene, pneumonia, fungal infections, bronchitis, flu, respiratory tract infections and tuberculosis. A good immune stimulant, it is edible and contains a high level of vitamin C. It can also be used in textile dyes, cosmetics, deodorants and as a bushcraft fire starter. However, due to possible toxicity to the liver, most use is topical, and it should not be used in any form during pregnancy.

Beard lichen is highly sensitive to air pollution, and grows abundantly where the air is clean.

There is a peculiarity to living on newly disturbed ground. Slow-growing habitats do not exist. At least, not at first. When we move into our new home, the only thing growing in the garden is perennial ryegrass, sown over a thin substrate of topsoil. The rocks, newly excavated from the waste of this industrial ground, are barren. The concrete slabs are freshly laid. The grey render on the house walls, recently sprayed. Nothing grows where it should not. Into this sterile world, my son wants to add moss.

Moss has a magical quality. It lives where sprites and fairies, and all things hidden, exist. When the sunlight catches, it softens the drystone walls, billowing and folding its sensuous flesh over the angularity of rock, the slowest of dances between stone and spore. It appears fragile, but it is resilient and strong; given enough time, it can turn granite into soil. A nun once said to me, when I challenged the patriarchy in the Catholic Church, that change would come 'in God's time, not our own'. It is the same with moss. For over four hundred and fifty million years, it has slowly shaped this world, surviving burning, drought, ice and the fiercest heat. With the ability to die back into itself and wait for better climes, it can go to the edge of death and be revitalised with the first rains. Always among the first life to colonise scorched ground, moss can turn the most barren rock face into a biodiverse world. It grows on the hardest stone, and the softest forest floor, turning both into an echo of an ancient realm. It can also save a life.

When botanist Isaac Bayley Balfour and military surgeon Charles Walker Cathcart identified sphagnum moss as an effective remedy to staunch bleeding and cleanse wounds,

Methuselah's Beard Lichen

they may not have known how many lives this little bryophyte would go on to save. By 1918, over one million sphagnum dressings were being used by British hospitals each month. Its unique structure of cells, combining high-absorptive properties with the inbuilt ability to create a low-pH, sterile environment, helped prevent thousands of deaths from sepsis on the front line. The success was such that across the UK, communities were rallied to take part in voluntary 'moss drives'; sent out with sacks to collect moss to send to the front line.

Our intentions are less noble than that. When my son and I read about moss graffiti, we decide to have a go for ourselves. We find a recipe for the paint in a permaculture magazine, and head out on a hunt for starter-moss to make our slurry. A pleurocarpous moss can double its size within six months. Acrocarpous moss is slower, taking two years to fully adhere to the rock, but grows in soft, tight cushions that are easier to sculpt. Both have their merits, and their demands.

We take out our foraging bag. Within a ten-minute walk of our house, we discover thirteen different kinds of bryophytes: dew-filled pixie cup lichens, flaming torches of redshank, and mosses that make miniature, glittering forests, delicate fern-like fronds, and pillows of springy turf. Each habitat is a slow-growing world, home to thousands of microscopic invertebrates busy out of sight.

Careful not to disturb too much, we remove a small fragment of each, gently coaxing it from the stone. At home, we wash the moss under running water to rinse off the soil, then put it into the blender, adding in two cups of plain yoghurt, half a teaspoon of sugar and two cups of water to the mix. My son presses the button, and watches as the mixture whizzes and pulses until it transforms into a thick sludge.

The opposite of the instant claim of paint, moss art has the patience of Zen. All it needs to grow is time, and the right weather. I see pictures of elaborate, swirling text and imagine whole poems growing across our home, turning our house into a waiting page, but we are not allowed to have any plants attached to the outside walls, and I doubt I can claim it wrote itself. Instead, we settle for starting small, and choose a few stones. I write my words with care, conscious of my untidy hand. My son has no such fear, and paints a dinosaur, a daisy and a cow.

The next day, he goes to check his creations.

'Where have they gone?' he asks, unable to find a trace. He wants to see the rewards of his work now, but that is the thing: moss is slow to grow. Each day, we must tend to these invisible scrolls, not knowing if they will survive. In time, our words should appear, like spectral messages from the other side. For now though, we must simply stand back, and wait.

Red Campion

SILENE DIOICA

Adam's flannel, kettle-smocks, granfer-griggles, wake-robins, fadder-dies

Use the flowers and seeds in a spell to ward off loneliness

Red campion is associated with faeries, thunder and snakes. The seeds were traditionally crushed and used to cure snakebites, while the root can be boiled to make a soap substitute. The flowers are an important source of nectar for bumblebees and butterflies. Named after Silenus, the drunk Greek god of the woodland, it was said to protect the honey stores for the faery folk and was generally considered bad luck to pick.

Red campion is considered an edge-dweller, and grows prolifically on verges and waysides.

As we settle into our new home, my son is excited to make friends. It is one of the reasons why we applied for the house; we have chosen to home-educate, and the estate offers a safe place to play, and a group of children his age.

'How does a friend become a friend, Mummy, if I don't know them yet?' he asks. I find making friends hard, always shy of reading things wrong, my mother's voice warning in my ear. I don't want him to feel this way.

'Just begin with hello, and tell them your name,' I say. It seems a good place to start. He takes it to heart, and introduces himself this way to everyone he meets. Some respond. Some look confused. My son smiles at them all, and moves on.

When he sees a poster on the village noticeboard for the harvest festival, he wants to join in.

'Can we go, Mummy? Please, please?' he begs, hopping from foot to foot, eager to be part of everything that is going on. This is a struggle for me. My normal reaction to unknown social invitations is anxiety and avoidance. How much is mine, and how much is learnt, I do not know. Even though I grew up in a village, my family never took part in community life. We were a self-contained unit, used to living in places where we were on the outside. It wasn't any different in England. Our arrival was met with curiosity, and fear, the curtains twitching out the Morse code of village rumours – *outsiders, hippies, not-from-round-here*. We soon figured out that, like always, we were better off keeping to our own.

In the beginning, we tried to blend in, but this was rural England in the 1970s. We were different, and that made us dangerous. My father travelled abroad a lot. My mother wore hot-pants and home-made kaftans, had an art studio in the shed, and refused to take us to church. Her attempts at contributing to parochial life met a swift end after she suggested livening up the craft show with an exhibition of nudes. My sister and eldest brother came and went, one dressed in rainbow skirts and chanting on the lawn, the other in cowboy boots and flares, cigarette in hand, and frequently drunk. The younger of my brothers made his home in the barn, declining to live in the bourgeois house. He grew his copper hair long, talked revolution, and slept under a Che Guevara flag, but every morning my mother carried his breakfast out to him on a tray. As for my other sisters, two remained. At eleven and twelve, the older of the two was blonde and soft, baked in the house, and was labelled as *sweet*; the younger was all fire and mud, happiest when outside, practical but wild. Born fourteen months apart, they were simply called '*the girls*', and were as different as they were close. I loved them both.

Now we are grown, we joke that our father didn't so much have a family as a factory, each one of us the sum of our worth; not names, but labels: the artistic one, the reliable one, the talented one, the kind one, the practical one and me. The last. The one who tells tales.

Six of one, and half a dozen of the other; everything we had was divided into six equal parts. If there was food, it would be served in equal portions. If there were presents, each one had to have the same value. If there wasn't enough for everyone to have equal, then we would equally share in nothing. My mother was fierce about being fair, even when it hurt.

It was the same with people. In a family where none of us

felt like we belonged, others found their safe harbour, and a place to rest; our house a port-call for the lost and lonely.

'Everyone needs a friend,' my mother said. Her empathy for the outsider had a flip-side, though. The boy who lived with his granny and spoke strangely, and tied me up in the shed? I had to invite him to play. I knew being kind was the right thing to do, but his games hurt, and I didn't want to be his friend. When I look back now, I am both sad and proud: proud that my mother taught me kindness; sad that she didn't protect me from what was cruel.

This was the world in which I lived, the only one I knew. We were a unit all to ourselves. Two brothers, four sisters; my mother's brood. All my life, it was the same big, boisterous, living-on-the-margins family that I blamed and needed in equal measure; the same one I would lose with my sister's death.

Now, here I am after twenty-five years, living in a village again. I would be happy keeping my distance, but my son has other ideas. He looks at the poster again, and points at the pictures of vegetables and fruit.

'It's about gardens, Mummy! You like gardens,' he tells me, aware he is scoring a winning point.

'Maybe,' I say, hoping he will forget. He doesn't. When the topic comes up during a play date with a friend, another mother tells me that 'perhaps it would be the right thing to do, seeing as you don't send him to school', and I give in. I have my doubts that attending the harvest festival will do anything to improve our acceptability, but my son wants to go and I want him to be happy, so I agree. Six weeks after we move into the new house, we attend our first village event.

Red Campion

The hall is full when we arrive. Everyone appears to know each other. My son points excitedly towards the stage, where two rows of fidgeting children sit cross-legged, each dressed as a vegetable or fruit. To the side of them is a long trestle table bedecked with traybakes, dried pasta, biscuits and cans of soup. My son turns to me, panic in his face.

'Did we bring food, Mummy?' he asks. I think about the half-eaten bag of jelly babies gathering fluff at the bottom of my bag. Somehow, I don't think these offerings will suffice. It seems that I have already committed a social faux pas.

'Sorry, darling, I didn't. I'm sure it is okay, just this once,' I tell him, though I suspect this is not true.

The only available chairs are at the front of the hall, facing the little vegetable-and-fruit children. We bump and jostle with our coats and bags, apologising our way to the empty seats. Just as we sit down, the vicar stands up, and everyone in the hall rises to their feet. They begin to sing. I look at my husband in panic. I don't know the tune, or the words to the hymn. Heavy with awkwardness, I can't make myself stand up. My husband is laughing, barely managing to hide his amusement. He finds this hilarious. He has never lived in a village before. He thinks it doesn't matter what people think, or else doesn't care. I know differently. I am aware of every eye upon us. My head is filling with cotton wool. Heat rash rises up my neck and face. What on earth am I doing here? I want to escape, but my son wants to take part and I don't want him to feel like he doesn't belong. He pulls at my sleeve.

'I thought it was about gardens, Mummy?' he asks, puzzled by the singing. Raised without church, or school, he has no frame of reference for these public rituals of village life.

'We don't have to sing along, poppet. We can just listen,' I tell him, holding on to his hand. I make myself stand, counting down my breathing and hoping this doesn't go on too long.

When the hymns end, everyone sits down. The vicar, still standing, talks us through a PowerPoint presentation of global hunger, showing us photographs of starving children and refugees in flimsy boats. He reminds his audience that they have a lot to be thankful for in their lives. He is right.

'What gifts should we be grateful for?' he asks the children. My son sticks his hand high into the air, stretching up to be seen.

'Me!' he shouts, then grins, secure in the knowledge that he has this answer right. I smile. It is what I tell him every morning and night, and it is true. His little life, fragile in my hands; such precious gifts it brings.

Broad-Leaved Dock

RUMEX OBTUSIFOLIUS
Butter-dock, cushy-cows, kettle-dock, smair-dock

Carry the seeds to help you conceive a child

Broad-leaved dock is a traditional country remedy to counter nettle stings. The plant's energy is said to be helpful in releasing frustration, irritation and anger, and eliminating emotional waste tied to past problems, anxieties and old pain. High in antihistamine properties, it can be used as a poultice to treat insect bites, stings, skin irritations, blisters and general urticaria. A compress can be made from the leaves to relieve bruising, and the seeds can be prepared as a tincture to treat coughs and colds. The whole plant is edible and contains high levels of vitamins A, B and C, as well as iron. Young leaves can be cooked or used raw in salad, or as an alternative to vine leaves. Seeds can be dried as an alternative to pepper, or ground and used as a thickener for sauces and gravy, and the stems can be cooked as an alternative to rhubarb, or dried to create basket rope.

Broad-leaved dock grows abundantly on disturbed ground and wasteland.

Three months after my son is born, I go to my first parent and toddler group. I don't want to be here but the health visitor tells me I am at risk of what she calls '*the baby blues*'.

My ugly grief does not fit this pink-tinged world of motherhood. No one wants to hear about death, so close to birth. In my last trimester, there were no trips to buy baby clothes, no antenatal classes to learn breathing techniques for an easier birth, no numbers swapped with other expectant mums. When others were *nesting*, I stayed in my room and cried and, when the time came, I gave birth at home beside the coal fire, as snow fell from the January sky. Now, the snow has gone, the narcissi in the woods have bloomed, and my son is three months old. It is time to re-enter the world.

I try to find a comfortable way of sitting on the hard, plastic seat as my son roots at my breast, his hands reaching like a kitten into the air. I think it is okay to feed him here, but I don't know for sure. I hide him under my baggy smock, noticing milk-sick stains down its front. I wonder if they are visible, and if I have remembered to brush my hair. I hold my son closer, feel the heaviness of his warmth against my body. In this blown-apart land, I am kept rooted by his love.

I look at the other mothers in the room, with their casual carrying and easy air. These mothers are happy. These mothers are coping. These mothers are clean. They talk to each other, cradling infants in colourful rainbow slings, or bouncing them in compact, coordinated buggies. I try to read the language of the room. How am I meant to speak? It seems to come easy to them but every time I try to think of something to say, words settle in my throat like sand. What can I tell them about my world?

A woman with a clipboard approaches, and gives me a cup of tea. It is hot, and burns my hand, but there is nowhere to put it down. I try to keep it steady, away from my nursing son.

'Just the one?' she asks. I do not know what to reply, and so stay quiet.

'It's okay, we get quite a lot of older first-time mums,' she tells me, with a reassuring smile.

I have heard this phrase a lot. In medical terms, at thirty-six I am a 'geriatric mother'. When I told the doctor that I wanted to give birth at home, he looked at my notes and told me I was too high a risk. 'After all, with your history . . .' he said, implying that my choice would risk this baby's life. My mother tells me that when she was pregnant with me, the doctor told her to terminate at once. 'You never know what problems it will have at your age,' he said. She was thirty-nine. She told him she would love me whatever way I turned up, and left.

The woman moves on. I stand up and walk over to the tea table, carrying my son under my tunic, my baby bag over my shoulder, and the hot tea in my spare hand. A woman with a pink fluffy jumper and tight pale jeans stands chatting to another mother. She fetches a pink wafer biscuit from a plate, using it to distract her son from shoving a triceratops repeatedly into her thigh. Next to her, she has a baby in a pram. I smile at the baby, who sucks on a pink-tipped dummy, and stares back without blinking.

'Just the one?' the woman says, looking over my shoulder, as if I might have mislaid another child somewhere. I still do not know what to reply. How do we account for the ones who live with the dead? When people ask me how many siblings I have, I stumble over the answer. Two brothers, two sisters. This is a lie. Two brothers, three sisters – one dead. This is true, but what to do with the awkward silence that follows? It is the same with this. How many children do you have? The one living, or the ones who never birthed?

Fold back four years. On the night our first baby died, I had three dreams. In the first, a little boy with blond hair stood beside me on the water's edge. He took my hand and told me it was not time. In the second dream, a black dog came, eyes red as movie hounds', blood dripping from its teeth. It paced around my home, looking for the door. I hid my baby under an upturned flower basket, held my breath and prayed for the hound to leave. In the third dream, I carved a coracle from a turtle shell, placed it in the water with my six small turtle-babies inside, and set it out to sail. When I woke in the morning, I knew that my baby had died. I kept quiet, hoping I was wrong. I was not.

*

I lie flat on the bed as the nurse smears my belly with cold gel. We look at the screen. There is a pause; a moment's small breath between the looking and the words. She wipes the gel off my stomach, and tells us to go downstairs. She does not say why.

'It will be okay,' my husband says. I do not speak.

The process is repeated again. My husband and I hold hands, and wait for the heartbeat. It does not come. The nurse turns the screen away. We are not allowed to see this time. Without looking at me, she tells us what I already know: our baby has died.

Broad-Leaved Dock

A spider of grief crawls up and out of my mouth. I try to hold it back but fail, and begin to sob. As my husband guides me through the waiting room to the toilet on the other side, expectant faces look away, not wanting bad luck. I howl into a grey-flecked Formica floor. My husband sits at my feet, holding my hand. The tears pour into a lake between us. I pull rough paper towels from the dispenser, attempting to soak up the pain.

When we return to the room, with its flickering screens and its silent beats, the nurse smiles. She hands me a tissue from a floral box. It is soft and white. She tells me that miscarriage is very common in the first trimester, that one in four pregnancies fail to reach term. It makes me feel ashamed to be so distraught. I swallow hard to stop another howl escaping.

No one tells us what we are meant to do next, so we drive home. We do not speak. I touch my belly out of habit, wait to feel the butterfly flutter of life, but it is still.

After my husband goes back to work, I telephone the doctor. He tells me that he will make an appointment to have the waste products removed. I do not understand. Not yet a child, in death my baby is seen as only waste, but not to me. I tell him that I am not ready yet.

'You are on your own then,' he tells me, and hangs up.

Six weeks later, in the quiet of the afternoon, I give birth to what is dead. I wrap my shrunken placenta and tiny, unborn child in tissue paper, and place them in a takeaway box. When I get to the hospital, I hand the makeshift sarcophagus to the duty doctor.

'Waste products,' she says, as she throws it all into the medical bin.

They anaesthetise me and scrape away what is left, but I saw what was inside. Rotten and black; no life could grow where such dark was held.

The years cry by. We keep trying. I sit in the gynaecologist's office. Different consultant, but the same question every time.

'How many children do you have?' he asks, without looking up from my notes.

'None,' I reply. The medical profession does not class my dead babies as children.

He tells me to lie on the examination couch. When he comes closer, I can smell pine and citrus, not the kind you get in lavatories but the essence-of-the-forest kind that comes in expensive bottles at the airport. I do not look at his face.

'Everything appears to be normal,' he tells me, but I know the truth: *I am not good enough to carry a child*.

*

'Just the one?' the woman in pink asks again, this time more slowly, pointing at my son and smiling in a way that suggests she thinks I do not understand what she is saying.

Snap back.

The room fills up with noise, and mouths all talking, talking, talking. I do not know why I am here. My skin prickles with heat. I need to get out.

'Yes,' I reply. I put down my cup, and walk out.

Great Mullein

VERBASCUM THAPSUS
Hecate's torch, Devil's tobacco, hag's taper, candlewick plant

Place mullein and lavender under
your pillow to help ward off nightmares

Great mullein is connected with crone and death magic. It was thought to encourage the manifestations of spirits, and help communicate with those who dwell in the Otherworld. Because of this, it is considered a good plant for those who have gone through traumatic or life-changing events, and can assist in processing experiences. Expectorant, antiseptic and mildly sedative, it can be prepared as a tea or balm to loosen phlegm, soothe coughs, aid relaxation and also treat burns, bruises and minor wounds. Before cotton, it was used to light lamp wicks, which gives it its common name of candlewick plant.

Great mullein grows abundantly by roadsides and on wastelands.

For a year after my sister drowns, I have a recurring dream. We are travelling together in a car, but she does not understand that she is dead. As I drive, she talks but, even though her mouth is moving, I cannot hear her speak. Her voice has disappeared. She begs me to take her home. The car keeps moving forward, but we cannot escape. We just keep moving forward, unable to change.

Then I wake and, for a small moment, I find the world is whole again, with my sister alive, but memory always floods in, like water into sand, and she dies all over again. Every morning is the same, her death tumbling into the day; my palms spotted with blood where my nails have dug in, the pillow damp with tears. I am left with only the impossible to understand: my sister went out one day, and did not come back. I repeat the moment of her death on a play-rewind, attempting to slow down time, to stop it before she spends her last breath. In this way, I try to keep her alive, looped on the axis point of her crossing, from being to not-being. It hurts me to stay in this place, but it is harder to leave.

As my son nurses, I try to piece together the events around the moment of her death. In the face of an unbelievable truth, I search for facts. I scroll through online forums, where experts and hobbyists discuss the risk of leg-lock pinning in old-style canoes, and the odds of someone so experienced dying on an easy stretch of grade-two rapids. I read a news report that tells me the rescue was 'hampered by the poor mobile signal in the rural area', and another that tells me my sister was trapped for over fifteen minutes, facing against the current, the full force of the river pushing into her mouth. I look up the chances of survival in cold water. After four minutes, there is a forty per cent chance of resuscitation; after fifteen, it is almost zero.

The death certificate lists primary cause of death as acute cardiac failure, and secondary as drowning and hypothermia, but these only tell me what killed her, not how she felt as she died. I research the physics of water, and find out that it is around seven hundred and seventy times denser than air, the result of the combined weight of water and atmosphere. The coroner's summary concludes that the pressure of the water at the time of her drowning was equal to two metric tonnes, crushing her lungs. But the facts still don't tell me how she felt. Did she understand she was going to die? Did she realise she was trapped? Did she lose consciousness before she drowned, her head striking the rocks as the river tossed her like a broken stick, or did she stay conscious throughout it all, the water pushing in on her lungs as her heart gave out?

I search for the facts, so that she does not have to be alone.

Fact: my sister is dead.

Fact: I will not see her again.

Selfheal

PRUNELLA VULGARIS
Heal-all, heart-of-the-earth, woundwort

Use to help bring hope and healing to those who feel wounded

Selfheal has been traditionally used to alleviate sore throats, lower fevers, reduce inflammation, speed the healing process and stem the flow of blood from wounds. High in vitamins A, B, C and K, flavonoids and rutin, it is antibacterial, antioxidant, astringent, diuretic and styptic. Both leaves and young shoots can be eaten raw in salads, added to soups and stews, or used as a culinary herb.

Selfheal grows in grasslands, wood clearings, rough ground and lawns.

Selfheal

Motherhood is made of sugar-milk and sweet dreams, but grief is the dark hag that lives in the woods. She does not invite tenderness, she does not ask for love. She is a mud-dweller, feral and fierce, and will not leave. The wound she tears in me is pink and raw, unable to heal.

I do what I have to do. I stitch myself together, shore up my crumbling centre with pins of practicality. I wash clothes, read stories, feed, change, bathe, care. I keep going. Sometimes I cry, but I must try to stand with the living. In the rain, I clean windows, to let the light in.

It is hard to hold a person who is grieving. We are not fluffy. We are not pliable or gently vulnerable. We do not swoon. When I hold my baby in my arms I feel whole, but when my husband tries to touch me, I shrink away. This grief-body feels alien to me, as if I am walking in someone else's flesh. The world seems harsh and abrasive, with too many sharp edges, too many clawing hands.

'What's wrong with you?' my husband asks. I hear it as an attack, and shrink further away.

I am angry. I am sad. I am consumed by love, and full of rage. I am exhausted. I feel betrayed. I am terrified of losing my son, of having him stolen from me when I look away. I am staggering between maternal love and fierce grief, my heart shredded by this sharp, strange landscape.

'I'm just tired,' I reply. It is a small word to describe the hurricane of grief that batters my bones, but it is all I have.

Yet, my grief-hag also protects. In the dark, she watches for monsters as I sing my son to sleep, snarling her sharp teeth to keep us safe because she knows that where death resides, so life must also exist.

When I hold my son against my breast, his body soft against my skin, I find hope. I am determined he will not suffer by my broken-edged self. Even though I am held together by spit and soil, he will know only love.

As the grief-hag paces the perimeters of my world, keeping the monsters at bay, another voice calls out.

'Hold me, keep hold of me,' it says, hoping someone is listening, hoping someone is brave enough to break through.

I do not want to be held, but I need someone to hold on. I need my husband to find a way to me. I need him to love the unlovable she. I need to find a way to love her too.

Field Poppy

PAPAVER RHOEAS
Flanders poppy, blind buff, head waak, thunderclap

The poppy offers rest and relief from pain

Field poppy is believed to grow where men have died in battle. Now commonly associated with the fallen soldiers of World War One, the poppy symbolises eternal sleep and was presented by the Ancient Greeks and Romans as an offering to the dead. Used in spells to release buried anger, it is gently antispasmodic, sedative and good for pain relief. The flowers and seeds can be used as a syrup or infusion to ease coughs, catarrh and other respiratory disorders, and to relieve headaches, neuralgia and shingles.

The field poppy thrives on disturbed ground.

Each day, we cut, and turn, and shift scrub-turf. Mounds grow like giant turtles in every corner. I dig down into the industrial bones, pull out rocks and rusted metal from the soil until the garden beds begin to take shape. When it rains, they become waterlogged, not able to drain away through the compacted ground. My son and his new friends play in these muddy puddles, laughing as the brown sludge fills their wellington boots. He is delighted with this new game. I add drainage to my list of things to learn.

The garden will be our classroom. When neighbours ask why my son is not in school, I tell them that we are home-educating instead. Together, we research permaculture, plant medicine and sustainable gardening methods. Each morning, we head out onto the building site to see what we can find. In the rubble, we find what can be transformed, and what has been. We root out smooth black granite that glints in the sun, to turn into hotplates and chopping boards for our kitchen. I load up large chunks of sandstone, limestone and river rocks into my salvaged, squeaky wheelbarrow, to shore up the edges of our vegetable beds. My son, a self-declared palaeontologist, finds discarded segments of carboniferous sandstone laced with crinoid stems, brachiopods and gastropods. He loads these discoveries into his little green barrow to add to his geological display beside the back door, reciting names and facts, an endless vault of knowledge that he somehow stores in his young brain.

Together, we strip back the layers of sod, and mulch it into mounds. We till the thin topsoil for stones, and chip away at compacted bedrock left by a century of industrial use. We

Field Poppy

forage fields for strange harvests of rotten branches, and autumn leaves that smell of dark. We scavenge sharp sand and jagged gravel from the building site, staining our hands and chafing our knuckles raw. Each day, we fill our wheelbarrows with rocks to shape the beds and ponds, saving broken slabs of granite to make stepping-stone paths. Into the gaps, we stamp down rescued leylandii clippings that smell of forests and make my son sing Christmas songs. When the rains fill our dug-out beds with sludgy water, my son dances his muddy-puddle jigs. Neighbours peer over the fence. Some complain. Others see the promise of what might be revealed. Everything gathers in wait, taking shape.

My days are simple again. I stop searching for a better place to be. Against the noise of grief, the silence of stone and soil soothes me. These are the routines of our days and in them, we grow. The bones of my body ache, and my hands are cracked, but we keep going and, at night, I finally sleep.

Sow Thistle

SONCHUS OLERACEUS
Milkweed, swine thistle, turn sole, hare's colewort, soft thistle

Hang sow thistle in the home to drive out melancholy

Sow thistle has similar healing properties to the dandelion. Cooling and astringent, it was traditionally used to regulate the menstrual cycle, encourage milk production in new mothers, and treat kidney and liver complaints. The 'milk' can be used as a skin tonic or as relief for sunburn. In Greek mythology, Theseus eats sow thistle to gain power before slaying the Minotaur. The whole plant is edible and high in vitamin C, calcium and iron. The young root can be peeled and roasted, and the leaves steamed and served as a vegetable, but the plant will increase in bitterness as it ages.

Sow thistle grows abundantly on rubbish dumps, wasteland and roadsides.

Sow Thistle

To turn this waste into fertile land, we have to start by growing soil. We find four wooden pallets and a length of blue plastic rope on the building site, which we use to build a makeshift compost heap. Then we wait, and watch the fat pink worms as they turn our waste into what we need.

It is not long before a letter arrives from the housing association. It has a traffic-light picture in the top corner, highlighted amber, to help us understand the urgency of its notice. We have seven days to clear our garden of rubbish, or be served an eviction notice to leave. I try to work out what they are talking about. Our garden contains rocks, mud, and the salvaged wooden pallets that make up our compost heap. The pallets are the only things I can think of that could be classed as rubbish.

I reread the twenty-page tenants' handbook, trying to find the clause we have broken. It states that we have to keep the outside space 'free from rubbish'. It also states that, as the estate is a social enterprise, the landlords aim to 'improve green credentials and encourage the practice of recycling'. I get the dictionary out.

> RUBBISH (noun)
> *worthless, unwanted material that is rejected or thrown out; debris; litter; trash.*
>
> RECYCLE (verb – used with object)
> *to treat or process (used or waste materials) so as to make suitable for reuse:*
> *to alter or adapt for new use without changing the essential form or nature of.*

We cannot risk getting evicted. We have nowhere else to go. This house is our new beginning, and our last chance. We are trying to make it our home. It is not just about affordable rent. This house offers us a chance to get back up again, somewhere safe to heal and grow roots. My son paints a picture that I hang on the wall, of three smiling stick people, a rainbow and a blue door.

'Our new home,' he tells me, and it is full of light.

I write my reply, explaining the principles of permaculture, plant medicine, and the benefits of backyard biodiversity. I lay out our plans for the coming year, and include a diagram of the Hügelkultur beds. I describe to them my son's magical garden, so they can see it through his eyes. I tell them about the grief and illness that has brought us here. I tell them that sometimes what is broken can be beautiful again.

Lady's Mantle

ALCHEMILLA VULGARIS
Bear's foot, dewcup, woman's-best-friend, nine-monks, fair-with-tears

Carry in your pocket to overcome
fears associated with childbirth

Lady's mantle draws its botanical name from the art of alchemy. Energetically, it is considered helpful in transforming painful experiences into something better. Associated with the goddess Freya, it was traditionally used as a tonic for the female reproductive system, and to encourage fertility in later years. It can be used to strengthen the uterus and encourage contractions, and can be applied topically as a wash during labour to reduce perineal tearing and to speed up the healing post-partum. It can help balance hormones, reduce premenstrual symptoms, and ease menopausal complaints such as sweats, anxiety and mood swings. A poultice made from mashed young leaves is good for hands that are damaged from gardening, and topical use is said to improve breast elasticity and reduce visible signs of ageing.

Lady's mantle grows well on unimproved grassland, roadside verges and banks.

Body as beautiful. Body as a place of pain. Body of death and of birth. Instead of learning to see my body as beautiful, as strong, I grew a skin of shame around my womb that I could not name. When my son arrived into this world, there was no hiding from this dark blood inside. It came roaring out with my spent womb, bound itself with the fury of grief, and broke me open. Out of this wound, my birth-body was born, stinking and foul, and I could not stand to see it, or be seen.

Yet here he was: this tiny miracle of being, made from my cells. When I lifted him into my arms, his body still attached to mine, the cord pulsing blood between us, I felt a love so fierce, it scared me. I promised him that I would keep him safe. I could not promise myself the same.

When my husband took him from my arms, only moments old, I felt myself disappear. In the darkened room, the coal fire fading in the grate, I held the light while the midwife stitched my ripped body back together again. As she stitched, I sang to scare away the emptiness that grew inside me. It was a terrible, lonely pain that I kept to myself.

We are not meant to mention these feelings. Birth is swaddled in rosy glows, sanitised and made safe, but it is not. It is bloody, and it can break you. How is a woman meant to reach inside herself and find strength to bring her baby into life, and then come out unchanged?

Once, curious to know the stories of my own birth, I asked my mother if my father had been there when I was born. She looked at me, puzzled.

'He wasn't at any births. Why would I want him to see me that way?' she said, shocked that anyone would. For my mother, birth was something 'other' that lived in the shadowed world. It was something women understood, and endured. Not having a mother or a sister, or female friend in her life who could be by her side, my mother birthed six children alone, with only the obstetrician and midwives to guide. But when my eldest sister, twenty-six and alone, asked my mother to be at the birth of her first grandchild, she agreed. After the delivery, she refused to hold her grandson, and retreated into a furious sadness that spilled out over us all. At the time, her reaction made no sense to me. Now, I think I see. Our sexual bodies were a dark mirror she did not want to see.

My mother taught me how the body works: the ovum, the sperm, the egg. What she didn't tell me, I gleaned from watching my sisters grow, or from the soft-porn books hidden at the back of the bookshelf and never openly owned, or from playground taunts and games where boys forced kisses and put their hands in my tights. When my first period came, on the day of my best friend's eleventh birthday, my mother handed me a pack of fat, white sanitary towels, and told me I would need to use them once a month from now. I stuffed one into my knickers, pulled down my daisy-patterned party dress, and hoped no one would be able to see. A few months later, on a sleepover with girls from school, I started to leak blood. The towel was soaked through, and I didn't have another one to use. I locked myself in the bathroom and filled my pants with toilet roll. Not knowing what else to do, and too ashamed to let anyone know, I hid the used sanitary pad behind the potted plant. I still wonder who found it, and whisper a small apology for my eleven-year-old actions, even now.

Two years forward from this first blood, I sit on the edge of my bed. The buttercream sun slips through the closed curtain, the December day not fully dawned. I turn my hands palm up, palm down, noticing the bloom of bruises on my wrists, the scuff of grazes across the knuckles of one hand. My white pants lie crumpled on the floor at my feet. The cotton is stained pink. I push them under the bed with my bare toes. I do not want my mother to see.

'Is something wrong, darling?' my mother asks, as she sits down beside me with my morning cup of tea. I keep staring at the floor, and try to pull my nightshirt over my wrists. I want her to make things better again but I don't know how, because I haven't got the words that my body needs to explain. The sounds stay caught in my mouth.

. . . The girl watches stars ripple in the skylight above, distant silver fish caught in a pool of black. She can taste vermouth, and blood, and the cloying smell of pine disinfectant in her throat that makes her retch. Beside her head, a diamanté necklace coils itself on the grey gloss floor; cheap paste jewels stolen from her mother's drawer. Somewhere far off, she can hear music, as if through feathers. She knows she must make herself get up, make herself leave. Standing on shaking legs, she walks out, beyond the boy with kohl on his eyes and scars that thread his arms like runes, beyond the people in the doorway who laugh as she walks by, beyond the noise of rooms and the thick of smoke; out into the midwinter night, into the silence of snow, its bright-light glitter, all sparkle-sparkle-sparkle in the dark . . .

My mother stares at the wall, her hand clasped tight around the handkerchief. She looks so sad.

Lady's Mantle

'I knew I shouldn't have let you go,' she says, banging her fist against her thigh. She is hurting, I can tell. I don't want to make it worse, so I tell her another truth, one that is easier to share.

'I lost your necklace. I'm sorry,' I reply and then, even though I don't want to, I start to cry.

When the sobs stop, she takes a white cotton hanky from her pocket, wraps a corner around her finger and licks it, smudging away the tears. I pull a face.

'I'm not five!' I complain, but this little act of mother-love feels okay today.

A shadow slips across her face.

'When a man says he loves you, he will expect things,' she says, then pauses, frowning as she tries to find the next words. They do not come. I don't understand what she means but I pocket it anyway. In a world where no one talks about sex, this is my only advice. She stands up to leave the room. At the door, she pauses.

'Don't worry about the necklace,' she says.

We never speak about it again.

My mother taught me how my body worked, but she never taught me to make it my own, how to celebrate it, or speak its desire. How could she, with no language for her own? When, years later, we finally speak about the boy with the runic arms, and the glittering stars, and the pain, she tells me a story of her own: of the young men who followed her into the park that night as she walked home, and the police who came to her flat the next day.

'Did you do these?' they said, sneering as they looked at her charcoal nudes, pinned to the wall.

'They're from my life drawing class. I'm at art school,' she explained, proud of her work.

'Perverted,' they said, and laughed. She didn't understand why they said that, but she knew she was somehow to blame: for the boys in the park, for the pain, for the way those policemen looked at her that day. She was sixteen.

She pushed it down, and survived, but the lesson stretched out in time. When I turned to her for protection, she did the only thing she knew. She taught me to survive in a world where being a woman meant being hurt. It was all that she could give. That, and her shame.

In birth, I was magnificent and powerful; terrified and confused. Bad blood, hidden blood, dark blood, lost blood, blood magic, blood moon. A woman's blood is born of power, and of pain. Psalm 139 says, *'You knitted me together in my mother's womb. I praise you, for I am fearfully and wonderfully made.'* As we grow, we are taught to clothe our body in the borrowed robes of shame, but the truth is, from the blood of our mothers we are born; beautiful, and strong.

Creeping Cinquefoil

POTENTILLA REPTANS
Five-finger grass, witches' weed, bloodroot, crampweed

Bathe the forehead and hands nine times
to wash away hexes and curses

Creeping cinquefoil is an all-purpose magical herb, used in medieval times as an ingredient in flying ointment, and in spells for blessing, protection, divination, love and prosperity. It is said to stimulate memory, eloquence and self-confidence.

Used for centuries to cure fevers and infections, it is antispasmodic, astringent, anti-inflammatory and antiseptic. The leaves are high in tannins, iron, magnesium and calcium and can be prepared as an infusion to treat sore throats, toothache, mouth ulcers, gingivitis, sunburn, shingles, stomach ache and menstrual cramps. The root can be applied as a poultice to reduce joint inflammation and bruising. The bark is styptic and can be used to staunch nosebleeds. The root can be dried and ground, as a coffee or flour substitute, or roasted, boiled, or eaten raw, with a similar taste to parsnip or sweet potato.

Creeping cinquefoil grows widely on wastelands and roadsides.

All My Wild Mothers

Sometimes, the place that breaks the hardest is where new life comes through. At fifty-three, my mother was trying to remember the woman she had been. At thirteen, I was trying to discover the woman I might become. As I stumbled into the fecundity of my body, she was letting go of her own. It was a time of life, and a time of grief, and some things broke, and some things grew.

*

My father, having spent so long striving to reach this part of life called Success, is frustrated that it is filled with tears. Needing to try to fix what is broken, he maps a route between Cairns and Melbourne on the east coast of Australia. Just over two thousand miles; the guidebooks warn against breaking down. 'Be prepared to wait,' they say, but my father is impatient. He hires a pale-blue, 1958 split-screen VW campervan, packs the cases with information about the Great Barrier Reef, and heads out on the long tarmac road.

It doesn't work. I am thirteen. I don't want to be here. Neither does my mother. The van is small, and uncomfortable, and doesn't have air conditioning. The route stretches out, endless and hot. My mother has stopped bothering to be nice, and has started to scream 'Fuck off!' A lot. I sit in the back of the van, with my Sony Walkman switched up loud, Prince's *Purple Rain* drowning out the sound of their shouts. Five hundred miles ago, they stopped speaking at all. Now, each day is just hour after hour of silence, my mother staring out of the side window, my father telling us to 'look at the view'. I fold myself into my baggy black clothes, and write furious poems.

Creeping Cinquefoil

We make camp beside a long silver beach. At dawn, my father wakes us up. Already dressed, he tells us we are going for a walk. He leads the way. It is a fierce, furious affair; a beautiful nature-cure aimed at forcing the depression from my mother, and the rebellion from me.

The sea sparkles silver and gold, as one hour becomes two, becomes three. We keep walking, until my legs stiffen with sunburn. I begin to cry. My mother sits down, and refuses to go any further. My father walks on a bit further, then turns around.

'This way,' he says, pointing back the way we have just come. We walked this way; now, we will walk back. My mother walks in silence next to me. I stare at my father's footsteps in the sand, retracing our own.

By the time we get back to the campsite, my skin is blistered, my lips are cracked and my limbs will not bend. Concerned neighbours offer us pink calamine lotion, tomatoes, butter and vinegar for the burn. My mother slices, smears and washes, willing to try it all. Heat radiates above my stretched, angry flesh. I seethe silent, dry tears, my body boiling with rage.

We do not speak for the rest of the day. My father reads his maps in silence. My mother weeps on a foldaway stool, but not for me. I watch them both but do not speak. Tomorrow, we will head out on the road again and I will swim with bright-coloured fishes in a turquoise sea, and watch the silver-dollar eucalyptus leaves shine in the shimmering heat. At night, I will listen to the bush-stone curlew, as it screams its high-pitched call, and in the morning I will hear the kookaburra laugh, just like we used to sing in the song at school; all these wondrous things of beauty, but what I will remember most is the sunburn, and the sound of my mother, quietly crying in the dark.

When we finally reach Melbourne, the blisters have dried, the skin has started to peel away, and none of us are speaking to each other any more. We are dusty, tired and miserable. All I want to do is have a bath, sleep in a soft bed, and be alone. The company my father works for has booked us into the executive suite of the hotel. I have a room to myself, with a queen-sized, massaging bed, Jacuzzi bath, fluffy bathrobe, and a private exit to the roof pool.

I throw down my bag, go into the bathroom and close the door. There are several little bars of soap and bottles of shampoo, neatly lined up along a marble shelf; I choose one and put the rest in my bag to take home. Over the running water, I hear shouts. I ignore them and undress, ready to sink into the bubbles and heat.

There is a loud knock on the locked door.

'Get dressed. We're leaving!' my father shouts. I wrap myself in the soft white bathrobe, and go into the lounge. My mother is perched on the edge of a sand-coloured sofa. She is crying again.

'Your mother doesn't want to stay here,' my father says. I resign myself to not having the bath, and go back into my room to get dressed.

A porter arrives, and tries to explain to my father that there are no alternative suites in the hotel.

'We only have the basic family room available,' he says.

'We'll take that,' my mother says. The porter looks surprised, but helps us load our bags back onto the brass trolley. I look at the floor, wishing I could be anywhere but here, with my angry father and my crazy, crying mother.

The new room has a double bed, and a single pull-out, pushed up against the window. The covers are orange, the carpet is brown, and there is an upright trouser press beside the teak-veneered drawers. I go straight to the bathroom and run another bath, listening to the silence and the slamming door; the guttural sobs of my mother through the wall. I sink down into the foam, and close my eyes. At least I got the soaps.

There is no escape from the arguments though. By the fourth night, my mother has still refused to go out. My father, unable to understand why his plan hasn't worked, or why she is still depressed, loses patience with us both.

My mother doesn't want to be here any more. She doesn't want to be anywhere any more. She grabs hold of the brown metal window and pulls it open, the light and hum of the city pulsing far below.

'You wouldn't care if I jumped!' my mother yells. I grab hold of her legs.

'Please, come down, Mum. It will be okay,' I say, reaching up and taking hold of her hand. Her body softens and she steps back down, crumpling onto the bed. I sit there in silence, smoothing her hair.

'There, there,' I say, whispering the mother's prayer.

After that, my father has to go away to work for a few days.

'Look after your mother,' he says. I order up room service, and we dine on cheeseburgers and processed chips, and watch *Neighbours* on the colour TV.

On the third day, she sees an advert in the paper – *Pop Art, 1955–1970, National Gallery of Victoria.* She gets dressed, brushes her hair and puts on her purple shoes.

'Come on. We're going out,' she says, picking up her handbag. For the first time in weeks, she smiles.

My mother grows increasingly excited once we get into the exhibition. She grabs my hand and pulls me through the bright colours, offering a potted lesson in art history as she points out Warhol, Hamilton, Hockney, Rauschenberg. It is only when we reach the Lichtenstein that she goes quiet. The dot-painted, blue-haired woman calls out in speech-bubble tears. '*I don't care! I'd rather sink – than call Brad for help!*', her hand held up as the waves threaten to swallow her down. When we leave the gallery, my mother buys me a poster of the *Drowning Girl*.

*

A fortnight after our return, she enrols to do a two-year diploma in fine art. It has been thirty-six years since she left art college, and many years since she painted for herself. She buys a new portfolio, stocks up her oils and heads off to class. Her first painting is a portrait of me. I wear a long red skirt and red jumper, pulled down to cover my arms. My hair is cropped short. Behind me, the poster is pinned to my red bedroom door. I sit without moving, as my mother paints in silence, filling the six-foot frame with red and blue, and tiny, endless dots; the nameless girl, forever drowning, refusing to call for help.

Spearmint

MENTHA SPICATA
Lamb mint, mackerel mint, Mary's herb, sage of Bethlehem

Drink mint tea to add strength to your words

Mint is associated with Hades and was widely used in ancient rituals involving the Underworld. The Ancient Greeks rubbed mint on their arms to give them strength. Magically, it was used to protect against hexes and bad luck, and in spells to increase fortitude and assist in overcoming difficulties. It is anti-fungal, expectorant and antibacterial, and can be used to treat odours and infections of the feet and mouth, relieve digestive disorders and colic, ease headaches, clear congestion and soothe coughs. The menthol is good for treating inflammation of the muscles and joints, and makes a good insect repellant.

Spearmint grows well in roadside ditches, along the foundations of buildings, and between cracks in concrete.

'Why can't we make her better?' my son asks, when our cat takes ill. The vet has told us that it would be kinder to let her go. He knows not everything can be fixed but still, he wants to know why.

'Everything living must die. It is how it is,' I reply, aware this is a hard truth to give. There is a pragmatism that comes with sudden and repeated grief. It strips away the sentimentalism of wishful thinking and hollows out the euphemisms and death-disguise.

Yet, as her breathing slows under my hand, I find myself crying for the cat who was a stand-in for the children we could not keep; for the loss and loneliness of this time. My tears, pushed down by the unrelenting insistence of life, slip out before I can fold them away.

'It is good to cry,' my son tells me, a tiny grown-up holding my hand.

We dig a hole in the garden, and place her stiffened body in the ground. Over this, we plant a small, purple lilac, rescued from the end-of-line shelf. It has seen happier days, but might pull through.

'Boo needs flowers,' my son says, as he scatters a handful of calendula seeds over the earth. Marigold, merrybud, flower of grief. Latin for 'little clock', it blooms in early summer, and dies when the first frost comes. Throughout time, the little marigold appears, to remind us of the fragility of this life. Yet it also serves to protect. When my son was newborn, I made a balm from calendula, to protect his tender skin. This summer, I will gather its petals to heal his needle wounds. Life and death; this little clock ticks out our hours, but also brings us light.

Spearmint

Rain begins to fall, to water the seeds. We go inside, and hide under blanket castles in a land of make-believe. As night comes and the moon rises, we point to the sky and lay our wishes on faraway stars before we sleep.

These are our passing days. Sometimes we cry, and sometimes, we say goodbye.

Common Nettle

URTICA DIOICA
Stinging nettle, nettle leaf, burn hazel, sting weed

Use nettle to protect against negativity,
break curses and offer protection

Common nettle is associated with motherhood and transformation. The energy of nettle reminds us that even when a situation appears hard and unloving, we have the power and strength to turn it into a place of nurture and fertility. An excellent plant for convalescence and to help find inner strength. Long used in traditional medicines as a wound healer, it is antioxidant, anti-inflammatory, detoxifying, diuretic and coagulant. High in calcium, iron, vitamins A and C, potassium, silica and protein, it is good for breaking down uric acid and is a frequent remedy for gout. It strengthens and supports the body, and can be used to relieve joint pain and inflammation, reduce eczema, staunch nosebleeds and as a detox for the liver and kidneys. Some studies have shown potential to aid blood-sugar control. The leaves and seeds are edible, and the fibre can be used to make rope. Combined with plantain, it makes an excellent remedy for hayfever. All parts of the plant are edible and provide a rich source of food and shelter for butterflies, ladybirds and seed-eating birds.

Common nettle grows well on ground that has been disturbed and littered with rubble, and can be used to increase nutrients in the soil.

Common Nettle

Although our request to grow a garden is finally agreed, there are stipulations. We cannot hang our washing in sight, we must not place a shed beyond the house-line and, when we leave, we must remove everything we plant, and return it to its original state.

The first thing my son wants to plant is nettles. Nettles give him soup, and string for boats. Before cotton, the common nettle gave us cloth to weave, as well as tea, beer, rennet and dye. They are also good for easing inflammation and pain. We investigate further, and find that nettles support over forty kinds of insects, including the small tortoiseshell and peacock butterflies, and provide food for house sparrows, bullfinches, hedgehogs, shrews, frogs and toads. Now, we call it a weed.

'Happen the birds like nettles almost as much as me,' my son says, a wise gardener for his age, adding a nettle bed to his garden map. With his trowel and bucket, he heads out to search, finding a cluster of woody nettles clinging to the kerbside out the back of our house.

'Here, Mummy. These are good,' he calls out.

'Watch out! Don't touch!' I shout, worried he will grab hold. He steps back and cries, afraid of their bite.

'It's okay, they won't hurt you if you take care,' I reassure, pulling on my gardening gloves and loosening the tough, white roots that reach deep under the concrete and soil. Handling with care, we replant them against our fence. What others dig out, we dig in.

'Can we make soup today, Mummy?' my son asks.

'Not today. They're too old now. See?' I say, pointing to the delicate catkin-like seeds.

'But nettle soup is tasty,' he says, disappointed that he has to wait.

'In spring, the nettles will give us food but right now, they're making food for the birds to eat. That's okay, isn't it?' I reply. He smiles, and turns to his new crop.

'You live in our garden now, Nettle. We put you here so we can make soup but first, can you feed the birds? They are hungry. I like soup, but I don't mind sharing,' he explains.

I smile. To my son, these weeds are a prize to find. He understands, without knowing why, that the nettle will bring new life to the garden, even though at first, it may sting.

Oxeye Daisy

LEUCANTHEMUM VULGARE
Poor-land flower, dog daisy, maudlinwort, moon-penny, poverty weed

To dream of your future lover, place daisy root under your pillow and your shoes outside your door

Oxeye daisy is associated with the goddess Artemis. The plant is similar to chamomile and was traditionally used to treat 'women's complaints', including menopausal symptoms and night sweats. It can be applied topically as a poultice or wash to treat wounds, burns, bruises, conjunctivitis and chapped hands. Antispasmodic, tonic and diuretic, it can improve appetite and has been used to treat liver and gallbladder complaints, reduce fluid retention, relieve chronic coughs, colds and fevers, and soothe sore throats. The unopened buds can be pickled like capers.

Oxeye daisy grows voraciously in disturbed ground.

We cannot afford to buy new plants, so my son and I search the housing site for weeds to plant in. When he spots an oxeye daisy, pushing up through the rubble, he shouts out. We loosen its roots from the rock, and take it back to plant. Bright and bold, like the goddess Artemis who rules it, this woman's weed is wild, and strong. It grows where things are broken, resilient to survive.

'Welcome to my garden, lovely flower,' he whispers, bending down to give its yellow and white face a kiss. Poverty-flower, common weed; our garden refugee. Where did its journey start, from seed, to stone, to here?

When people ask me where I am from, I never know what to respond. My husband's family live in the same small town where they were born, but mine? Even when we were staying still, we were always moving, looking out for the next life, trying it on for size, as if the one we lived in did not fit. In a way, it never did.

For my family, life was a windblown, scatter-seed affair, no sense of root or route; and yet, those roots were there. My father's were grown in Cumberland, deep in a seam of iron and coal, but when the mines closed, poverty forced his family south, three hundred and forty miles to the mouth of the Thames. If it had not, my own story would not have begun.

At first, they were housed in the slums near Tilbury Docks. On the day of my father's tenth birthday, the Blitz began. The German planes targeted areas of strategic importance, including the docklands. The slums were hit, but my father survived. By the next morning, one thousand six hundred people were injured, and four hundred and forty-eight had died. The history books remember it as Black Saturday.

What wasn't cleared by bombing was bulldozed by the clearances that followed. My father's family was rehoused in a new council estate. For the first time in their life, they had a garden, and an outside privy of their own. My grandfather dug potatoes in the lawn, built a wire pen for his hens, and caught rabbits, which his wife turned into stew. At forty-five, he'd saved enough to buy himself a Bantam motorbike, the only thing he ever owned, but by fifty-four he was dead, killed by a falling sack of cement when he was loading the ships. It took him a week to die from the invisible bleed in his head. 'Plant cauliflowers on my grave. At least you can eat them,' he said.

My father does not like to talk about the past. Even so, certain seeds grow through. When I was small, he showed me how to eat the berries and leaves from the hawthorn tree, to keep the hunger out. 'Bread-and-cheese,' he called it. I still pick the leaves and berries from the tree, and when we walk, I show my son the same.

How do the roots of this past find their home in my soil? In 1945, seven days before my father's fifteenth birthday, the war in Europe came to its end. Year Zero, they called it; a chance to reinvent the future out of the waste of what was lost. My father had left education at thirteen to take a job on the docks, but it was not where he wanted to stay. As politicians set about redrawing the boundaries of power, my father and his best friend mapped a way out of the poverty of their past. After work, they studied at night school to qualify as mechanical engineers. My father would be the first in his family to step out of the manual labour of blue-collar work.

All My Wild Mothers

My mother was studying fashion illustration at the art school opposite where my father was taking his class. She was the first to go to college in her family too. Her people spoke to horses, brewed strong dandelion wine, and had words on their tongue from a language lost to my own. My skin is like hers: olive and weathered, like the tanner's hide. They were the makers and menders, sifters and sorters, the ones who walked carts calling 'rag an' bone'; but she had talent and her mother had ambition, pushing her to reach for a different life.

My mother started to date my father's friend, and my father had a girl of his own. The four of them would catch the train up to town every Friday, to go dancing at the Lyceum on the Strand. My mother danced the jitterbug, while my father stood on the sidelines, looking on. But, like all good love stories, there was a twist of fate. One night my father, taking a corner too fast, crashed the Bantam bike into a wall. His best friend saved his life, but it would be a long stay in hospital before he was well again. My father's girl didn't like the smell, and asked my mother to visit in her place. My mother agreed. As he lay there, his body fighting the gangrene that was spreading in his leg, she described the walks she took along the chalk pits near her home, and drew him pictures of the wildflowers that colonised its abandoned industrial past. In return, he wrote her love poems, and promised he would show her all the wonders in the world. Six months later, he had gained a shiny scar that covered his inner thigh, and won the hand of his best friend's girl. It was 1948, and she was sixteen. A year later, they got engaged, and set off cycling through the Alps.

In the aftermath of the unimaginable, all things are possible. As they cycled through the mountains, they conjured up a plan

Oxeye Daisy

to build a wood cabin in the Canadian Rockies, where my mother would paint pictures, and my father would write poems, and they would grow a garden and grow old among its flowers.

My mother got a job at London *Vogue*, and started saving for their dream. A year later, my father passed his engineering exams with distinction, and was conscripted into national service. His newly gained qualification enabled him to apply to officer rank. At the officer training camp, the other cadets came from Eton and Gordonstoun. It was a world of privilege and class my father had never known. He learnt to adapt and passed out top of the class. Soon after, he was drafted to the Suez Canal for eighteen months, but he still wrote my mother love poems to send home.

They married during a three-day leave, at the local Methodist church. It was 1952. My mother's mother did not approve. 'That's your future ruined,' she said. It was the last conversation they would have for many years. A week after the wedding, my mother's family took the Pom ticket to New Zealand, and didn't come back. At twenty, my mother started married life alone.

When my mother ran, she wasn't running from poverty. She was running from a life pre-owned, where her days had already been spent. Her mother had wanted to be a singer, but at eighteen had got pregnant. Unmarried, she chose security as a carpenter's wife, and passed down her glitter-dreams. If she could not be a star, my mother would be. At the age of three, she twisted my mother's wiry black hair into Shirley Temple curls, painted her nails, and sent her onto the stage at the local working men's club. Though my mother loved to dance when she was older, when she was young she was pigeon-toed and shy. That shyness spread a shame through her that would never release, but with my father, she felt beautiful, and free.

Years later, when I ask her why she chose my father, she tells me it was because he didn't have their future written; but, of course, he did. By the time my father had seen his service out, he had grown a moustache, changed his voice and left behind his past, and his poet's pen. He had spent his life poor, and his sight was set on success. His time in the army had shown him what wealth could afford, and opened up a door to a different life. He told her he didn't want to live the rest of his life broke and hungry. They would find a better way to pay for their dream. His army rank rewarded him with a management-level engineering apprenticeship with a Canadian extrusion company. 'Just for a while,' he told her, but he stayed until he retired.

Choice and chance gave us the privilege of our lives but it didn't shake out the roots. As he tried to stay one step ahead of being caught, an imposter in this carved-out world, what parts of him did he leave behind? And though he made a point of cutting ties with all that held him there, no matter how much he tried to change the past, somewhere deep inside was the hungry boy; the one with the wrong vowels in his mouth, who stared through the window of the bric-a-brac shop on Bridge Road, marvelling at the giant seashells carried back from far-off shores. By his side was a girl who drew wildflowers, and dreamt of a cabin in the woods where she would be free.

How much of this is true? Memory is an unreliable narrator, and most of this is second-hand romance. My parents walked away from their pasts, and into mine. Like the dog daisy, I grew in this ground, and called it home.

Wild Thyme

THYMUS SERPYLLUM
Mother-of-thyme, creeping thyme, elfin thyme

Burn thyme to leave the old behind and begin anew

Thyme has been used for centuries as a medicinal and magical plant, from Ancient Greek purifying rituals to Roman protections against poisoning and Egyptian embalming processes. Worn as an amulet, it is said to bring courage to those heading into battle. During the Middle Ages, it was commonly used as a strewing plant to disinfect houses against the plague. Antibacterial, expectorant and anti-fungal, it is now more commonly used as a digestive aid. It can also be used to soothe sore throats, coughs and colds, relieve mouth ulcers, reduce bad breath, and treat minor burns and wounds. An excellent companion plant, it will protect brassicas from cabbage flies, beetles and aphids.

Thyme is drought-resistant and thrives well in soil that is low in nutrients.

When my mother gardened, it was an act of quiet rebellion. Where others tried to tame nature, she encouraged it. In her bag she carried a small pocketknife to dig out weeds that caught her eye, planting them into the flowerbeds at home. Throughout the year, she gathered wildflower seeds into unmarked envelopes, and in autumn she would throw their contents, guerrilla-style, into the borders. She wanted to be surprised by the flowers. She planted old pot onions in among the lavender, and trailed purple-tipped ground ivy and snow-in-summer across the paths. A rusting, wrought-iron chair stood in the long grass below the pear tree, its blue paint delicately peeling, impossible to sit on but perfectly in place. Cracked Victorian bedpans housed rosemary and sage, and cranesbill tumbled from wicker baskets that had long outlived their original use. Like everything she did, it seemed to me effortless, a summoning of senses that enveloped my world.

The house I grew up in was one of the oldest in the village, and had originally been a slaughterhouse. Built in the sixteenth century, and surrounded by three acres of fields, it was named Lilac Cottage, though there was no lilac tree. My mother thought this twee, and renamed it Shambles, after its origins. She left the old meat wheel hanging in the rafters of the barn; a macabre reminder of a past that she refused to take down. To those who disapproved of the disorder of our home, the name was taken at its more contemporary meaning: a mess.

This was a landscape influenced by people who broke the rules, yet nothing was by accident. She was constantly shaping nature to fit her vision of beauty. Like William Robinson, my mother believed that 'every plant should look as if it planted itself'. Inspired by the Impressionist artists, she followed a wild aesthetic, composing in light and colour, an homage to the gardens of Monet and Bonnard. In a world where so much was constrained, it was my mother's *jardin sauvage*. To me, it was my home. In this garden of magic and mystery, I could be anything I dreamt. Perhaps she felt the same.

There were treasures to be found in the soil: ancient bovine thigh bones that became dinosaurs bleached by time, Victorian sheep shears that I cleaned with wire wool and oil to sell, broken shards of blue Willow pottery that my friend and I traded as coin. Of all these finds, the clouded glass bottles, with their elaborately written names – Boots, OXO, Lemonade – were the most prized. At once familiar and strange, they became our wares. Little witches, we decanted potions made from rose petals, nettles and lavender to peddle to my mother for pennies, waiting anxiously to see her sniff each one and be cured. She always declared them 'lovely', despite them smelling of rank water and slime. In darker corners, we made poisons from crushed laburnum and yew, nightshade and tansy. These we would not drink, though we threatened enemies with our brews.

My mother, fearing the danger of strangers, had rules about where I could roam. Outside was out of bounds but within the garden, I was free. Long days of summer heat were spent playing in the back field with my best friend, the rash of seed and pollen on our skin, our legs grazed and brown. We climbed the rough-barked apple trees, camped out under the stars, toasting bread on the fire, soot smeared across our greasy chins. We built dens under the branches of the laburnum and, if we were hungry, we helped ourselves to the pod-peas and radishes that grew in the walled vegetable garden, breaking off stalks of rhubarb to dip into white sugar, or feasted on sweet, sticky plums. When winter came, we towed the makeshift sledge my father made me from an old ironing board and a broken pair of wooden skis, up to the top of the field, and set sail. Racing too fast down the slope, we screamed as the cold night wind snapped at our cheeks. As teenage years replaced our childhood games, we sneaked sweet alcohol and gold-tipped cigarettes into the caravan parked in the drive, and stayed up late swapping stories of the futures we would lead. We were as close as sisters through those years, and stay friends now.

When she and I were fourteen, we lay in the long grass and watched the sky explode in iridescent ripples of violet, emerald, rose and gold. We held our breath as this strange beauty pushed through into our world, not sure whether we were witnessing magic, or the end of the world. When it started to fade, I ran inside to where my father sat working at his desk, hidden away on the top floor.

'The sky, the sky is on fire! Look!' I urged, breathless with the excitement of the unknown.

'It's the aurora borealis,' he said, without looking up from his work, his disinterest like a pinprick in a balloon. I went back down the stairs, and into the dark night. The sky was tame again. No sign remained from the wonder we had seen.

After that, I assumed the Northern Lights must be something commonplace. As the years went by and we didn't see it again, my friend and I came to doubt if we had seen it at all, and I have never seen it since. Now, it is the stuff of legend, and I tell my son of the time I saw Aurora's dancing lights and thought the world was ending.

'Will we ever see them again, Mummy?' he asks.

'One day, if we are very lucky,' I tell him, whispering a silent thanks for that witnessing, when my fourteen-year-old self drew back the veil on wonder, and watched in the long grass with her best friend.

That garden was my mother's masterpiece, and my world, but life moved forward and the house was sold. The commuter couple who bought it said my mother's rusting chairs and wildflowers had a 'rustic charm', but after they moved in they mowed down the flowers, landscaped the grass and renamed it Mulberry House. The rattling, leaded windows, with their imperfect hand-blown glass, were swapped for triple-glazed imitations. The vegetable garden that had kept our family fed was dug out to lay foundations for a new house, its mock-Tudor beams and specially aged, pristine stone kept gleaming clean. The creaking barn, transformed from slaughterhouse to childhood sanctuary, got transformed one last time into a deluxe holiday home, and the butcher's wheel that had hung in the rafters for over four hundred years was finally taken down. My mother returned there once, to revisit the garden she had grown, and cried. She would not find herself there again.

Common Fumitory

FUMARIA OFFICINALIS
Hedge fumitory, earth smoke, wax dolls, fumaria

Carry fumitory to protect against dark spirits

Common fumitory is frequently used to cleanse and clear, both physically and spiritually. It produces a yellow dye that is used in cosmetics and facial tonics. All parts of the plant that grow above ground are used in remedies. Antispasmodic, laxative, anti-inflammatory, hepatic, stimulant and mildly diuretic, it has been used in remedies to treat scurvy, skin conditions, bleeding gums and conjunctivitis, and as a tonic to cleanse the liver and kidneys.

Common fumitory grows well on dry and disturbed soil.

Common Fumitory

Time strips away my sister's hours, but there are small moments when I stumble over her in some familiar act of living, her life grafted into mine, my body reshaped around the space that she once filled. I carry her within me, just as I carried my son, blood of my blood, cell of my cell. Is this what they mean by the dead live on?

As I live out the years she could not have, she begins to inhabit mine and when I look, it is her that I see, staring back from the glass. All these faces, traced into my skin: my sister, my mother, my own.

Meadowsweet

SPIRAEA ULMARIA
Dolloff, meadsweet, Queen-of-the-meadow, bridewort

Burn the dried herb in your home to get rid of negative tension

Meadowsweet is a traditional flavouring in wine, beer, vinegar and jams. Its primary active ingredient is salicylic acid, later synthesised to form the basis of modern-day aspirin. Aromatic, astringent and diuretic, it has been used to treat fever, flu, rheumatism, arthritis, stomach ulcers, heartburn, gastric disorders, urinary infections and headaches.

Meadowsweet favours wet habitats such as ditches, damp meadows and riverbanks.

Meadowsweet

All through summer it has rained, until the year seems to have seeped direct from March into grey-washed autumn days. I used to love this time of year; the way the trees push against the fading light, the colours sharpened by the snap of cold. It is the time of birthdays and new pencil cases, and the possibility of unknown things. Those shortening days were never about endings, but anticipation. When my husband and I married, over two decades ago, I carried a bouquet of autumn branches. Now, October is long, and our anniversary is forgotten. I hold my breath to make it past the milestone of death.

I am glad then, of this year of rain, the way it mutes the colours and gives us sodden leaves. It does not expect me to be happy. As dulled leaves rot in the roadside, my son and I gather handfuls of sodden beech and sycamore, oak and ash, to mulch down over winter in the dark. Neighbours may rake and blow against the inevitable, but we want them to land on our ground. In time, these cast-offs will feed our soil.

After one long night of rain, my son is excited to find that one of the vegetable beds has filled with water, too compacted to drain away.

'The garden made a pond, Mummy. We can have ducks, and fish, and frogs!' he tells me, as he fetches a small wooden boat from his toy box. I do not think it will support grown ducks or fish, but a bog garden would be a good way to make use of this waterlogged patch. We look up what will thrive, and find out that a small wetland area will attract butterflies, bees and damselflies to pollinate our flowers and fruit. It will also provide a habitat for toads, frogs and newts, and a water source for hedgehogs, bats and birds. All this gain, from rain that would not drain away.

We gather in flag iris, water mint and willowherb from the beck at the bottom of my mother's garden. A friend from the Wild Women group brings us meadowsweet from her garden.

'It will like it here,' she tells my son. She has spent a lifetime gathering weeds, and shows me how to make a tea from the flowers, useful to soothe inflammation and to support times of painful change. Later, when I look it up, I find that meadowsweet contains salicin, the root of aspirin. It seems it takes a long time to find our way back to what we know. This wisdom, once hidden, begins to take root.

Lungwort

PULMONARIA OFFICINALIS
Wolf's lung, Jerusalem sage, bloody butcher, Our Lady's tears

Drink lungwort tincture to release grief

Lungwort was primarily used to treat pulmonary disorders such as tuberculosis, based on its visual resemblance to lung tissue. It is a good example of the doctrine of signatures, which connects the visual and physical properties of the plant to the remedy it can offer. Mildly astringent, anti-inflammatory, antiseptic, coagulant and high in vitamin C, iron, silicon and allantoin, it has been used as an alternative to iodine, and is a common treatment for coughs, whooping cough, bronchitis and mild pulmonary irritation, as well as being used to treat diarrhoea and haemorrhoids. Associated with the lungs and the heart chakra, lungwort is used to shift stagnant situations, and release trapped emotions.

Lungwort grows well on damp ground, often in areas of limestone.

All My Wild Mothers

Tomorrow is All Hallows' Eve, a day of sugar and sweets, when the veil is thinnest between the living and the dead. We have avoided it so far, but now my son is old enough to want to take part. As he sleeps, I spend the dark hours hanging cobwebs, cutting out black-paper broomsticks, and creating bat wings from recycled cardboard and signwriter's vinyl for his fancy dress.

He wakes early, pulling on my hand before the sun is full up. 'Hurry, Mummy – Nana and Grandad will be here soon,' he says, with urgency. My parents are not due for another twelve hours, but I let myself be wrapped in his delight. There is magic afoot.

When the girl from four doors down comes round to play, he shows her his wings.

'I am going as a witch,' she tells him.

'My mummy is a witch,' he says, matter-of-fact. He is used to seeing me making potions, gathering berries and herbs.

'Your mummy is not a witch,' she replies, flatly refusing what he has said. He doesn't know what to do with this, and tries again.

'Yes, she is. She makes Mummy Magic happen. I can make magic too. When I go to bed, if I think really, really hard, I can make my toys come alive,' he tells her, decisive in his belief. I smile, glad that my secret has not yet been discovered; that when he sleeps, I move his toys around so that in the morning, he believes he has made them come alive. Sometimes, if I have enough to spare, I slip a small treat under his pillow for him to find. He calls it Mummy Magic, and I am lifted up by his surprise.

LUNGWORT

Their conversation shifts to other things, and I go about my day, but after the little girl leaves he pulls a stool up to the kitchen counter, to help peel apples for a pie.

'Why do people say witches are scary, Mummy?' he asks. I must decide now what to tell him. Even though I want him to keep hold of the magic, I will not let him keep hold of the lie. The witches, the misfits, the wild women, the crones; these were the ones that didn't fit in, didn't obey, and they were tortured, and burned. To be a woman of this land is to carry that legacy in our bones. At one time, not so long ago, the state and church sanctioned the mass torture and murder of our kind. If I had been born at a different time, that fate would have been my own. I take a deep breath.

'Well, a lot of them were the healers and midwives. They knew about plants, and nature, and magic, but some people said they were evil. They appointed witch-finders, and these men killed lots of people, mostly women, who they said were witches. Sometimes people are scared of what they can't control, or what is different, or what they don't understand. I think that's why people still say witches are scary, because they don't understand. What do you think?' I say.

He thinks about this for a while, eats a piece of apple, and gets down off the stool.

'I think it is okay to be different,' he tells me. 'Can we go outside now?'

On our walk, we gather up fallen twigs and russet leaves from the sycamore trees. My son carefully arranges these finds on the windowsill. We tie star anise and slices of wrinkled, long-baked orange onto the branches, to represent the night sky. He finds red tinsel and left-over Christmas crackers to add to the display. I give him a pair of gold taper candles, then change my mind as a vision of my sister rises up from memory, frantically trying to extinguish a velvet curtain set alight by the cotton-wool-and-candle Christmas log. A small laugh escapes my heart, and lifts itself into the room. I find two small night-lights instead, to put in the window to guide the way home for the dead.

'Maybe these will be better,' I say.

When the decorating is done, we stir and sweeten ginger-bread and treacle cake, and bake it with soda bread and apple pie. The kitchen smells of cinnamon, cloves, nutmeg and heat. We carve out the flesh of pumpkins for soup, setting it to roast with onions and carrots, seasoning with fresh rosemary and thyme. My son picks out the largest pumpkin shell, and draws on awkward eyes and a toothy mouth. He wants to cut it himself. I recall an article I read on how to raise a confident child, in which a woman sat in her soft-lit garden. *'Children should be allowed to handle knives from an early age. Accidents are opportunities to learn,'* she said. I know that accidents happen, and some can kill. I keep hold of the knife.

When evening comes, my son dresses up in his bat wings, ready to go out to trick-or-treat.

'Take a picture for Daddy,' he tells me. He smiles a big grin, holding the pumpkin up proudly, its wonky eyes glowing with candlelight. I press send on the phone; a small glimpse into our little world while my husband works away.

The rain falls heavy and cold as we walk from door to door, but my son doesn't mind the weather. He is excited to be out after dark, with the pumpkins burning, and the smell of candle-wick in the air.

Lungwort

'Happy Halloween! Would you like a treat?' he says, holding out a plate of gingerbread stars and sticky treacle cake. He knows that Halloween is about treats and wants to share. His offering is given without expectation of anything in return, and he is thrilled when he is given lollipops, little toys and a small bag of penny coins in exchange.

'Thank you very much!' he says, surprised by each gift, their kindness like a seed in his heart.

When we get home, he adds the pennies to his garden jar.

'People are very kind,' he says. Sometimes, it feels hard to know the truth of this world I am handing down, but these small things help him see the good that it can hold.

The table is laid with a red cloth and the golden candles, hot soup and soda bread ready for my parents to arrive. For my son, it is a day of sugar and colour, spiced biscuits, and gifts. He wants to share it with the people he loves most. This may be a day of ghosts, but his joy fills the evening with life.

Later, after my son has lost himself to dreams, I creep outside to light a candle in the dark. It is raining heavily now, and my matches sputter as I strike. I don't know if my sister will see it, if it will lead her home, but I light it just in case, and I sit, alone in the dark, beside its tiny flame. A face watches from a neighbouring window, peering from behind the glass. I breathe out embarrassment, close my eyes and say her name. I know magic cannot return her, but maybe, when the veil is thinnest, I might hear her again.

Comfrey

SYMPHYTUM OFFICINALE
Grow-together, knitbone, slippery root, bruisewort

Hold comfrey under the tongue to still
chaotic thoughts and help with grounding

Comfrey is used magically to offer support for healing, protection and endurance. Often referred to as 'knitbone' because of its ability to 'knit' broken bones back together, it is high in calcium, vitamin B_{12}, iron, silica, calcium, potassium, phosphorus, inulin, alkaloids, tannins, amino acids and allantoin. Allantoin is also found in breast milk, and encourages cell reproduction and regeneration after trauma. It can be applied as a topical remedy on sprains, pulled muscles, swellings and fractures, and on joints affected by arthritis and rheumatism. The leaves may be prepared into a poultice to draw out infection, or used as a wash to reduce the appearance of wrinkles, and soothe sunburn, eczema, dry scalp, acne, callouses and other skin irritations.

Comfrey grows well in ditches, roadside verges and wastelands, and is an excellent compost plant.

Comfrey

As the days darken, we plant for the coming year, and the return of light. I give my son a brown, unmarked paper bag, containing narcissi, bluebell, snowdrop, grape hyacinth, tulips and crocus. He peeks in at the dry, brown bulbs.

'They don't look very tasty,' he says, wrinkling his nose.

'They are not for eating. These are bulbs, and next year they will be flowers,' I say, as I take a handful and throw them in the air. He laughs as they fall down, then takes a small handful and copies me, tossing them upwards.

'Now, we dig where they land. If we plant too deep, the flowers won't show. If we plant them too shallow, they might freeze,' I tell him, kneeling down and pushing a stick into the ground. First try, and I hit rubble. I prise out the broken concrete and shale with my fingers until the hole is deep enough to hold the tulip bulb that waits nearby.

'You put it in like this, big bottom first,' I say, popping it in.

'Big bum, in you go,' he says, repeating the move.

'Remember to cover it up with a blanket. That way it will stay warm when it snows,' I say, tamping down the soil.

We repeat this act of throwing, digging, burying until all the bulbs are hidden in the ground. There is a magic to it that delights us both.

'Goodnight, bulbs. You need to sleep because you will be flowers next year,' my son says, before we head back inside, our hands sticky with mud and our fingers cold. Evening draws in quick, and the sun is gone. We make cocoa and tea, and curl up on the sofa to read. He chooses a book about a kind giant. I read up on the principles of green manure. As I watch him flicking through the brightly coloured pages, reading out words he remembers but does not know, I realise we are both quietly growing, under this wintering soil.

SEED THREE

Creeping Buttercup

RANUNCULUS REPENS
St Anthony's turnips, Meg-many-feet, crazy cup

Hang buttercups around the neck as
the moon wanes to restore sanity

Creeping buttercup is an analgesic and was traditionally used to treat sores, aches and rheumatic pains. Mixed with wild garlic, it has been used as an insect repellant against midges, although buttercup can cause skin irritation in some. It was thought that applying buttercup to the udders of cows would increase the yield and richness of the milk. All parts of the buttercup are poisonous unless heated or dried.

The creeping buttercup grows well in wet meadows, pastures, woods and wastelands.

When the local school organises a concert by a visiting flamenco guitarist, I ask if my son and I can go. He loves music and, living rurally, we don't often get the chance to see musicians play live. Even though my son does not attend the school, they agree to let us join in the event.

When we arrive at the village hall, the schoolchildren are already seated in neat lines, two teachers to each row. My son recognises other children from the estate. As we make our way to sit at the back of the room, he smiles, and waves hello.

The guitarist plays each tune with passion and soon the music pulls my son up out of the chair to dance. He clicks his imaginary castanets high in the air. A little girl turns to watch as he stamps and twirls his dance. When he notices her, he smiles and holds out his hand.

'You can dance too, if you like?' he says. The girl grins and stands up, wriggling and stomping to the sound of the guitar. It is beautiful and fun, and I laugh.

'Sit back down in your seat!' the teacher shouts. The girl sits down immediately, hands on her lap, face forward, eyes down. My son stops dancing.

'Did I do something wrong, Mummy?' he asks me.

'No, darling. Of course not,' I say. The teacher looks at me, unsmiling.

'The children are not allowed to dance. It will get out of control,' she says. I wonder what is wrong with losing a little bit of control, and go to tell her so.

My son rubs away the tears from his face, and sets his mouth firm. He is trying not to cry.

Creeping Buttercup

'Mummy, let's go. Let's go now,' my son whispers, tugging at my top. I keep quiet, and help him back into his winter coat.

Once outside, he runs off, angry at the invisible rules he did not understand his dance could break. When he calms down enough to talk, he comes back to me.

'The music made me fizzy inside. I had to dance, or I would go pop! Did I do that wrong?' he asks.

'There is nothing wrong with dancing. You are a beautiful dancer,' I tell him, taking his hand and dancing with him on the grass. I do not want my son to be reprimanded for being himself, for loving music, or making a mess, or singing loud. So much of his life is about rigid control: what he eats, when he eats, how he medicates, what checks to do. He needs no more hard lines in his young days.

I don't always get it right. Some days, I am tired, and quick-tempered from lack of sleep. I struggle to find the energy to run around the village dressed as a pirate, or to offer enthusiasm at his latest exploration. My mother used to call it 'the arsenic hour', and it is all I can do to keep my eyes open and my body moving.

Sometimes, he gets frustrated that I cannot let go of the demands of this adult world. He wants me to play as he does, and tries so hard to help me enter his games. When I do, when I remember that the world won't fall if I let loose the ropes, I discover such delight that I am left in awe of this little person. He doesn't need a teacher to tell him what is important to learn; he is finding that out for himself. His own curiosity drives him to want to know how the world was formed, what the universe holds, what is buried under the soil, how plants grow, how his body works, what language is, what faith is; how life begins, and ends. His days are a constant flow of explorations and discoveries. My role is to answer as best I can, and show him that it is okay not to know the answers sometimes.

Alongside this, I am his carer. Before he was born, I was his blood and bone. I stripped my cells to build his body, and gave him safe harbour in my womb. When he was a baby, my milk gave him sustenance to grow. When he was diagnosed with type one diabetes, I had to learn to be his body once again, in order to help him survive. Three years on, I still make mistakes. I miss the warning signs of hypoglycaemia, and end up having to force-feed him glucose as his eyes lose focus and he goes limp and starts to shake. I chase the highs, holding him tight as he thrashes his small fists against my body, his blood thick and raging with sugar. Every day, I end with a promise to do better tomorrow.

I can teach him numbers, so that he can count the carbohydrates in all that he eats and drinks. I can teach him how to check his bloods and how to inject, and what to do if he is low or high. I can teach him all these things, and more, but I am not just his teacher. I am not just his carer. I am here to nurture the space around him, to create the right soil for him to grow. I do not want him to feel afraid, or ashamed. I want him to love his body, and feel confident in his skin; to race over fields, climb across the rocks, ride his bike too fast along the lane without hearing my fearful voice. I want him to follow his dreams, to believe he can live in this world as he is, and not apologise for who that is. When the music lifts him up out of his seat, I want him to dance, and not worry about losing control.

There is a vocabulary of domination that comes with

diabetes. People talk about *getting it under control*, but we cannot fight what is part of ourselves. It is not a battle; we are not at war. We are not in control. We are learning to dance and diabetes is a tricky partner. We must learn the steps and routines, then turn up every day and dance with our eyes shut; responsive, pre-emptive, synergistic. It is without respite but the dance, that can teach us something too.

We are discovering it together; his hope giving light to my sadness, my courage giving support to his faltering steps. In this trip, slip, hit and misfire way, we are learning to dance the stories of our lives.

Feverfew

TANACETUM PARTHENIUM
Bachelor's button, devil daisy, nosebleed, vetter-voo

Plant around your house to prevent illness from entering

Feverfew was widely planted in the gardens of medieval Europe to protect against the plague. Although bitter to taste, the leaves can be made into a tincture or infusion to relieve migraine, headaches, inflammation, dizziness, tinnitus, menstrual symptoms and symptoms caused by perimenopause.

Feverfew grows prolifically in poor soil.

Feverfew

For my father, life was something to be conquered by will. Any success is equal to the effort we make. In this way, every failure is a fault. I *should have* worked harder. I *should have* done better. I *should have* made a different choice. Some things, though, are out of our control. Still, when my son became sick, it was easy to blame myself.

*

'Come along, it will be fine,' I say as my son clings to my body, begging me to let him stay at home. He is two years old and believes Mummy can kiss everything better, but I know that this is not true.

For six months, I have been trying to tell the doctors that my son is not well. They tell me that it is a childhood virus, teething, the *terrible twos*. Only, he doesn't get better. He doesn't grow out of it. I spend hours cutting every label out of his clothes, because he does not like the way they feel on his skin. I carry him screaming from crowded places, because the loud noises hurt his ears. I stop going out, because his body stiffens in fear when I try to get him into the car. I hold his fists as he thrashes against himself, panic in his eyes. I wonder if he is autistic.

Then, I start to notice other things. The cold he just can't shake off. The sores that take too long to heal. His clothes don't fit and I pack them away, not because he has grown but because he has lost so much weight, they have become too big again. *Lost his puppy fat*, people say, but when I bathe him, I see his ribs pushing against his pale skin. I change bedsheets, nappies, clothing – four, five, six times a day – because he keeps wetting them through. He is thirsty, hungry, tired; wanting all the time and never satisfied. His eyes are ringed with a purple bruise. His smile has gone. He becomes listless. He sleeps more and more. I listen to his chaotic breathing, wipe the sweat from his skin.

For five months this goes on. I ask the doctors and the nurses to tell me what is wrong with my son who, up until this year, has never been sick. They tell me it is *common for older mothers to over-worry*, and send me home. I ask the alternative healers, and they tell me to detox his soul and give him herbs. I ask the grandparents, and they give me syrup of figs. All the time, I watch my son slip away, not knowing how to help him, the words lost as he holds on to me, a lifeboat in this terrifying sea. I must fight for him. I must fight and make them listen. I must save his life.

When I call the surgery, the receptionist triages us as non-urgent, and tells me to calm down. The first available appointment is at 5.30 p.m. I have to wait until the end of the day. My son stops crying and starts to scream, pointing to his stomach and telling me he has a pain. I wait for my husband to return home. I am afraid.

'Back again?' the doctor says, letting out a sigh as I walk into the consulting room. It is the end of the day. He is tired. He wants to go home. I am nothing but an overanxious older mother to him. I sit with my son on my lap. My husband holds my hand, as I repeat the liturgy of symptoms again. I add in the constipation that has been ongoing for two weeks, and the strange, pear-drop odour on my son's breath. I describe the way he seems to pant instead of breathe, how he is unable to stay awake, unable to walk, and screams in pain. All the while, my little boy sits patiently on my lap, holding my hand.

Feverfew

The doctor takes out a thermometer to check my son's temperature, and listens to his chest. Then he turns to me and smiles.

'I am sure it is nothing to worry about, Mrs Bennett,' he says.

'Ms,' I reply, reflexively.

'You really must stop worrying, Mrs Bennett. It's just a virus, maybe a little chest infection. If you are concerned, you can give him infant paracetamol to help with the fever,' he tells me, handing over a prescription. My husband and I look at each other. We checked our son's temperature before we came out. It was normal.

'Are you sure his temperature is raised?' I ask. The doctor sighs again, and looks at his watch.

'Children get these sorts of things at his age. A couple of days, and your son should be right as rain,' he tells me. This time, I am not backing down. I speak back.

'Can you check his temperature again, please? Only, I don't think he has a fever. I think he may have diabetes,' I say. I have searched online, and his symptoms fit the warning signs. Inside, I am shaking, but I try to keep my voice steady and firm.

The doctor checks my son's temperature again. There is a pause. He hands us a sample pot for my son to wee into. When we return it, the doctor dips a paper stick into the urine. It changes to a deep purple. He takes my son's tiny finger and lances it with a needle. My son pulls back in surprise, but does not cry. The doctor does not speak. He checks the results, then turns to look at us, a change in his face.

'Your son has diabetic ketoacidosis. He needs to go to hospital at once. I will call ahead to let the paediatric ward know you are coming. It will be quicker for you to take him yourselves,' he tells us, avoiding eye contact as he speaks.

'Mummy, I hungry. Go home now?' my son says, pulling at my arm.

'Can I get him something to eat first?' I ask. I still don't really understand what is happening.

'No. You must go straight to the ward,' the doctor replies, standing to open the door.

At the hospital, we are greeted by nurses who are there waiting, ready with questions and machines. It is then that I realise that we are not going home. I send my husband home to get an overnight bag.

'Food, Mummy. Food now?' my son asks. His chart says *Nil By Mouth*. I am still breastfeeding, but they tell me that this counts, and so even this comfort must be denied. A nurse applies thick cream to numb his hands and arms. My son thinks cream is something that heals you, and assumes that his hands are poorly. This is something he understands.

'Hands sick, Mummy,' he tells me, holding his bandaged paws up so that I can see.

They take us to a different room, where colourful plastic fish bob up and down in a plastic tube. My son points to them and smiles. The nurses try to find a vein to insert the cannula. He needs insulin and fluids urgently, but he is too badly dehydrated and his veins have collapsed. I have to hold him down as they push the needle in, again and again, his eyes widening with fear.

'Mummy, why you let them hurt me, Mummy, why?' he sobs. He trusts that I will protect him, and does not understand why I am letting these strangers hurt him in this way.

'It will be over soon, my love. You must stay still and let the nurses help you,' I say. Each time they try to insert the needle, he tries to be brave. I am trying to do the same.

'What is happening, Mummy? Mummy, take home, please,' he cries. After an hour of trying, they finally manage to get the cannula inserted between his toes.

Two hours after the first insulin is administered, my husband walks into the room. For months, my son has screamed whenever his daddy has come near. Now, he looks up and holds his arms wide for a hug. I can see the wrist bones protruding against the skin where his hospital tag has been tied.

'Daddy, love,' he whispers, his voice croaky from the crying. My husband reaches down to him, and holds him tight. We are both crying. Our son has come back.

The machine blips his vitals through the night. Nurses come and draw blood, administer fluids and insulin, and test, test, test. When they think I am out of earshot, I hear them discussing his case.

'He's lucky to be alive, that one, another hour . . .' they say. I turn away, and cry. I listen to his shallow, uneven breaths, and will him to fight. Despite it all, I could not protect him. I tell him that I am sorry that I cannot kiss it better this time.

My son is two and a half, and has type one insulin-dependent diabetes mellitus. It is lifelong, life-threatening, and incurable. Our lives are not the same as we began the day with. I look out of the hospital window, over the orange city sky, and make a wish on the long-dead stars.

Please, let him be okay.

Sweet Woodruff

GALIUM ODORATUM
Wild baby's breath, master-of-the-woods, herb Walter, ladies-in-the-hay

Place woodruff in a leather pouch and keep it on
you to protect against harm

Sweet woodruff is associated with protection, money, fertility and abundance. It was commonly used as a strewing herb in churches and in pagan spring festivals. Containing the anticoagulant coumarin, it has been used to treat blood clots, general digestive and heart problems, anxiety, hepatitis, varicose veins and insomnia. It makes a good addition to potpourri or scent bags, having a similar base-note scent to benzoin.

Sweet woodruff thrives in semi-shade and sheltered spaces.

Sweet Woodruff

My son opens his eyes, and smiles. Then he remembers and fear fills his face. He reaches down to his chest, and rips off the monitor pads with surprising force. Then he notices the red light of the clip attached to his toe, and plasters on his feet. He starts shouting again, words glottal with sobs.

'What happening, Mummy? What happening me? Go home, Mummy, go home,' he cries. The machines send out emergency bleeps. A nurse runs in. She notices the pads and disconnected monitors. To our surprise, she doesn't rush to put them back on just yet.

'Shall we keep them off for a wee while then?' she says to him, smiling as she gently takes his arm to do his checks. From that moment, he is in love with the nurses.

It is not the case with the doctors. When the consultant arrives, my son recognises him from the night before.

'What is Bad Man doing in my room, Mummy?' he asks in a low voice.

'This is the doctor, poppet. He is here to help you,' I tell him. Two more doctors arrive, carrying clip charts. These three men tower over my son, who looks up from the hospital bed. They begin to talk about the pancreas, and beta cells, and the autoimmune response, but I am unable to take any of it in because my son is crying and pulling at me.

'Just walk away, Mummy, just walk away,' he pleads. I have taught him that if anyone does something to his body that he doesn't like, or if anyone makes him feel scared, he must walk away and get help. He is just doing what he has been told.

The consultant is losing patience. He has a ward round to do. He tells me that I must stay and listen to what they are saying, but my son's anguish is physical to me. I decide that the adults in the room must wait. I pick up my son and we go for a walk, up and down the corridor, just as I used to do when he was newborn. He rests his head on my shoulder, and I sing quietly to him.

'. . . I like the flowers that blossom in January. The witch hazel blooming so gold in the woods. I like the flowers that blossom in January. They tell me that life can be good . . .' It is a song I have sung since his birth, made up for him during the long hours of sleepless nights, as we walked, my arms aching from the weight of his little life.

I look at his face that used to be so full of joy. It is pale, and broken with sadness. I want to explain to him what is happening, but I don't know how. Until now, my son believed I could kiss all things better. Now, he knows this is not true. Everything in his world is having to rearrange itself. He is learning how to endure.

When we return to the room, the doctors have gone. My husband is reading the pile of leaflets they have left behind. He is arming himself to protect his family. At that moment, I am so grateful to be married to him, this man who stands like the oak through all our storms.

My son sleeps in my arms. For now, he appears free. Then, he startles.

'No, no, no, Mummy, no!' he cries out, and I know then that he will never be free of it, and neither will we.

Field Scabious

KNAUTIA ARVENSIS
Pins-and-needles, curl-doddy, lady's pincushion, gypsy flower

Used to protect against illness
or accidents caused by dark magic

Field scabious has long been valued as a medicinal herb. It was traditionally used to treat bubonic sores, scabies, boils, abscesses, bruising, worms, typhus fever and infections of the heart. More contemporary uses include the treatment of eye inflammations, eczema, rashes, coughs and sore throats. Both the fresh and dried plant are used in dye-making.

Field scabious grows especially well in poor, sandy soil.

I know that we have to go home but, when it comes time to leave the hospital, I realise that part of me wants to stay here. I want to stay where it is safe. Where I can still hold on to the illusion that my son will be cured.

Before we are allowed to leave, we have to show the paediatric diabetes nurse that we can manage his medical care. Today, I am learning how to do a cannula change. First, I must remove his insulin pump. Then, I must prime and measure the insulin, replace the new vial in the pump, and insert the attached tube and cannula using a large needle, fired at high speed into fatty tissue. This will need doing every two to three days, more if the cannula fails.

My son listens by my side. I am shaking. I don't want to hurt him, but I have to prove I can do this. My husband has already done it, twice. Both times, I have had to hold our son down.

'Diabetes is not your friend. If you get this wrong, your child's life could be ruined,' the nurse says. I try to hide my tears. She softens her voice, and places a hand on my arm.

'I know it is hard. You came in with your son, and you leave with a different child,' she tells me. My son tugs frantically at my arm, face full of panic.

'Why, Mummy, why leave me?' he begs, crying. I glare at the nurse, and reassure him that I will not be exchanging him for another child. His fear reminds me that he is trying to make sense of this all with a two-year-old's logic. I put the pump supplies to one side and walk up and down the corridor, holding him in my arms, his body hot and damp with stress and rising sugar levels.

Field Scabious

The pump must not be disconnected for longer than an hour. I have run out of time. We go back in, and when he sees the medical equipment on the bed he begins to cry. There is no way to ease him into it. I hand him a little yellow digger to hold.

'Here, Yellow Digger will help you be strong,' I say, as he takes the toy into his hands, his focus briefly held by the scoop that goes up and down. I release the infusion set with a loud click-snap, pull out the insertion needle and rip off the old cannula.

'There, there, hush, all done,' I say, repeating the age-old motherhood mantra again.

'All finished now?' he asks, wiping away his tears with the back of his hand, before driving his digger over the make-believe land of pillow and sheet.

A while later, my husband and I take him outside for some fresh air. As we walk the hospital grounds, I notice he is shaking and pale. We do a finger-prick check. Too low. This is our first unsupervised hypoglycaemic episode. I fluster as I try to get the straw into the juice carton.

'Drink, darling, that's it, drink it all up,' I say, holding it to his mouth.

'Not thirsty,' he says, pushing it away.

'You must, sweetheart,' I tell him, trying not to let him hear the fear in my voice.

When we go back to the ward, he starts to cry.

'I don't want to go home. Home made me sick, and the nurse-mummies made food work,' he tells me.

'Poppet, you got sick because we didn't know what was wrong, but now we know. You have diabetes and Mummy and

Daddy will look after you, just like the nurse-mummies do,' I tell him. I hope it is true.

They let us stay an extra night. At the end of the day shift, the diabetes nurse gives us a large carrier bag filled with supplies. As my son sleeps, I unpack the contents onto the bed. Blood glucose monitor, ketone monitor, testing strips, lancets, infusion sets, insulin pen, tiny syringes, leaflets, inch-thick manuals, a fabric pump carrier, a yellow sharps bin, a set of medical scales, an orange box containing a single glass vial of glucagon powder and a two-inch syringe needle that we must insert into muscle in the event of a severe hypoglycaemic episode, tubes of gel for rubbing into his mouth if his cognitive function is compromised, a diary for monitoring his activity, insulin doses and everything he eats and drinks, and boxes and boxes of needles, needles, needles.

As I look at all these things laid out on the bed, I start to cry. This is his life now. Our lives. I try to tell myself I am lucky, that at least we got him here in time, that he is not dying, but still the tears come. My husband holds me.

'It isn't fair,' I whisper.

It never is.

Ivy-Leaved Toadflax

CYMBALARIA MURALIS
Mother-of-thousands, herb of the Madonna, creeping-jenny, rabbit-flower

Use as a wreath to protect the home from evil spirits

Ivy-leaved toadflax was a traditional remedy for jaundice, liver complaints, skin diseases and scrofula. Astringent, anti-inflammatory, hepatic and detergent, it can be prepared as a poultice, ointment or infusion to treat haemorrhoids, skin irritations and eye inflammations, or boiled to make a liquid fly-deterrent. High in vitamin C, the leaves are edible and have a similar flavour to watercress. The seeds can be pressed to make a substitute for olive oil, and the flowers can be used to make yellow dye. It is thought to have made its way into the wild after escaping from the Chelsea Physic Garden sometime in the seventeenth century.

Ivy-leaved toadflax grows abundantly in walls, pavements and stony ground.

A man arrives to replace the wire-and-post boundary with a four-foot-high wooden fence. It has been decided that our garden, with its Hügelkultur beds and nettle crops, does not give the '*right impression to prospective buyers or homeowners visiting the estate*', and so we are to be hidden from sight.

Our garden occupies the exposed corner plot, and is overlooked on three sides. What we lose in privacy we gain in garden size, but when the north-east wind whips around the gable end, there is little protection for the things that grow. The fence that they erect to hide us will serve to protect our fledgling plants as well. When the job is done, I will repurpose the sturdy posts to support raised beds, and the wire will make a cage for our peas. Nothing is lost in this exchange. I don't object.

What they fail to mention is that the fence will only be erected on the sides visible to those visiting the private part of the estate. The parts not bordering the access road are left untouched, the wire-and-post remaining in place. We are left with a three-quarter fence, a façade of respectability over what is not approved.

My son and I decide to plant a wildlife hedge to fill the gap. The hedgerows of my childhood were full of heavy sweetness that scented the long summer months. Running alongside fields of barley and oats, they were woven with honeysuckle, dog rose and bramble thorn. In June, my friend and I drank nectar from the honeysuckle flowers. In late August, we stained our lips purple from the blackberry fruits, gorging on those last hot days before returning to school.

Here, the hedgerows are full of hawthorn, elder and sloe. In

Ivy-Leaved Toadflax

May, they flounce like brides against the green before they let their petals fall, like summer snow, all down the lane. Come winter, they will give us berries, crimson and wine, to protect our hearts and souls.

My son chooses three native blackberries to begin. We dig them in, bare-root, beside the gate.

'The hedge is very small, Mummy,' my son says, not convinced these little sticks will grow at all.

'That is because it is young. It won't take long. I bet that by next year, it will be as tall as you,' I tell him. He seems amazed at this possibility. For him, it has taken all the time he has known to get as tall as he is.

'Like my tree! That is as big as me now,' he says, smiling. He knows the story of the conker that I planted when he was waiting to be born, and loves to check himself against its growing height.

'Yes, like your tree. Only these will grow more shoots, and more, and one day, we will get lots of blackberries to eat,' I tell him.

'Yum! Jam!' he says, licking his lips in anticipation. 'Will Mister Robin like blackberries?'

'Yes, and yellowhammers, and thrush, and blackbirds, and even little mice,' I reply, making my hands into little mouse paws, and sticking out my front teeth. He laughs at my goofy face.

'I am going to build them a house in our hedge!' he decides, busying himself with finding stones and sticks to build. He selects the smooth, rectangular sandstone offcuts that he has squirrelled away; the upside of living on the old stoneworks site is the plentiful supply of materials for construction games.

Before long, his hedge-house has a door, lintel, two windows, stone steps, a flagstone hearth and a slate flat roof. It is better than where we live.

'It needs a bed, Mummy. Can we make one now?' he asks, pulling at my hand. We choose a little square of blue felt from the fabric box, which he lays down over a small pile of leaves.

'There! Now the animals can have a house to keep them safe and warm, just like us,' he declares.

The fairy stories taught me that thorns were bad but that sometimes they can help. This little blackberry hedge will grow and spread, and, like the briars that grew around Snow White's bed, it will protect.

Wild Columbine

AQUILEGIA VULGARIS
Crowfoot, culverwort, granny's bonnet, sow-wort, lion's herb

Use to invoke courage, wisdom and clarity in making choices

Columbine has been used in folk medicine since medieval times. Traditionally fermented into a wine to restore a woman's strength, it is immune-boosting, astringent and antiseptic. The root can be used to treat eczema and heal light wounds, the leaves can be used to help soothe a sore mouth, and the seeds can be dried and crushed into a topical paste to kill ticks, or as a shampoo to treat head lice and scabs.

Wild columbine is found growing in meadows, ditches and around old house ruins.

All My Wild Mothers

When I was eight years old, my parents nearly died. We were staying in northern Spain, in the Picos mountains. My parents wanted to go for a hike, their two teenage daughters did not. My mother, deciding it was only a short walk, left me in their care at the guesthouse, with a promise that we would not venture outside the room until her return. At first it was exciting to be left alone but when dark fell, and they had not returned, the excitement turned to fear. When I ask now, my sisters tell me they were not scared, but I remember the way that fear grew, like a hunger, as the hours passed.

This story is not a tragedy though. This story is a *could-have-been*, the kind of story we tell to reassure ourselves that everything works out okay in the end. Here is the end then: our parents made it back alive. The mountain fog had come down too quickly and my father, trying to look brave in the face of fear, had got them further lost. Instead of a short walk, they were out for over twelve hours, with no warm clothes, no map, no equipment, no food and no way of calling for help. When my mother remembers the walk years later, she recalls the ridge they crawled along, the stones falling from its side, and the way the white closed in front of her eyes. She tells me that she expected to die that day and just kept thinking of her children, left in the guesthouse alone.

Our family stories are tinged with a danger that we only see in the retelling. At the time, it was just life. My brothers, not even fourteen years in age, sent to canoe the length of the River Wye alone. A camping trip in Death Valley in mid-July, with no water in our trunk. My father, surfing for the first time on a remote Hawaiian beach, pulled out to sea as my mother looked on. It is only later in life that they admit how close to risk we had often been. Why did they risk so much? When I asked my father why he did these things, he laughed.

'Life is an adventure, and I've always been lucky,' he said. This was a world to be explored and conquered, each mountain demanding to be climbed. My memory is full of scenes of epic beauty that play like David Attenborough films. Look closer, though, and what you will see is my father up ahead, telling us to 'keep walking', or 'look at the view', and me walking behind, legs chafed, belly hungry and, often, very scared.

Luck, or maybe ignorance, seemed to keep them safe. Was it a challenge to death, as if to say *come and try*? The warning tells us not to tempt fate, but what if we tempt it close just so as to feel in control? *I am invincible*, the challenger says. *Catch me if you can*, the child cries, thrilled by the chase, secretly longing to be caught. I know now that there is no such game to play. Fate is fickle and swift, and sometimes cruel. We can plan, or we can leap, but we are never in control.

For my father, fate came in the middle of the night; an invisible aneurism flowering in his brain. At the age of sixty-seven, on his way to use the toilet, he had a stroke. The rest of us slept on in our houses, unaware.

'Your husband was very lucky,' the consultant said, as he prepared my mother for the possibility of permanent and significant disability. My mother smiled and listened, and when the consultant left the room she turned to my father, who could not reply.

'You're going to have to do better than this. Don't think I'm going to spoonfeed you for the rest of our lives,' she told him. She was never one for bedside sympathy but, for the next six weeks, she drove to the hospital every day, and found out everything she needed to know about stroke rehabilitation and care. When my father went home, the first thing he did was walk up the stairs. It took him two hours.

'Where there is a will, there is a way,' he said. It was a phrase I often heard growing up. To my father, the stroke was just another challenge to be conquered.

Despite this determination, he never regained full use of his legs. Not long after this return, frustrated with his body and furious from an argument, he left the house without asking for help. My mother told me later that she sat with her arms folded, until the worry overtook her anger and she went out to look for him. She walked for two hours, calling his name. She knew his deafness meant he couldn't hear her, but she kept calling, all the same. When she returned, sure that my father was dead somewhere on the fell, she found him waiting. He had fallen a short distance from the house and had crawled back, dragging himself along the ground with his good arm. My mother, choosing to turn left outside the house, rather than right, had missed him. A different decision, and she'd have found him straight away.

'That was rather silly of me,' he said and, even though he'd trekked across the mountains of the world, he never walked on his own again.

My father saw life as an adventure, to be shaped by his will, yet the life he led seems so different from the one they'd planned.

'I'll still show you the world. It will be an adventure,' he told her, when they were young, but he stayed with the company until he retired, and the dream was gone. It was a decision that changed their whole lives, and mine. My mother told me she had married a poet but lived her life with an engineer, and from that point our stories unfold.

Life is made up of the big and little choices that we make. When my father chose to take the engineering job, he changed the story of our lives. When my mother made the choice to surrender her dream, she did the same. These are the choices we remember. Sometimes though, it is the mundane choices that change our lives.

In the months that followed my sister's death, my mother repeated a litany of different ways to save her daughter that day. If only my sister had decided to stay at home. If only she had decided to walk past the rapids, instead of staying in the canoe. If only she had chosen a different river, a different companion, a different day. Further and further back the choices go. What if she had stayed working as a gardener, instead of becoming an outdoor educationalist? What if she had never moved to Cumbria? What if she had taken fewer risks with her one, precious life?

What if/if only. These are the bookends of our regrets. Yet, there must always be choice. When I was a young girl, my father scribbled two poems on the inside of the airing-cupboard door: Robert Frost's 'The Road Not Taken' and Ezra Pound's 'And the Days Are Not Full Enough'. He did so to remind us that life was an open adventure, and quickly lost, but maybe he missed the point? What if it was never about the road, but the choice; never about the big picture, but the quivering grass?

Perhaps the truth is that there is no road less travelled, just those small and passing moments in which we decide? Every choice shapes our lives, in ways we can never know at the start. When it doesn't turn out the way we expected, we seek to blame. We cry out, *'what if?'*, instead of *'what is'*.

German Chamomile

MATRICARIA CHAMOMILLA
Ground apple, chamaimelon, scented mayweed

Use to protect and purify the home

German chamomile is ruled by the sun god Helios. The Egyptians used chamomile in the embalming process. One of the nine sacred herbs, it was a popular ingredient in both medicinal and magical practices. Antimicrobial and mildly sedative, chamomile is now more commonly used to treat insomnia, tummy ache, stress, rheumatic pain, rashes, fevers and inflammation. It can also be used as a hair rinse or a tonic for the skin. It is commonly used in drinks and teas, and as a flavouring in beer.

Chamomile helps poorly plants to thrive.

German Chamomile

After the hospital, returning home is strange. The toys are still on the floor. The washing is still in the basket. Everything is the same; only now my son has an incurable and life-threatening autoimmune disease. I listen to him laugh as he plays with his godfather, rushing trains along the wooden train track that weaves around the living room. It has been so long since I have heard that sound.

In the kitchen, I sort out the pantry and fridge, putting all the high-carbohydrate snacks out of his reach. Food feels threatening now. I weigh out the ingredients for supper, and try to calculate the ratio of insulin to carbohydrates the way the doctor has shown us how to do. My brain feels slow, and I struggle with the maths. Even though I am just weighing potatoes, I start to cry.

When the meal is cooked, I give my son his insulin dose, then put his food down on the table. He pushes it around the plate. I watch the clock. The insulin will start to work in fifteen minutes.

'Come on, darling, just a few mouthfuls,' I beg, choo-chooing the loaded fork towards his mouth. He looks up at me with tired, sad eyes.

'Mummy-food not as tasty as hospital food,' he says, and refuses to open his mouth. I scrape the meal into the bin, and give him jelly babies instead. It is a back-to-front Wonderland world we live in now.

My husband and I take it in turns to test his blood glucose throughout the night. When they drop too low, we coax sugary foods into his sleepy mouth. An hour later, and his blood glucose runs high in rebound. We work out the insulin correction to bring it down, and get the measurements wrong. We lance his tiny finger again. Too low. We wake him, and feed him glucose, then repeat the whole process again. When we wake him this time, he grumbles back.

'No, Mummy, this is all wrong,' he slurs.

He is right, of course, it is. We are exhausted, but the threat of him not waking is very real and terrifying. We are back where we were when he was newborn: inexperienced, and overwhelmed with love, and fear.

Borage

BORAGO OFFICINALIS
Starflower, bee bush, bugloss

Use borage to bring hope in dark and difficult times

Borage is particularly good for those who are highly self-critical and, as a result, become exhausted. It stimulates breast-milk production and can be used as an adrenal gland tonic for nervous exhaustion and adrenal depletion, including the symptoms of depression, anxiety and general fatigue. It is a useful medicine for those who suffer chronic long-term illness and hormonal issues. It has the highest known plant source of GLA, an omega 6 fatty acid, and is a good source of B vitamins and trace minerals. Excellent at repelling pests and attracting pollinators, it also makes a great compost and plant food. The leaves and flowers can be eaten raw as a salad, cooked as a vegetable, or used as a herb in soups, salads, drinks, preserves, jellies, sauces and desserts.

Borage grows well in gardens, fields, wasteland and dumps.

In the months that followed my son's diagnosis, we tried to find our way. Sometimes, as we struggled to make sense of it all, we forgot his world was changing too. Friends and family attempted to reassure. *He is so young*, they told us, *it will just seem normal to him soon.*

I am hanging up the washing on the line. The autumn is drawing to a close, but it is still warm enough to be outside. My two-year-old son plays at my feet. He is creating a new compound for his dinosaurs. He holds up a small plastic digger. The scoop is hanging off.

'Can you fix Yellow Digger, Mummy?' he asks. I kneel down and take a look. Even with the magic he imbues me with, I cannot fix it this time.

'I am sorry, darling, I don't think I can. It is too broken. I think this one will have to be thrown in the bin,' I tell him, putting the droopy digger to one side. He picks the toy back up, turning it over in his hands. This digger is important to him. It helps him feel strong when he is scared, reassuring in a growly digger voice that he can be brave. To him, it is more than a broken toy.

'We can have a go at fixing it, if you want?' I ask. I don't think I can, but I can at least try.

He doesn't reply at first. Then he looks at me, and I know it is something more than the digger.

'What is wrong, poppet?' I ask.

'Can the doctor fix my diabetes?' he asks me. I look at my son, sitting on the ground in the mud, his broken digger in his hand. We all want to believe in miracles at times. It is

Borage

important that he knows the truth of his body, yet how do I explain to my small child that diabetes is not the endgame, that this lifelong disease could leave him blind, or that he might lose his limbs, or end up on dialysis; that if the blood glucose goes too low, or too high, he could end up in a coma, or die? That even if we 'manage' it, we are at best, a third-rate hammer slamming down on the pinhead complexity of the human body, and we will fail?

'No, sweetheart. They are working on it but right now, they can't fix it,' I tell him.

His smile falters. I watch as his little hands ball into tight, white fists. He is trying to hold in the feeling but it is too big for him, and it pushes out.

'You should throw me in the bin!' he shouts. I am stunned by his words.

'Why, darling, why?' I ask, tears cracking my voice. He exhales a loud breath, and his body slumps.

'Because I am broken, Mummy, and when things are broken, you need to throw them in the bin,' he tells me. What can I say to that? He has coped with so much in his small life. I see it buried deep within his body, silently shaping him into the man he will become. His illness makes him strong, but it also makes him sad. I do not have the answers that he seeks. My little boy, my bruised and needle-punctured child, what answers can I give? I am afraid. I cannot make this all right with a kiss, and I am sorry. I am sorry.

I know what it feels like to feel broken. No child should feel this way. I take his mud-smudged face into my hands, and look him straight in the eyes.

'You hear me now. You are not broken. You are beautiful and

amazing, and I am the luckiest mummy in the world to have you as my son. You remember that,' I say, with force. I need him to hear it, deep down inside his heart. I need to hear it as well.

Enchanter's Nightshade

CIRCAEA LUTETIANA
Sorcerer of Paris, witches' grass, great-witch herb, wood-magic herb

Use to heal from bitter memories

Enchanter's nightshade was traditionally gathered on Samhain and used in rituals to honour the dead and invoke the spirit realm. A member of the willowherb family, it is not edible but is frequently found in spells for enchantment, hexing, shapeshifting and transformation.

Enchanter's nightshade grows in damp, shaded areas and is considered a problem weed.

We are each shaped by stories told. Which do we hide, and which ones show? Fast-forward, or rewind, depending on where you stand, and I am fifteen. It is dark, and my body shakes under the thin material of my nightdress. A neighbour, walking home late from the pub, sees me lying out on the cold ground. She knocks on the back door, calling for help, but my father is deaf and my mother, who is usually a light sleeper, sleeps deep that night and does not wake. The neighbour lets herself in through the unlocked door, walks up the stairs to their room and shakes them awake.

'Your daughter is outside. She is hurt,' she says.

In the Accident and Emergency ward, the triage nurse sees bruising and asks me what has happened. I do not want to admit that I have done it to myself. The bruises go back too far, inflicted night after night in the dark, the heavy stones smashing down onto my arms and legs, again and again. If I managed to hit with the right pressure, it was a relief to feel the white noise inside my head recede, to feel the pain that tangled my body focused onto a specific place.

'It was an accident. I fell out of the window,' I say. I don't know that a nurse can tell things like the age of bruising, or the type of impact. There is hushed talk behind the curtain. I am discharged, and referred to a psychiatrist. *Self-harm. Suicide risk.*

'How could I not know?' my mother says, as we drive home.

Every week, my mother drives me to a white-walled clinic, where I sit on the other side of the large teak table and look at ink splats on cards. I tell the pin-shaped woman that I can see a butterfly, a demon, a flower. After three months, she asks my family to attend. We sit in a circle in the white room. The psychiatrist asks if there is anything that I want to say. I tell them about the exhaustion that swallows me up, the way I always seem to be viewing the world from outside, never able to connect. I tell them about the pain and the hurting, and the way my head screams all the time. They stay silent.

The problem is me.

Alkanet

ALKANNA TINCTORIA
Pheasant's eye, dyer's bugloss, orchanet, hoary puccoon

Burn with patchouli to lift melancholy

Alkanet has a long history in herbalism. A strong astringent and powerful diuretic, it was traditionally used to treat pleurisy and lift depression, and can be used to clear toxins from the body. The leaves can be prepared as a tea to reduce fever and ease bronchial congestion, or applied topically as a salve to soothe bruised, sore or wounded skin. A red dye can be prepared from the root and has been used for centuries as a colourant in cosmetics, furniture staining, and in beverages and food, although it has some liver toxicity. It is popular with pollinators, high in nitrogen, and can be steeped to make plant food.

Alkanet grows well on roadside verges, disturbed wasteland, and in abandoned fields.

Alkanet

By twenty-six, the world had become a scary place and I was not able to live in it very well. It felt like an ending, but it wasn't.

It was 1997. My not-yet-husband and I had moved into a two-up, two-down brick terrace house in the roughest part of Nottingham. We had graduated not long before, and had plans to set up an arts company, but funding cuts made it difficult to find work, and we were broke. Every week we handed over fifty pounds in rent money to the sallow-faced man in his crumpled brown suit, and he ticked it off in his leather-bound book. When the wind blew in through the hole in the back wall, we fixed it with cardboard and tape. At night we slept on a mattress by the fire, and during the day we signed up for free, council-run training courses in business skills, just so we could get a hot lunch. I read a book on colour therapy that said orange and yellow helped clear the creative chakras and encourage positivity. I bought cheap emulsion, and painted the walls with sunset stripes, but mould blossomed up each one, like black roses creeping through abandoned wrought-iron bars. This life was meant to be bohemian, but really, it was just hard.

My parents came to visit. We heated soup on our camping stove, and ate it sat on an old rag rug in front of the small coal fire.

'From rags to riches and back again in two generations,' my father said, before they left. They didn't visit again. Not long after, someone painted *'Everything Is Fucked'* in lurid yellow letters across our front door. I stopped going outside.

The doctor prescribed medication that made my words dissolve, and my brain too slow to read or write. The psychiatrist asked me lots of questions about why I thought something bad would happen if I went outside. He told me I had to 'recondition my behaviour' in order to overcome my agoraphobia, and suggested I take repetitive walks around the block each day to train my brain. He called it 'Cognitive Behavioural Therapy'. I asked him where he lived. He closed the lid on his expensive, gold-tipped pen and told me the problem was in my head. I didn't go back after that. I'd had enough of being told I was mad. Instead, I threw the pills away, cleared the yard of rubbish, bought some plant pots and tried to make a garden, but it was dark and not much grew but blown-in sow thistle. It was not going to work. I started to cry, and did not stop.

Not knowing what else to do, I went back to be close to the women who raised me. We handed in our notice to the man in the crumpled suit, packed our empty thistle pots into the back of our jalopy car, and drove north to Eden.

The day we left, it was the general election. The Conservatives had been in power for eighteen years of my life. Still registered at our city address, we stopped to cast our vote. The queue stretched three streets, a sense of collective determination drawing people out. By the time we reached Eden, the Conservatives had lost. Perhaps change was possible, after all.

The old estate cottage we moved into had cheap rent, no heating and damp walls, but all around it were fields and fells. With no money for furniture, we sat on cushions on the floor, and kept our food cold in a stone trough by the back door. In the summer, we swam in the river. In winter, we collected fallen wood to burn on the fire. I read a Zen proverb that said, *'before enlightenment chop wood, carry water. After enlightenment chop wood, carry water'*. This was the rhythm of our life. We told our friends we had retired to the country; it was easier than trying to explain something had broken inside. But it felt like there was hope in that home, and I began to heal.

I kept my days simple to survive. In the mornings, I wrote in a journal, ate breakfast and took a long walk. In the afternoons, I painted pictures I would never show. Usually, at some point, I cried. On Thursdays, I went to a writing group at the local college, and sometimes I cried there. Once a week I went to see a psychotherapist, who asked me questions about the past, and usually I cried there too.

I thought this was going to be the hard part. I thought if I could find out what made me this way, I would be happy, and not hurt any more. I was yet to understand this was just another passing through.

Herb Robert

GERANIUM ROBERTIANUM
Stinking Bob, death-come-quickly, dragon's blood

If the plant is picked and taken
into the home, a death will soon follow

Herb Robert was traditionally used to strengthen the blood, balance the mind and ease heartbreak. The flower, leaves and root of the plant can be used either fresh or dried. It is antibiotic, antiviral and antioxidant and provides a good immune support. Medicinally used to treat toothache, conjunctivitis, jaundice, nosebleed, gout and dysentery, it can be applied topically to wounds and bruises, or rubbed onto the skin as an insect repellant.

Herb Robert has the ability to absorb and break down poisons in the soil, and grows abundantly in areas of high radiation and heavy metal pollution.

Herb Robert

Life and death have no balance sheet, or fair-promise to keep. It is not luck, good or bad. It is as simple as this: sometimes, terrible things happen. And then sometimes, they happen again.

A year after my sister drowns, my sister-in-law is diagnosed with advanced, inoperable lung cancer. Before we know this, she loses her voice. At first, the doctors do not seem concerned. She is young, healthy and has never smoked; but her voice does not come back and the months pass. My brother tells me they have done scans. I say that just because the terrible thing happened before doesn't mean it will happen again. I tell him not to assume the worst.

I am wrong. Fifteen months after my son is diagnosed, and four years after my sister drowned, my sister-in-law dies. She is forty-nine.

On the day of her funeral, it rains. It rains on our faces, our clothes and our shoes, as we walk through the suburbs of Exeter to the cemetery. My brother reaches his arms wide, like wings, to shelter his halfway-grown twins. Our mother watches, struggling to know how to comfort her son. This death comes too soon after burying her own daughter, but she knows that he needs her now.

'It's worse for you,' she says, walking by his side. There is a hierarchy that hides within the rituals of death. After my sister died, I looked it up. According to contemporary Catholic codes of mourning, a husband or wife is due a year of mourning, a parent or child is allocated six months, a grandparent given three. Siblings, friends and distant cousins are granted just one month. Thirty days; the acceptable grief for losing a sister. A parent loses a child. A husband loses a wife. A child loses a mother. This death is worth that, that life is worth this but how do we measure what sorrow a single life is worth?

'It isn't worse,' I tell her, and take her hand.

A wet and straggling line of mourners fill up the pews in the small, non-denominational chapel. One family arrives with a small baby and toddler. They push a three-wheeled buggy past the pews, and make themselves comfortable on the floor beside the wicker casket, bringing out colouring pens and paper for the toddler, and a rainbow mat for the baby. I wonder if I should have allowed my son to come, but he is only three. I am not ready to share the strange world of funeral rites with him, and choose to do this grieving alone.

There are no priests, or prayers. Knowing death was coming, my sister-in-law prepared her funeral in advance. People stand to share their stories. A man plays folk songs on a guitar, and people sing along. It is lively and full of colour, and like her. I remember the first time we met. She was wearing rainbow dungarees and Doc Marten boots. Her head was shaved and when she smiled, it was like her whole face was laughing. I watched her as she teased my copper-headed brother. She was confident, and beautiful, and fizzing with fun. Everything about her was made of exclamation marks – all *darling!* and *yes!* and *amazing!* – exuberant with life, and very different to my awkward self.

My brother bows his head to hide his tears. Those whose lives are left truly empty remain silent; their sorrow too raw to give sound. In this moment of grief, I want to find some words to let them know I care. I am worried whatever I say will seem pointless to their pain, but I make myself stand and

Herb Robert

begin to share a story, of travelling through a storm, flying high above the rain-filled clouds and the rainbow that broke through. It shone so bright that I knew, in that moment, it was her leaving this world. It is a small tale of hope, though I do not add the moments after landing, the soft buzz of my phone; the single text message that said 'she no longer has to hold on'. These small words that cradled such sadness, and such love.

When all the speeches are over, and the singing is done, we watch the coffin being lowered into the ground. The rituals of mourning are almost complete. One by one, the white flowers are thrown. One by one, the living turn away. Over her body, the rain continues to fall without malice or praise. As I watch my brother falter and pull himself up strong again, it seems to me that it doesn't matter that she had time to tell her family that she loved them. It doesn't matter that there has been singing, or that she is free now from the pain. This is the truth of death: my sister-in-law must stay, and those who loved her most must turn away and carry on.

Back at the house, I stand close to the edge of the room, attempting to be invisible. It doesn't work. A man in a primrose-yellow shirt approaches.

'What is your relationship to the deceased?' he asks. I am confused. It feels vaguely competitive, as if assessing the value of one's loss. The peculiar hierarchy of grief is here as well. I mumble, inarticulate, trying to find the appropriate words.

'Brother,' I blurt out. He walks away. I see my husband and son at the other side of the room and wave. Their arrival offers me refuge. My husband, understanding my social discomfort without me having to explain, moves through the crowded space with ease, offering condolences; the front face of our little unit. I take the chance to escape, and go out into the garden with my son.

'This is a strange party, Mummy. Everyone is sad. Why is everybody so sad?' he asks.

'Do you remember the rainbow up in the sky? Do you remember what I said?' I ask.

'About Auntie Rainbow?' he replies. I like this name. It fits, and makes me smile.

'Yes, well, Auntie Rainbow died and this is a party for us to say goodbye. We all loved her very much. When people we love die, we feel lots of things, both happy and sad. Do you understand?' I ask, but he has wandered off. He has found a small patch of garden at the base of an old apple tree, where traces of flowers remain into November. He takes some small stones from the nearby path and arranges them in a circle, placing in two stone eyes, a nose and a wide stick smile.

'Auntie Rainbow isn't inside. She wants them to come outside. She says the flowers will make them happy,' he tells me, softly. I cuddle him, and try not to cry too much. I want to tell my brother the wise words of this little boy. We go inside to find him, but there is a slick of people all around and I don't know how to break through.

I look for my husband, but can't see him in the room. My son pulls away from my hand, and runs straight for the chocolate cake. I need to do a glucose check but I don't want to shout, so I wave my hands instead, gesturing for him to put it down. He grins, and takes a huge, sticky bite. His insulin pump alarms. I see people look around, trying to identify the sound. I apologise as I push through the crowd, but as I reach to take the plate, my son runs away again.

Herb Robert

I am suddenly very tired. I want to cry but somehow, even though this is a wake, crying seems out of place. Someone hands me a cup of tea, which I gratefully take. I spy a seat on the burgundy velvet sofa in the conservatory. It looks quiet in there, and I need to sit down. My brother built the garden room for his wife, when she was too ill to go outside. I like it in here. It is calm, and warm. I close my eyes a while, let the sun fall soft on my upturned face, breathe in a small space of quiet.

Then I hear an aeroplane sound, and open my eyes to see my son hurtling around the crowded room, arms outstretched as wings.

'Slow down, darling!' I call, trying not to yell. He hears me, turns, and runs full speed towards the sound of my voice, crashing into my arm just as I lift up the cup to take a sip. Tea spills everywhere, all over my lap and down onto the sofa below. My son runs off laughing, unaware of what he has done. I go to call for him to come back, but my words disappear as I see my brother walking across the room.

'You've ruined her sofa!' he shouts. I try to help him wipe up the stain with my sleeve.

'It doesn't clean,' he snaps, and pushes me away.

I shrink away from the sharpness of his pain, a small child again, afraid of getting it wrong. I look at his hands as they scrub at the velvet, and I want to reach out and hold them; to say that I am sorry, to tell him that I wish he had not been so wounded, that I wish he was not so alone, but I don't know how. Instead, I stay silent, my words tumbling unspoken into the space between us.

I move away from the sofa and stand on the other side of the room, silent as I watch others come to my brother's aid.

The room floods with noise and heat. I cannot focus any more; everything is colliding, until I cannot breathe. My husband looks at me and understands. He gathers up our son, and we leave; unnoticed and unseen.

I do not speak as we drive away. I am thinking about my brother. In childhood, he was magical to me; a long-haired, copper-headed rebel who drove a yellow van covered in CND signs, and read Marxist manifestos by candlelight in the barn. I kept a photograph beside my bed, and cried when he went away. I wanted so much to tell him about the garden my son made, about how he needed to go outside and see the flowers, but I was afraid of getting it wrong. So many things we never learn to speak about, our hidden hearts seeding silence in our mouths.

Rain falls across the windscreen. The windshield wipers swish and slide.

'Paint a picture, wipe it off, paint a picture, wipe it off,' my son sings, in time with their rhythm. I close my eyes, wipe away the picture of the casket, and the sofa, and the pain, and replace it with another picture, five years before.

My brother's wedding day. Over twenty years together, and the birth of two children, this day is about being witness to the journey they have shared. Vows have been made, promises offered, and now we celebrate. The night is lit by fairy lights, sparkling the dark. Someone puts Sister Sledge on the stereo, and we drag my brother up to dance, his four sisters and his new wife encircling him, laughing, our hands linked as we raise them upwards, singing loudly to the chorus of 'We Are Family'; none of us wise to the future that will soon be here.

Hedge Woundwort

STACHYS SYLVATICA
Whitespot, clown's all-heal, red archangel, hedge dead-nettle

Place woundwort in your home to
rid yourself of overwhelming sadness

Hedge woundwort has a long history in herbal medicine and is a powerful healing plant. It is antispasmodic, anti-inflammatory, antimicrobial and sedative. The flowers can be made into an infusion to alleviate sadness, clean and heal wounds, and staunch blood flow. The leaves can be made into a topical salve to treat menstrual cramps, ease gout, relieve rheumatic pain and reduce joint stiffness.

Hedge woundwort grows well in hedges, woods, and on disturbed ground or wastelands.

It seemed everyone wanted to tell me why my son got sick. Some told me I should avoid lactose. Some told me I should look to see where his energy was blocked. Some told me that his 'sweetness' was caused by an overabundance of sorrow in my womb. Others wanted to tell me how it could be worse. They said, 'at least it isn't cancer' and 'it will be easy once you have it under control'. I felt ashamed for feeling so overwhelmed. I needed time to mourn, not for his life but for the life he would not have, the motherhood I would now never know; but how can a mother mourn a child who is not dead? After all, my son had survived.

And yet, here I am: a year on from his diagnosis, sat alone in the spare room. I want to be able to say that I am taking time out for myself, but that is not the reason. The truth is, I am hiding. I don't really understand, but I know I am doing it. I hear him laughing with his daddy as they build a tower across the hall, and I feel jealous of its ease.

My husband tells me that he doesn't understand why I find it so hard, that it isn't 'normal' to be so stressed. I want to cry out, 'I don't want to feel this way,' but I don't make a sound. Instead, I crumple quietly inside. My heart breaks in places only mended with sticky tape and paper glue. When my son asks me, 'Mummy, where has your play gone?', I cannot answer. How can I let down my guard when the monster might come back at any time? I hide, not because I don't love my son, but because I don't want him to look for love in my eyes and see fear.

Every night when I go to bed, I silently promise that tomorrow I will laugh with him more, play with him more; be the mummy he used to have. He deserves gentle days and joy.

Hedge Woundwort

When he struggles to hold back the tears at each needle insertion, it breaks something in me. When I have to hold him down as he screams, the guilt gorges itself on my self-recrimination. Every time I watch him disappear inside his illness, I see the light he carries slip a bit further into the shadow, replaced by a tired acceptance that is too old for his young heart. He holds out his love to me, in hands that are scarred by needles, and I am afraid to take it.

'Mummy, I love you. Mummy, remember I love you,' he sings to me, when the anger and grief swallow me up. His trust makes me want to promise to be better, to love more in these broken days, but I am so tired. Instead, I try to keep up. I clean the house, instead of splashing in puddles, trying to be the mother that I think I should be.

Last night, instead of cuddling him under the blankets, I cut his hair. When he cried and wriggled, straining against the scissors and rising blood glucose, I kept going, determined to get this one thing done in a day where it seemed all else had failed. Later, when all the tears were spent and we curled close for sleep, he stretched his little fingers out in the dark to seek my face.

'I get scared, Mummy, because I can't find you any more,' he said, so quietly I could hardly hear. I held him tight, knowing he was right. I have been afraid to show him my feelings because they make me feel ashamed. In doing so, I have hidden my heart as well.

The truth is, I am angry at this disease that has entered our home uninvited. I am angry at my own impotence to do the one thing I promised I would do: keep him safe. His vulnerability makes me scared. Each morning, I listen out for the proof that he has made it through the night, terrified that one day, he might not answer my call. To my young son though, I am simply angry. The mummy he knew has gone away when he needs her most.

My son lets out a satisfied exclamation. His tower is built.

'Wow! I am very good at building. Come see, Mummy!' he calls. I go into his room, and see bricks of all shapes and sizes, precariously balanced to create a fabulous, impossible tower. His daddy lifts him up to place the last brick on its peak. He stands back on the floor, and nods in satisfaction at his creation. I admire it, amazed by its unfeasible reach. Then, he grins and smashes his hands into the tower at full speed.

'Wind too strong!' he shouts, laughing as the bricks tumble into a heap. He turns to me, offers me a hand.

'Now we do it again. Mummy, you can help too, if you want?'

I get down onto the floor beside him and start to rebuild, brick by brick.

Dog Rose

ROSA CANINA
Dogberry, witches' briar, hip fruit, hogseed

The rose teaches us that both joy and challenge
are needed to discover our true strength

The rose holds an ancient and special place in the apothecary garden. It has a variety of medicinal, culinary and beauty uses. High in vitamins A, B_3, C, D and E, as well as calcium, phosphorus, iron and zinc, its petals are mildly astringent and diuretic. They can be prepared as a tea to ease respiratory complaints and soothe sore throats, as well as to treat kidney irritations, gout and bladder infections. A syrup made from rosehips is a traditional remedy for colds and coughs. A tincture made from rose petals is said to improve male virility and stimulate the female reproductive system. According to Christian legend, the thorny rose grew to remind man of his imperfect nature.

Dog rose grows in hedgerows, along roadsides and at the edges of woodland.

Change happens quick, and change happens slow, and through it all, we grow. Most days, my son leads the way. Two years after he is diagnosed, he helps me find a way through.

'Nana and Grandad will be here soon. Would you like to bake some biscuits with me?' I ask. I have avoided baking with him so far, afraid he will lick the sugary spoon or dig his fingers into the mix, but today, I decide we will give it a go.

'Biscuits!' he yells, running into the kitchen. I take this as a yes.

I show him how to measure, weigh and mix the ingredients. As we do, I write the carbohydrates on a chalkboard. Everything he eats and drinks must be measured this way, so I might as well use it to help him learn to count. We make a mess of the kitchen, and ourselves. It is delightful and silly, and so very needed right now. The biscuits we bake are meant to be Scandinavian vanilla swirls, but come out of the oven looking more like miniature baked vaginas. I tell myself it doesn't matter, and keep this observation to myself. One day he will learn that I am not a very good baker, but for now he is still young enough to regard me as the Queen of Magical Things.

When my parents arrive, he runs to greet them at the door.

'I made biscuits for you!' he tells them, with pride. He pats the sofa for them to sit, then runs to the kitchen, returning with a plate of misshapen biscuits to offer around.

'Mmmm, nice cup of tea and biscuit,' he says, smacking his lips together in exaggerated pleasure, and holding out his finger for a blood glucose test. His old-man joy makes my mother laugh out loud.

Dog Rose

Later, when they have gone home, he asks if we can play in the puddles outside. It is raining, and getting late, and I go to say no. Then I remind myself he has diabetes, not pneumonia, and the sun is still up. I pack the testing kit and apple juice into my coat pocket, help him into his all-in-one red rain-suit and green dinosaur wellies, and head out onto the road.

We chase rain-rivers down the hill, racing sticks as we go. I let him clamber, slip, and fill his wellingtons with muddy water. I feel the cold seep through the holes in my broken boots. His face is spotted with mud, and rain drips from his hood. He laughs so loudly that the sheep turn their soggy heads to watch.

After an hour, I decide I am as wet, and as cold, as I can cope with. We turn for home, taking the long and winding route of childhood up a supposedly straight road, stopping to examine how the water changes the shape of the verge, how the leaves collect in eddies, how rivulets form and force through new streams. We observe which type of stick floats fastest along the road edge. I listen out for cars. Through all this, I am constantly checking his speech for signs of slurring, his movements for indications of failing coordination that might signal a dangerous low. I have one hand on the apple juice, but I do not tell him to stop.

Then he stumbles and falls, and diabetes takes centre stage again. I run to his side and lift him up, juice at the ready.

'Do you feel dizzy? Are you low?' I ask. The internal reprimands line themselves up to accuse me of neglect. I should not have stayed out in the cold so long. I should have tested his levels before we set off back up the hill. *I should, I should, I should . . .*

And then, he smiles.

'No, Mummy. I am muddy,' he replies, holding up his filthy hands.

In this perfect, simple moment he reminds me of something so incredibly important: he is not his illness. He is my son, a wild and mud-soaked little boy exploring his world. As much as I fear the very real threats that come with this disease, I must stand to the side and let him play in the rain. I will be here, ready should he need me, just as I have always been. The contents of my pockets may have changed – where before I might have carried wet wipes and toy trains, I now carry a glucose monitoring kit, insulin and high-sugar snacks – but I must let him live, and celebrate the muddy hands. It is time to find a way for me to do that too.

Fox and Cubs

PILOSELLA AURANTIACA
Tawny hawkweed, Devil's paintbrush, grim-the-collier, missionary weed

Use to help you see beyond the veil

Fox and cubs is antioxidant, anti-inflammatory, diuretic and high in vitamins A, B and C, calcium, phosphorus, iron, potassium and magnesium. It was commonly used to treat jaundice and dropsy, and to cleanse the urinary tract. The leaves are edible and can be eaten as a salad, or cooked like spinach. It was believed that hawks gained their superior vision by eating these flowers, earning it the name hawkweed. Used magically to help a person see beyond illusion, the sap was used as a remedy to strengthen eyesight.

Fox and cubs is attractive to pollinators and grows prolifically on stony wasteland.

It has been just over two years since my son was diagnosed. In that time, one thing has become clear: the idea that diabetes can be controlled is an illusion. It is like sitting on top of an angry dinosaur and expecting the ride to be smooth. It is a complex and constant management of mathematics, science and guesswork, all carried out with a potentially lethal drug.

My son has hit a growth spurt. Growth hormone increases insulin resistance, and makes his blood glucose erratic. During these points, we have to adjust the insulin ratios and background rates on his pump, to try to find a better way to achieve this ever-shifting mirage of control.

'What would you like to do today?' I ask him, hoping the added autonomy of choice might help to balance out the didactic control of his body that I will need to impose.

'I want to watch television all day long,' he tells me. It is not something we usually do, but I agree. He is delighted, and somewhat surprised, when I do.

The cartoon family are having a picnic of juice and cake. When my son was newly diagnosed, he loved to watch *Peppa Pig*. He liked the predictability of the happy outcome, but worried that they must be low. He had juice when he was low, so they must be low too. He understands that he is different now, but when he watches the cartoons, he still frowns.

I watch the glucose line on his insulin pump; my screen into his body. The aim is to keep it steady as I monitor and adjust. This is theoretically possible, so long as we don't do anything unexpected.

'Mummy, television is not that fun. Can we go for a walk?'

Fox and Cubs

he asks. I make changes to the pump levels to compensate for the unexpected exercise, and we set out, wooden swords in hand.

Halfway around the village, he stops.

'Mummy, can we have a picnic?' he asks.

We return to the house, and make a picnic of sandwiches and tea. I change the levels again, to accommodate the extra food, and we set off across the fields. We talk, and walk, and it is beautiful.

Then there is a horse. My son is afraid of horses. He begins to cry. Nothing will make him walk through the field. He tries to convince me to walk across the river instead. I need to calm him down, and avoid extra stress. We sit down by the riverbank, and discuss the relative merit of choosing the known risk of deep, cold water over the feared risk of the horse. He still won't cross the field. We return home, and set up our picnic on the floor of the living room. I check his blood glucose. My son is now smiling and happy. Things have most definitely not gone to plan, but the line remains steady.

In the afternoon, we settle down to study. He reads a book on dinosaurs, teaches himself the Roman numerals from one to twenty, then has a go at making butter with double cream and a jar of marbles. When his blood glucose is out of range, he finds it difficult to concentrate. His brain, starved or flooded by glucose, struggles to focus or comprehend. Today though, he is engaged throughout.

'That was really fun, Mummy. Can we do more tomorrow?' he asks, when we are done. I check the line. It is steady.

And so the day goes on until bedtime. We curl up under the covers and read a bedtime story about soup, and cats, and wayward ducks. When it is done, we cuddle down under the duvet.

'This day has been lovely, Mummy. I have been able to eat all day, and not feel scared at all,' he whispers to me in the dark, before drifting into sleep, a small smile on his lips.

His words remind me that this is not how a normal day feels to him. Normal, for him, is to feel an almost constant state of anxiety. I look at his face. It is flushed a healthy pink, not the sallow, grey sweat I see so often in the night. He does not kick out his legs, or whimper, in the way I have come to understand are the warning signs of highs or lows. He is simply dreaming.

It will not remain this way. We have been doing this long enough now to know this calm will not stay; but for the moment, he rests easy. Together, we have given ourselves the gift of this day. I check the line. It is steady.

Wild Cherry

PRUNUS AVIUM
Gean, mazzard, merry tree, sweet cherry

Plant cherry to bring good fortune and love into the home

Wild cherry is used in wand-making to ground spells and add power. It is high in calcium, potassium and iron. Its bark was traditionally soaked in whisky as a mild sedative during childbirth. Now, it is more commonly used to treat chronic coughs, asthma, whooping cough and bronchitis, as well as to alleviate stress and tension, regulate palpitations and calm skin ailments. Sap from the tree can be chewed as an alternative to chewing gum, and is a rich source of vitamin C. The fruit twigs can be steeped to make an astringent tea or wash. The cherry fruit is widely used in pies, preserves, cordials and other kitchen recipes, and both the fruit and bark can be used to flavour alcohol. However, the leaves, twigs and bark all contain prunasin and amygdalin, which convert to hydrocyanic acid when added to water. In small doses this acts as a respiratory stimulant and mood enhancer, but can be fatal in larger quantities.

Wild cherry grows often grows in hedgerows, graveyards and disturbed areas.

Although there are trees planted on the communal green, we are not allowed to plant them in the garden. Without trees, there is nowhere for the birds to hide. At our last house, there were lots of birds. They lived in the copse that grew between our garden and the railway embankment behind. In spring, we gathered lambs' wool and threads of my son's blond hair to leave out for their nests, and during the winters we made fat-balls from lard and chopped fruit, which we tied to the holly tree outside our window. As they came to feed, my son and I checked in our *Pocket Guide to British Birds* to find their names: nuthatch, woodpecker, goldfinch, yellowhammer, sparrow, coal tit, fieldfare, robin. We miss watching the birds.

A garden needs trees. Without them, there is nowhere for us to make-believe. When I was a young girl, a plum tree grew in front of the kitchen window. In summer, it sagged heavy with fruit, and I would sit under it and eat the sweet plums, the sticky juice coating my fingers and chin. In autumn, wasps would come and with them, warnings to look before I bit. I can still smell the sugar fermenting in the late September sun. My mother said it was on account of my name that I loved them so much. I was born with hair the colour of ripe Victoria plums, or so the story goes. My mother, convinced I would be a boy after giving birth to two boys and three girls, had no name for another daughter. She took one look at my hair and named me after a tree.

One summer the plum tree broke in two, its bough split from the trunk. My father cut the whole thing down, in case it fell, and there were no more summer plums.

Wild Cherry

I decide to plant trees. Sometimes, it is good to break a few rules. My mother digs out a sapling damson and a wild cherry from the hedgerow at the bottom of her garden. She gives these to my son, a clump of sleeping snowdrop bulbs still clinging onto the soil. I tease the bulbs away to plant in later, and stand the two spindly twigs to soak in a bucket outside. To these two trees, we add an apple, apricot and plum, salvaged from an end-of-line sale.

The gardening books tell me a sapling fruit should be planted in a hole twice the diameter of its roots, and at least two feet deep. I manage ten inches down, digging out stones, before I hit compacted hard core. It will have to do, though I have my doubts that fruit will grow.

As we dig, a robin watches cautiously from the fence post. My son sees the bird, and pulls on my sleeve.

'Mummy, my robin has come to see me! He must have found out about the trees!' he says. A robin often visited the garden of our old house, sitting near to him as he played. My son called it his friend, and was sad when we had to leave it behind. I explained that wild things cannot be caged and he'd understood but still, he'd wished it wasn't so. Now, he greets this robin as his long-lost friend, delighted to be reacquainted again.

'Welcome, Mister Robin. We are planting you a tree,' my son tells this curious little bird who watches us work. They're messengers from the spirit world, folklore says; when a robin appears, a lost loved one is near. They bring signs of new life and new beginnings. In Norse lore, they protect against the coming storms. It is good that this little bird is here.

We wait until the cover of dark to plant our contraband trees, dropping each one into its hole, watering in, and covering the roots with compost and soil. My son stomps in circles around each one, tamping down the loose ground with his dinosaur wellington boots.

Our hopeful orchard; this planting is our first act of faith, a promise we will stay long enough to see it bear fruit.

Garlic Mustard

ALLIARIA PETIOLATA

Jack-by-the-hedge, hedge garlic, sauce-alone, poor man's mustard

Plant by the door to increase abundance

Garlic mustard is rich in vitamins A and C, sulphur, iron, chlorophyll, trace minerals and enzymes. It has been used as a remedy to disinfect wounds, relieve itching and skin irritation, ease sore throats and bronchial congestion, and treat mouth ulcers. The whole plant is edible. The roots can be pickled or used as an alternative to horseradish, the leaves can be used as an alternative to garlic in cooking, and the flowers as an alternative to mint with roast lamb. It is an excellent food source for slugs, snails and butterfly larvae.

Garlic mustard grows easily on wastelands and between broken tarmac.

Before the winter sets, we must ready our vegetable beds for the coming year. We have been promised a delivery of farm manure from a friend of a friend. My son is very impressed when she arrives in a large, shiny blue tractor, towing a huge trailer filled with steaming, well-rotted manure.

'Amour, Mummy, the lady with the amour is here!' he shouts, as she reverses the trailer alongside our fence. My son cannot say 'manure' and calls it 'amour' instead. I don't correct him. I like that his joy turns crap into love.

As we shovel it over our fence, she asks us what we are planning to grow. I tell her that we are creating an apothecary garden from weeds, wild and biodiverse, and need the manure for our food beds to grow vegetables and fruit. She owns a large, fellside farm. She looks at our small, bare plot and raises an eyebrow.

'Bit of a *Good Life* thing, eh?' she says, and laughs. I smile, remembering the television sitcom from when I was young. I always liked Barbara and Tom.

'I'm going to get chickens, and make blackcurrant jam!' my son tells her, excited to share his plans.

We shovel, slip, load and pile the manure over the fence. Steam rises into the cool air as two blackbirds hop and chatter close by, waiting for the prize find. By the time it is finished, the farmer knows a bit more about permaculture and the history of wortcunning, and we have learnt about her time as a soldier in Kosovo before she began to farm. There is always something more to people than we first understand.

Before she leaves, I offer her something for the muck, and her time.

Garlic Mustard

'Just give me a pot of jam from those blackcurrants you're going to grow,' she says, pointing at my son. He nods his head, serious about this bond.

At last, we have the bare bones to build our Hügelkultur beds. Not quite to the traditional design; we adapt to the space we have. First, we lay the sand and gravel to encourage drainage. Then, we layer in rotten branches and mulched leaves, which will slowly release nitrogen and retain moisture for the roots during the summer months. We tuck this in with a blanket of upturned turf, to create warmth and break down into new soil, and shovel on a sticky, stew-like feed made from half-composted kitchen waste that my son calls 'the smelly layer'. Then, we sprinkle over a fine mix of eggshells, chicken poop, pine cones and pips that we have collected from friends, and pile on a thick layer of rich, warm manure, our fingers digging deep to split the clumps, revealing writhing red worms.

'These will help turn all this into lovely soil for our food,' I tell my son.

'Thank you, worms,' he says, gently laying them down in the dark, leaving out a few for the patient blackbirds that look on. Lastly, we close the beds with a two-inch layer of topsoil, gathered from the disused vegetable bed in my mother's garden.

When we have finished, we stand back to see what we have created. Our arms ache, and we are covered in crap, but our smiles are broad. To those looking on, these are just mounds of earth, but we know what lies underneath. Things are mixing, turning, transforming. We are the garden alchemists, and this is our gold.

SEED FOUR

Lemon Balm

MELISSA OFFICINALIS
Heart's delight, bee-balm, cure-all

Use lemon balm to ward off evil and promote good cheer

Lemon balm was known as the Elixir of Life, bound to the moon and water. Named after the Greek nymph Melissa, protectress of bees, it is antibacterial, antiviral, sedative, and has antihistamine properties. One of the earliest known medicinal herbs, its use dates back over two thousand years. It can be used to treat colds, influenza, fevers, eczema, insect bites and wounds, and to bring relief from anxiety, depression, insomnia, migraine and shock. It can be made into a tea or tincture, used as a herb, or added to wax to bring a good shine to wood. It is highly attractive to pollinators.

Lemon balm can be difficult to establish but will grow prolifically once it is settled in.

Where the south welcomes cherry blossom, we wake to find hard frost and snow. We use this time of long nights and cold days to prepare for planting before the season starts. We let old potatoes chit in the basket, and set back the sprouting garlic and onions from our vegetable box. Family and friends donate left-over seeds for our vegetable patch. Cardboard toilet rolls are saved for planters. We source mismatched trays, a pop-up decorating table and three bags of potting compost from the local free pages. Slowly, our nursery takes shape.

Now, the snows have gone and the first of the narcissi have bloomed. It is time to begin. With great delight, and a lot of mess, my son fills the tubes with compost. Into these we poke peas, runner beans, kale, courgettes, pumpkin and sunflower seeds as a treat for the birds and bees. Hands deep in dark compost, we work side by side. As we do, we discuss what will grow, how a seed germinates, and the needs of each plant. Periodically, he breaks away to do a drawing, or conduct mark-making experiments with sandstone, water and soil. Sometimes he disappears to watch a favourite television programme, coming back after a short while to continue his task. It takes most of the morning, and the floor is covered in compost, but when we are done we have trays of toilet rolls stuffed with soil, and he has found out about the biology of a seed, and how to make pigment from stone.

Is he learning what he needs to know? When I am confident, this way of discovery seems the most natural way for him to grow, but it can be difficult to maintain that confidence in a culture that prioritises mainstream school. People question me about his welfare, in a way that wouldn't happen if he was not home-educated. 'Won't he be lonely, being an only child? What about socialisation? How will he learn to read and write? What about exams? How will he get a job?' I am asked. I ask them if they have met my son. He will talk happily with anyone of any age, is curious, and has a wide and rich vocabulary. At five, his social confidence is already greater than mine. As for the rest, life is long and childhood short; but the questions make me doubt my choice. I wobble, and fall. I *should have been* able to give him a brother or a sister. I *should* send him to school. Flip this over, and the underside is scored with darker words. I am a *bad mother*. It is a familiar fear, and a carried-forward shame. The *should-have*, *other-mother* chant of guilt. I try to let it go.

I worry that I am not good enough, that somehow the broken bits of me will break the best in him. Yet, this much I also know: I do not want to miss a moment of his little life that I am gifted with.

When he opens his arms to me and shares his world, with all its fears and delights, he doesn't ask me to be the *other-mother*. He asks me to be myself. *Trust that, if nothing else*, his love tells me. I give him what I have to give. My love, with all its messy parts, will be his soil.

Agrimony

AGRIMONIA
Cockleburr, sticklewort, garclive, fairy's wand

Place it under your pillow for a deep and peaceful sleep

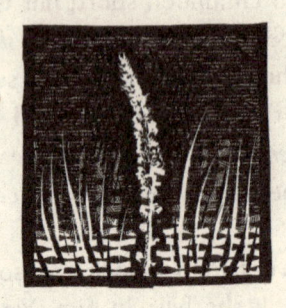

Agrimony is associated with protection spells. Used to help balance the emotions and banish negativity, it is a helpful aid for those who bury feelings deep. Mildly astringent, and rich in vitamins B_3 and K, iron and niacin, it is commonly used to treat colic, urinary infections, diarrhoea, skin complaints and ulcers. The flowers have a light apricot scent and can be made into a tea, tonic or infusion.

Agrimony grows abundantly in waste areas, hedgerows and open ground.

Agrimony

April's end brings storms, and blows the blossom from the blackthorn trees. My son and I sit tight inside, listening to the wind as it sings through the letter box. When the sun breaks through, we venture outside, like fieldmice waking from sleep.

'Do you hear the bedspring bird?' I say, listening to the *squeak-squeak* of the great-tit song that signals brighter days. I take up my spade, and start to dig into the storm-soaked sod.

Over the next two weeks we weather the seedlings outside, bringing them in at night until they are strong enough to stay the cold. Into the soil, we scatter gathered seeds of borage, cornflowers, corncockle, poppies. We dig dead-nettle and water mint into the bog garden, and gather burdock leaves from the beckside below the bridge, to lay over as mulch onto the vegetable beds. As they rot, the leaves will improve the soil for future growing. These changes come slowly, but what breaks down will give us what we need, balancing out the biodiversity of our backyard from the soil up. Together, we fill each space, each patch of barren earth. And then, we wait.

Grief lives with us, but I will not let it claim these days. Each morning, we walk our small and winding paths, the scent of cypress rising under our step. My son hugs his trees and currant bushes, encouraging each living thing to thrive. Under the lengthening light, our garden grows. We welcome rain and sun as gifts, and give witness.

Slowly, the ground begins to change. Invisible underneath, our winter work feeds the roots. Leaves and stems unfurl, and soon it seems all life is birthing. Bees find us, butterflies and birds, calling curious about this ripening ground, as life arrives, reckless and determined, to grow wild over what was once stone.

Field Horsetail

EQUISETUM ARVENSE
Bottle brush, mare's tail, shave grass, pewterwort

Use horsetail to resolve boundaries
and strengthen a sense of self

Field horsetail was commonly used by goldsmiths to polish gold. It is rich in silica, potassium, manganese and magnesium. Because of its ability to increase the absorption of calcium, it is useful during menopause to increase bone density and help prevent osteoporosis and osteoarthritis. It is good for strengthening connective tissues and improving skeletal stability. Taken as a tea, it stimulates the immune system and flushes out toxins. Topical application can help reduce wrinkles, ease sprains and inflammations, cleanse wounds, staunch blood flow and repair bleeding gums. The young plant is edible. It can be cooked as a substitute for asparagus, and the cooking water can be reused as a fungicidal spray to treat mildew and rust spot on roses.

Field horsetail grows well in damp meadows, gardens and on wasteland.

Field Horsetail

I am trying to meditate. The man on the app tells me to '*Be at one with the space you are in – let all distractions melt away.*' I am not managing to do this because, as he speaks, I am listening to my son shouting in the room below. He is upset. He doesn't want his daddy. He wants me. I have been here for five minutes. I do not feel relaxed.

Where does my space end, and my son's begin? Friends suggest that I should take time for myself, but who is that self? The magazines tell me how to '*get my body back in ten easy steps*'. I look in the mirror, and wonder who has my body now; if it was ever mine?

I always thought I had to choose: writer or mother, not both. The writers I read were, like Byron, mad, bad or dangerous to know. They had lovers, drank hard, and, if they were women, took their own lives. Those who survived needed not just rooms but whole worlds to themselves. All the great poets and authors spoke of the need for uninterrupted time, a disciplined writing schedule and space away from the demands of the world. There was no room for a child.

A mother, on the other hand, was selfless, stable and good. I was selfish, and broken, and bad, or so I believed. I told myself I had to fix myself before I brought another life into this world. When my babies died, this fear became truth: I was not fit to be a mother. Even though I was raised not to believe, I imagined myself being punished by an invisible, disapproving God. Yet my son did come, and when he did I knew, if only for a moment, that I had to be willing to die to bring him to life; and I was.

The mourned hours slip out of synch with the world, as life

continues unaware. In that space of grief and love, I bathed him, soothed him, sang to him, fed him from my breast. He was my newborn star, in a dark sky of sorrow. When the demands of my marriage shouted for attention, I could not respond. I had no energy for grown-up needs. The world went spinning on, but not here, in this mother-world. My son, created from my blood and bone, asked nothing of me that I did not want to give, and I gave it all. Perhaps this mother-love must always be this way? A series of small relinquishing griefs, each moment gone before its known. At the end, if I do my job well, I will be left behind.

'. . . *Be present in the moment* . . .'

To the person who grieves, there is only the moment and in it, I must live. I am trying to let that moment be one of love, not fear. My son is teaching me. When I pull him back from the water's edge, when I stop him from taking his next leap, warning of what danger might come, he turns to me and smiles.

'Yes, Mummy, but it might not,' he tells me, letting go of my hand.

I want him to feel the shape of the sky around his body. I want him to know where his heart pulls; how to circle the air, sure of his flight. In order to teach my son to love the shape he takes, I need to love my own.

To do this, I must spend time with the me that I have become, listen to the stories of my body; where it is broken, where it bends. I must learn how to be a mother, and myself; to feel the tension tug between the two and, sometimes, fall through. There are days where I feel that I am failing at both. On these days, I must learn to forgive.

Field Horsetail

Outside my window, the swallows circle in the blue, their bodies buffeted by the guidance of air. They are returning to their nesting grounds, driven by a memory of where they belong, even though those nesting grounds are no longer here. Will my son remember the home of my body, when he has flown?

I listen quietly to the rise and fall of my breath, let myself feel the quiver of skin over my bones.

'... *Take a deep breath in, and exhale* ...'

Between the breath of birth, and the last spent breath of death, our life is held. This beautiful, terrible, missable moment as breath rises, and falls; this is all we have.

For now, I exist here, between the in-breath and the out. It is not Zen-like. I am not a lotus flower coming into bloom. I am. That is all.

Still, that is a good place to begin.

Lesser Celandine

FICARIA VERNA

Spring messenger, figwort, smallwort, cheese cups, pilewort

Burn at midsummer to give protection to your home all year

Lesser celandine was traditionally used in Cumbria to clean teeth. The whole plant is edible, but poisonous in its raw state. High in vitamin C, it was used to prevent scurvy. Bruised leaves and flowers can be blended into a balm to make a topical treatment to alleviate haemorrhoids. The roots can be cooked as a starchy vegetable, and the leaves cooked and dried to use as a herb in stews.

Lesser celandine grows at the edges of woodlands, riverbanks and damp ditches.

Lesser Celandine

In a cul de sac of homogenised green, our determination to grow wild is incongruent with the neatness of hard-mown lawns. Each week, the housing association adds a charge to the rent, to pay for a team of gardeners to mow the communal areas and spray weedkiller along the roadside paths. A neighbour grows a satellite dish in their front garden that sprouts like a solitary, metal mushroom from the grass. Even though we are surrounded by agricultural land, nature is something to be kept under control.

As we continue our garden research, we discover the Green Guerrillas. My son is excited by their name. He imagines superheroes, and, in a way, they are. Founded by Liz Christy in 1973, they have spent the last forty years using radical gardening to transform abandoned wastelands into productive community gardens, in some of the poorest areas of New York City. The word radical comes from the Latin word *radix*, meaning 'root'. Through direct action, the Green Guerrillas use seeds to create positive change from the root up. In doing so, they challenge the established social hierarchy with a fundamental question: who owns this Earth we walk upon?

Unsurprisingly, not everyone was happy to see them flourish. Prioritising profit and privatisation over community well-being, Mayor Rudi Giuliani did a lot to eradicate the seeds that their civil disobedience had sown. Between 1984 and 1999 he oversaw the destruction of ninety guerrilla gardens, but he could not remove them all. Through legal intervention, community action and some notable support, over five hundred gardens were saved. To this day, the very first Christy Garden, in Houston and Bowery, is still going strong.

Their story inspires us. The estate where we live was built *'to provide Social Housing and associated amenities for those in need by reason of financial hardship'*. We are lucky to have this house. As property prices are pushed upwards by second-home owners, holiday lets and affluent retirees, private rental availability is squeezed ever further; it grows more and more difficult to find affordable rural housing, especially for those on benefits. Those of us who live here do so because we can't afford to rent or buy. The reasons for this are individual, and common to us all: bereavement, divorce, single parenthood, caregiving, illness, old age, job insecurity, unemployment, low income. Whatever the reasons, they each place us in the same box: according to the meritocracy of capitalism, we have failed. But this isn't an end; it is a shared new beginning. Like the Green Guerrillas, we have the potential to create a community from the ground up. If it can work in New York, maybe it can work here? What was once brownfield waste could become sustainable land.

My son and I dream up plans. We draw out wildflower walkways and a willow heart bower where the elderly residents can sit. We add a micro-meadow, a climbing area made from giant rocks, and a nature pond. Around the edges, my son draws squishy trees to mark out a communal fruit orchard, and little circles to represent vegetable plots. We let our imaginations lead the way, conjuring into being a sanctuary for pollinators, people and plants.

Our suggestion is met with a flat decline. The rocks and pond are a safety hazard; the garden would require too much upkeep; it would be sure to grow out of control. I propose that we could manage it as volunteers, just as the New York communities did, but the answer is still 'no'. My son is disappointed by the refusal of adults to see the garden his dreaming has grown. I know that our idea will never be approved, but that doesn't mean that the seeds cannot be sown.

'Well, they can't stop a flower from growing, can they?' I say. *Radix*. Root. Radical. Sometimes, you have to begin somewhere small to change the world.

We choose a mix of native wildflower seeds that will support the butterflies and bees, and roll them up into lumps of red clay, copying the design from the original Guerrilla green-aids. When the day is quiet and no one is about to see our tiny act of defiance, we throw a couple of our bombs onto the green, hoping some will have a chance to take.

It does not work. Every fortnight, the contractors come and mow it back down to a neat, homogenised green. There is no chance for our little seeds out here. We must take a different route. We sow our seeds where the mower cannot reach, lacing the border of our home with oxeye daisy, foxglove, purple tansy, vetch.

Behind the boundary of our fence, we quietly transform.

Cow Parsley

ANTHRISCUS SYLVESTRIS
Devil's parsley, mother-may-die, gypsy curtains, scab-flower

Use to calm emotions and bring courage

Cow parsley is an important early source of nectar for pollinators. Antiseptic, antispasmodic and antiviral, it has been used as a remedy to treat minor fractures, strains, sprains and respiratory issues, as well as to relieve stress, anxiety, insomnia and depression. Although it is an apothecary plant, its lookalike hemlock is deadly. They are often found growing together, so caution must be taken if foraging this plant.

Cow parsley grows widely on roadside verges and at the edge of woodlands.

Cow Parsley

Where there was nothing, now there is a world made of colour. Spirals of lettuce, towers of beans, and fat blackcurrants grow from this ground. Beside the fruit and vegetables bloom bright calendula, scarlet nasturtium, paper-bonnet poppies, selfheal, scabious. Some are garden refugees, saved from the surrounding construction site, some have been donated, others have found their way here by way of wind or bird; and some have been reborn, unearthed by our excavation and returned to life. Bees hum around the lavender bush, and the orange-tipped butterflies flutter and land. All around, there are signs of life pushing through. We have made this, my son and I, and we are proud.

Feeling emboldened, we enter our garden for the 'Most Creative New Garden' award in the parish agricultural show. Judging for this sought-after prize happens in July, a month ahead of the event. We have been making ready all week. We choose twelve pieces of blue slate, and write out poems to hide among the wildflowers. On the largest piece of slate, we paint 'Our Magic Garden' in copper and gold, and place it at the gate. We are ready for the judgement to begin.

When the judge arrives, my son takes his hand and leads him along the treasure trail of poems. There are no straight lines, and its paths meander, with magic at every turn. Though the garden is small, to my son it is wide, and every step must be taken slowly.

As they walk, my son explains which flowers have been given by nature, and which we have grown. He lifts up the downy leaves of *Alchemilla vulgaris*, to show where fairy-dew can be found. He rubs mint between his finger and thumb, and lifts it to the judge's nose.

'Good for tummy pain,' he says.

The judge is the owner of a local, independent garden centre. With a background in theatre design, he transformed his acreage of fields into a series of ornate Tuscan walled gardens, Japanese Zen spaces full of water and stone, surrealist grottoes, Monet-inspired bridges and lilyponds. He is attentive to what my son has to say, interested in what we have done. He tells him when to prune the apple tree, and when to harvest the blackcurrants to make the best jam. He feels the soil with his fingertips to check the quality, as my son explains about the Hügelkultur beds, and the smelly layer, and how the farmer was a soldier before she decided to grow lambs. When they reach our little pond, they crouch down to watch the water boatmen skate by. Together, they are respectful of the gifts that the garden brings. I am grateful to this judge, who listens so intently. His interest lights up my son's curiosity with joy.

When the judging is done, my son and I sit, nibbling on pod-peas. We watch the blackbird pull fat worms from the compost pile, listen to the soft hum of bees, and the collared dove, singing its three-note call from the nearby chestnut tree. There is magic in this garden, and its gift is our reward.

Good King Henry

CHENOPODIUM ALBUM
Fat hen, smearwort, mercury goosefoot, bacon weed

Feed Good King Henry to the pigs and hens to fatten them up

Good King Henry was a staple vegetable until the sixteenth century. The seeds can be soaked overnight and ground as an alternative to quinoa flour, and the leaves and young stems can be cooked and eaten as an alternative to sprouting broccoli. Commonly used in farming and crofting to fatten poultry and pigs, it is rich in protein, vitamins A, B_1, B_2 and C, niacin, calcium, phosphorus, potassium, iron, omega 3 fatty acids, magnesium, fibre and saponins. The leaves were traditionally used to treat gout, scurvy and toothache, and the seeds chewed to relieve urinary problems. Roots can be crushed and boiled to make soap, and the oil from leaves applied topically as a skin emollient. It makes a good companion plant to protect against pests.

Good King Henry grows abundantly in wastelands, disturbed ground, roadsides and rubbish dumps.

Since my son was two, he has wanted chickens, and has kept a penny jar on the shelf to get some of his own. Now a friend has asked if we can rehome her two ex-battery hens. I am hesitant, concerned that the tenancy has a livestock clause, but the neighbours have dogs, and rabbits, and cats, and these will be pets, after all. My son begs and begs, insistent.

'Chickens need love, just like everyone else,' he says. I like chickens; they are full of character, and turn waste into food. I relent, so long as he finds out how to care for them first. His wish is about to come true.

Today is Chicken Day. He has named them Flora Ann and Rosalita. These seem very grand names for two hens that are more skin than feathers, but to him they are beautiful. He checks the little henhouse, which he has filled with straw and treats of blueberries and mealworms. I am worried about the cost but he tells me it is okay, that the chickens will swap the treats for eggs.

When they arrive, my son jumps around them like a collie, excited to show them their new home.

'You will be very happy here. I will make sure that Arthur doesn't eat you,' he tells them, with a solemn note of responsibility in his voice. I don't think our new cat would view these scraggy old hens as much of a dinner, but I don't say that out loud. As they scratch and warble over worms and fruit, my son sits beside the cage, whispering their names. I watch from inside the kitchen, the door ajar, listening.

'I have been waiting a long time to meet you. You will be safe now,' he tells them.

Good King Henry

A neighbour glances over the fence on her way to her car.

'Do those chickens belong to you?' she asks. I notice she isn't smiling. My son, on the other hand, does not notice this.

'They are Flora Ann and Rosalita. They were sad, but now they have come to live here, and it will be lovely for them,' he replies, excited to introduce his new friends.

'We don't need them here,' she tells him, before walking away. I can see that he doesn't quite understand her words or tone, but he shrugs it off with a grin and gets back to his hens.

'Don't worry, I will look after you,' he tells them. I smile. I have been told that having one child is cruel, that he will grow up selfish, that he needs a sibling to teach him how to share. I look at my son, and wonder that anyone could think this is true.

Four hours later, a small white car pulls up at the side of our house, and a young woman steps out. She is dressed in a grey skirt and jacket, and carries a clipboard. She does not introduce herself. She approaches our fence, looks over and writes something down. I stop what we are doing, and walk over to where she stands.

'What are you doing?' I ask her. She wriggles her back to make herself taller, in a way similar to the hens fluffing their feathers. I read the logo at the top of the paper clipped to her board. She is from the housing association.

'We have received a complaint about livestock at the property,' she says. I do not respond.

'Chickens. We have received a complaint about the chickens,' she clarifies. By now, my son has climbed up to the fence, wanting to be sociable.

'Hello, would you like to meet my hens?' he asks, smiling.

The woman ignores him. I am always amazed at how rude an adult can be to a child.

I am trying to understand how this woman has received a complaint already. The hens have been here four hours. Every complaint has to be processed through several departments before it is acted on. It will have taken her thirty-five minutes to drive from town to our house. This means that whoever complained must have contacted the agency immediately upon the chickens' arrival.

The woman fluffs herself again, readying to speak.

'The tenants' handbook clearly states that no livestock may be kept at this address. You are in violation of these terms. You must remove them immediately. Failure to comply will result in the implementation of an eviction procedure,' she tells me. My son looks up at me.

'What is the lady talking about, Mummy?' he asks. I look at his little face, and back at the woman, and I feel rage rising in my throat. I push it back down. It will do no good to shout. She holds all the power here, and we have none. I ask her who has made the complaint. She tells me she cannot share that information. I ask her if she can put their reasons in writing. She tells me that I have seven days to remove the hens, or we will be evicted. I try to explain to her that they are not livestock; that they are pets, no different from rabbits, dogs or cats, all of which live on the estate. Besides, free-range chickens frequently wander onto the estate from nearby homes. My son tries to help.

'You can come in and meet them, if you like. They are called Flora Ann and Rosalita. Just tell them your name and say hello. That is how you make a friend,' he says, holding his hand out over the fence. She does not respond.

Good King Henry

'Are you really willing to make a family homeless, just because of two pet hens?' I ask, in disbelief.

'Seven days,' she says, handing me the notice over the fence.

After she has gone, my son is full of questions.

'Why do they have to go away? Where will they live? Why does the lady not like them?' he asks, on and on, tears spilling out of him, as he tries to understand why someone wants to take away his friends. He suggests that we write a letter to everyone and ask them to tell the lady that the hens can stay. I tell him that we can try. I am glad that he feels he has the power to change the things that don't seem fair.

We sit down together, and compose a letter. He wants it to be neat and asks me to write it down, adding a drawing of the hens to the bottom of the page, each one with long, yellow legs, little black eyes, and a speckled brown egg by its side.

Dear Neighbour, this is Flora Ann and Rosalita. They are my pet hens. They lost their home and were very sad, so we said they could come and live with us. I love them very much. The lady from the housing says they are not allowed to live at our house. Everyone is really nice here, and they will have a lovely time. Please, can you tell the lady that they can stay?

He packs the letters into his explorer's bag and sets off around the estate, carefully posting one through every door. He is sure that this will work. I am not so convinced. Since one of them complained, I know at least one of them won't agree.

I look up the definition of livestock. In 'The Agriculture (Miscellaneous Provisions) Act 1968', the term livestock applies to '*animals being kept for the production of food, wool, skin or fur on agricultural land*'. However, Clause 12 of 'The Allotments Act 1950' overrides this, asserting that '... *it shall be lawful for the occupier of any land to keep, otherwise than by way of trade or business, hens or rabbits in any place on the land and to erect or place and maintain such buildings or structures on the land as reasonable for that purpose* ...' This includes tenants in social housing. The only exemption is where the landlord can prove that the chickens present a '*significant health issue or nuisance*'. I compose a letter of my own, explaining how the hens will be kept, and highlighting the fact that we live in the countryside, not a built-up town.

My son returns with a little girl who lives four doors down. Her family have built a house on the private part of the estate, but she often plays here. I give them some scraps from the kitchen, and watch as they crouch down to feed the hens from their hands.

'I am going to have hens too,' she tells him.

'You are not allowed,' he says.

'Why?' she asks, giggling as Flora Ann tickles her palm.

'It is the rules of the world out there,' my son replies, with the wisdom of one who knows.

'I can too,' she declares, and that is that. After she leaves, my son asks why she can have hens and he cannot. I don't have an answer for him but it seems like a fair enough question, so I add it into my letter.

Three days go by. My son wakes every morning and runs to the henhouse, returning to the kitchen proffering two eggs each time.

'These are the very best eggs I have ever tasted!' he declares as he dips his toast soldiers into the rich, yellow yolk. Then,

Good King Henry

after breakfast, he goes to the front door to check for post, which doesn't come.

'Do you think they got my letter, Mummy, and the picture?' he asks me. I tell him that maybe our neighbours are too busy right now. My husband tells me I am giving him false hope, but what is hope if it is not seeing the good in what may come? I want my son to hold that close as he grows.

On the fourth day, we receive three letters through the door. We sit down to read them. The first is from a neighbour, who tells us that she has written to those concerned to say she doesn't mind the hens staying here. The second is from another neighbour, who worries that *'if you break one rule, what's to stop everyone breaking the rules? Before you know it, the place will be overrun'*. The third letter is from the housing association. It informs us that the Board of Trustees have met, and our request for our chickens to be granted the right to remain has been denied. It highlights the threat to health posed by poultry, and that they will attract rats into the estate. We live in the middle of farmland; rats are everywhere. Lastly, it answers my son's question as to why his friend can have chickens, but he cannot: a private house-owner does not require permission to have chickens on the estate. So much for risking the rat-plague.

'Grandad has said he will look after the chickens, and you can visit any time,' I tell him, hoping our backup plan will help to ease the pain. My father had chickens when he was a boy, and cannot see the sense in why his grandson cannot do the same. Neither can I.

My son asks me to read the letter again. He listens, then turns to me.

'If we had enough money to build our own house, could I keep Rosalita and Flora Ann?' he asks.

'I suppose so, yes,' I say. He thinks about this.

'Mummy, do we have enough to build a house of our own?' he asks.

'No, darling. We don't,' I reply.

'Oh,' he says. And that is that. In this one act, he has learnt that society has one rule for those who have wealth, and another for those who do not. I think about my father, and I wonder if this is how he felt, to be so disempowered?

My son is very quiet. He does not cry. Instead, he places his hand on my arm.

'It's okay, Mummy. I don't need chickens now,' he says. Then he goes outside to the garden and sits down beside the henhouse.

'I am sorry, Rosalita. I am sorry, Flora Ann. I love you very much but you are not allowed to live here. Grandad will look after you. He owns his house,' he says, so sadly that something in me cracks wide. I have tried to teach him about sustainability, community and compassion; they have taught him that money equals freedom. In one stupid letter, they have taught my son to see the dividing line between those who have and those who have not.

I pick up the telephone and dial the housing association. I argue that there are chickens roaming free range around the estate already. I am told again that these belong to a nearby private dwelling and therefore, the rules do not apply. I highlight the Allotments Act. They reiterate the danger to health. I ask if they will reconsider their decision, for the sake of my son. It seems such a small ask for such big joy.

Good King Henry

'You have forty-eight hours to comply. Failure to do so will mean you will be found in breach of your tenancy and due process will begin,' the woman on the telephone says. I try not to swear. My son calls me from the garden, interrupting the call.

'Mummy, do you think they will let me have an elephant? An elephant is not livestock, is it?' he asks. And so I ask, somewhat flippantly, if we can have an elephant instead?

'Elephants are on the government list of restricted animals. You can't have an elephant,' the woman replies, in unbroken monotone.

I hang up. There is nothing more to say.

Dandelion

TARAXACUM OFFICINALE
Bitterwort, lion's tooth, swine's-snout, tell-time

Drink dandelion tea to give strength against adversity

Dandelion is associated with sorrow and grief, as well as growth and transformation. It can be used to aid prophetic dreaming. It is commonly used as a playful way of telling time, and the number of seeds left on the head is also said to indicate the number of children a girl will have in later life. All parts of the plant are edible, and have a range of culinary uses, including tea, wine, as a green vegetable, or dried and ground as a coffee substitute. Diuretic and tonic, the flowers can be brewed into a tincture to cleanse the liver, and the leaves can be made into a tea to aid digestion and cleanse the kidneys and urinary tract. The sap from the stems can be used to cure warts, and was considered a potent witch-deterrent.

The dandelion is adaptable to a variety of soil conditions, and seeds itself easily in most locations.

Dandelion

In December 1982, thirty thousand women formed a twelve-mile-long human chain around RAF Greenham Common. They attached keepsakes, ribbons and children's pictures to the wire fence, singing protest songs, to save the Earth and make a stand against nuclear weapons. My three sisters were there.

It wasn't long before the police came to break things up. The more the police shouted, the more the women refused to be silenced by force. When the police heavy-hauled my sisters into the van, they kept singing. My father told them they were being ridiculous, but I thought they were amazing. They were fierce, and unafraid, and most of all they were mine.

I wanted so much to be part of this close-knit circle of women, but I never was. My three sisters. *The Girls*. Their names all began with the same letter. Their hair was tinsel-blonde and flame-red, where mine was dark brown. I was the only one to inherit my mother's dark hair and olive skin. When I was older, I grew to love this about our bond but as a child, I just wanted to fit in. They teased me that I had been adopted. Sometimes, I believed them. When my eldest brother married, the photographer asked to take a picture of the sisters. I stood up. 'Just the sisters,' he said. As soon as I was allowed to, I dyed my hair red, and didn't stop until my hair began to silver.

Other girls might be made of sugar and spice, but I was raised on Keats and Kahlo, de Beauvoir and Neruda, Cat Stevens and the Clash. It was an eclectic world, but it was never boring. Boring was not something we were allowed. 'Boredom is just a lack of imagination,' my mother would tell me, before giving me a cloth and vinegar and sending me to clean the windows. I would soon realise I was not bored after all. I read voraciously, even before I could understand the words, escaping into the gilt-edged worlds of my father's antiquarian books. As I grew older, I progressed to back copies of my sisters' *Spare Rib*, and fusty, yellowing copies of feminist poets, foraged from charity shops. If I couldn't fit into the shape the world gave me, I would have to make my own.

Just like the village that raised its eyebrows at my mother's art, the one-roomed school had no way of accommodating my square-peg demands. Keeping quiet and not sticking out was the goal to which we were encouraged to aspire. Not sure where to fit me in, they told me to sit in the library corner and read. I was happy there, preferring the quietude of words to the loudness of play, but eventually the books ran out, and I wanted to learn.

After that, I was sent to a private girls' school for the next three years. I didn't fit in there either. Their fathers had old school ties, and talked about going 'up' to Oxford. My father had left school at thirteen. Their mothers had nannies, and referred to grown women as 'girls'. My mother wore handmade clothes, and had a son who lived in the shed. Their houses had pools, and tennis courts, and well-tended lawns. Our garden grew wild.

My mother refused, or else was unable, to be anything other than who she was, no matter who asked. When she tried, it broke her into parts that were impossible to glue. I watched her struggle against who she was supposed to be, and who she felt inside. In doing so, she taught me not to hide. But, first, I had to grow up.

In this world of etiquette and tradition, wild was not the way a young lady should be. We were being prepared for conformity, not rebellion; motherhood, not mutiny. My mother did not agree. When I was given detention for not having a perfectly ironed napkin, she laughed at the pointlessness of the task. When I was sent home for taking wine to cookery class, she scoffed, and packed me pears and brandy next time. I often found myself sitting on the bench outside the headmistress's room, my head full of righteous rage. I did not see the reason for the rules, and so I would not comply. It made me a target for bullies, young and old.

Those who bully are afraid of difference. The more vulnerable they feel under its threat, the more power they need to take. The police afraid in the face of women's songs; the father scolding the wilful child; the playground taunts towards the bookish child. I learnt not to hide from those who sought me out but, when my difference threatened the adults around me, I didn't know how to fight.

We trained every morning in the outdoor pool, even when there was snow on the ground. My father had taught me to swim almost as soon as I could walk. My mother refused to go in a public pool; she didn't like the open changing rooms. But I loved the way the water felt; the way my clumsy body would lose its rigidity, and be replaced with strength and grace. One winter morning, the teacher called me to the front of the class. She strapped my arms together with ties, trussed them up like chicken wings and pushed me into the pool.

'Come on, what stroke do you call that? It's supposed to be front crawl. You look like a drowning pig!' she shouted. She told the other girls to count to fifty. As they did, I swam each length, my face stinging with shame. When I got out of the pool, I did not cry. I pulled the latex swim hat from my tangled hair, dried the chlorine off of my skin and walked back to class. I had proved I could do what she asked.

For three years she singled me out for humiliation, and I never understood why. Something in me made her feel afraid, and she wanted to feel strong. She called me wilful when I would not break, and tried harder each time. What she didn't know was that behind me, a line of wild women stood, and they would never back down.

I am short, cannot jump, and have poor coordination caused by hypermobile Ehlers-Danlos Syndrome, but in childhood I was just called a clutz. It made me a poor choice for a netball team but this same teacher chose me for the annual National Schools' Netball Championships, to defend the goal against girls twice my height. She must have known that I would fail, yet her need to humiliate me was obviously greater than her need to win. The opposing team scored goal after goal, the shooter reaching effortlessly above my head to net the ball, her shiny blonde ponytail bobbing in the sun as I jumped like a lapdog around her plimsolls. Every time I failed to stop the ball, the teacher shouted from the side.

'What do you call that? Useless!' she screamed, turning to the crowd to garner support. The more I cried, the more she shouted, until I couldn't see the ball for tears.

Then, like the warrior queens of my imaginary worlds, out of the crowd came my three big sisters.

'Fuck off, and leave our sister alone!' they shouted. The game stopped as all eyes turned to see who had called out. There they were, dressed in the oversized jumpers my mother had knitted, Afghan scarves and patchwork dungarees, their Goldilocks and livewire hair shorn short at the sides. Pushing between all the parents, they walked onto the asphalt, grabbed my hands and marched me off the court, sticking two fingers

DANDELION

up at the teacher as we left. I loved them so much right then. I didn't care that I hadn't won. I didn't care about the shouting, and the shame. I had something better than a school cup, better than fitting in; I had my sisters. As I walked away, past the mothers and fathers, past the whispers of shock, I kept my head up and smiled. I was a Bennett sister, and proud.

But they were the sisters of stories and myths, always three, with no place for a fourth. Their world was one I moved alongside, but could never join; always just a bit too young to belong. I could not run with them, but like wolf mothers they watched over me, circling when danger came close.

As I grew into womanhood, they continued to be there on the sidelines, with the same fierce, protective love that had saved me that day. It didn't matter how hard I fell, they were there. When I told them about the boy with runic arms, they told me I would survive. The day I left my first husband at nineteen, afraid and alone, they helped me find a home. When I grew so scared of the world that I refused to go outside, they kept hold of me down the wires of a phone. When I lost my babies, they stroked my hair, and helped me to rebuild. These three sisters, who shone like copper and gold, came without my ever asking, to shore up the crumbling pieces of my world, stitching me back together with their crooked smiles and strong hands. Since my birth, they have carried me, fighting my corner in this world.

All wild women; sometimes bruised and wounded, but refusing to give in. Like my mother, they showed me how to be resilient in a world that can be unfair. More than that, they showed me that, despite its brokenness, it is a world worth fighting for.

Wood Cranesbill

GERANIUM MACULATUM
Blood-grass, storksbill, crowfoot, Odin's grace

Carry cranesbill and prosperity will follow

Wood cranesbill was thought to give Odin's strength to the wearer, and was used to dye the battle cloaks of warriors. Astringent, antiseptic and anti-inflammatory, all parts of the plants are useable. The leaves, flowers and root can be used to treat stomach upsets, irritable bowel, kidney infections, cuts, wounds and ulcers.

Wood cranesbill grows abundantly on wastelands, open areas, and in woodland that has previously been burned.

Wood Cranesbill

I pull on my scruffiest clothes, tie back my hair with a makeshift bandana and head out onto the building site, my son marching close by my side. We are equipped with our weapons of choice: a rusty wheelbarrow for me, and a large water pistol for my son. We are on the hunt for rocks, and fun.

He is quick to spot Shap granite, its delicate pink and silver flecks catching the early-morning sunlight. This is his favourite stone. He pushes his small fingers into the hard-packed ground to loosen the smaller pieces, while I use a trowel to lever it out. Soon, we have a good stack of rocks to shape the edges of our new vegetable bed. We add further finds to our haul: a large slab of metamorphic marble, its smooth surface patterned with cross-sections of fossils, and a thick piece of Kirkby blue slate, squared off and perfect for a kitchen hotplate. The old stoneworks is good at turning up treasures in among what has been thrown away.

Tired of collecting stones, my son runs up to the top of the rubble mound.

'Let's play now,' he calls, his water pistol raised. My hands are cut from the rocks, and chapped from the cold, but I down tools and charge towards him, fist raised in battle mode.

'I am the Queen of the Wasteland,' I shout. He shrieks with delight, and takes aim. He is a good shot, and the water is cold.

'I am the King of Rock Mountain. Keep away!' he proclaims, jabbing a stick into the resistant ground to plant his invisible flag.

We are both filthy, our hands stained red by sharp sand, and our clothes and boots clarty with mud, but it doesn't matter. We charge around the site, shouting our battle cries. This is my son's world, and he gifts it to me. When he cries his victory call from the top of the mound, firing the last of the water-pistol ammunition down at my damp and vanquished army, I fall to the ground, a hand outstretched in a melodramatic final gesture of defiance.

'You shall never defeat me,' I croak, and then die.

Which is precisely the moment that the local Conservative MP walks around the corner, followed by twelve smart-suited men.

'The estate is a wonderful example of Big Society at work, providing affordable rural housing for low-income families,' he tells them, and then stops. Cue the delinquent poor. We turn to face them; muddied, dishevelled, and appearing to be caught in the act of stealing a rusty wheelbarrow filled with rocks.

The MP looks on, unsure of what to do next. The moment hangs between us, awkward, bristling with charge. I look at my son, and smile.

'To battle!' I cry, fist raised. We charge down the hill, screaming, fire in our eyes. We are King and Queen of the Wasteland, claiming our territory with pride.

Wild Marjoram

ORIGANUM VULGARE

Joy-of-the-mountain, grove marjoram, pot marjoram, wintersweet

Place wild marjoram in your bath for seven days to bring relief for sadness and grief

Wild marjoram is a powerful plant for dispelling negativity. Associated with Aphrodite, the Greek goddess of love, it is used for relieving symptoms of menopause and premenstrual tension, and promoting the production of breast milk. The leaves and flowers can be made into a tea to relieve insomnia, migraines, back pain, dizziness and depression, and to treat coughs, colds, loss of appetite, stomach cramps and trapped wind. It is an excellent source of nectar and pollen for bumblebees and butterflies.

Wild marjoram grows well on dry, infertile scrub areas.

My son and I are busy drawing with his chalks, on the path outside our house. As we sketch out dinosaurs, an elderly neighbour stops to chat. She tells me about a 'diabetic story' she saw on the evening news.

'... The doctor had to take both his feet off. Not much older than your son, and he never played football again,' she says. I force a polite smile as I try to distract my son's attention from what is being said, but it is too late; the words have got in. Later, as he plays in the bathtub, he lifts his toes out from the bubbles, wiggles them, and tells me that he doesn't want the doctor to take his feet away.

When he was first diagnosed with type one diabetes, the nurse showed us pictures of necrotic toes, flesh-eating ulcers and amputated limbs, warning us to watch for injuries to the feet. Since then, I have been diligent about foot care. I tell him that will not happen, but make a mental note to buy him a new pair of shoes.

The next day, I take him to the charity shop. He is distracted, excitable, unable to focus on one thing.

'What about this, Mummy!' he shouts, picking up a ceramic wishing well with a tarnished brass pail. By the time I reach him he has moved on, lifting up spoons, puzzles, plates, beads. I am offered a violet fake-fur cushion, a necklace made from pink shiny shells, a woollen rainbow scarf and a miniature model of Big Ben encased in a snow globe. I pick each discarded item up from the floor, as he hurries onwards to find the next prize.

'Darling, are you high?' I call out, my voice slightly louder than intended. I catch the eye of the pepper-haired shop assistant, who looks from me to my son and back again, eyes widening, before looking away.

I feel the heat prickles spread up my neck, smell the hot, baked-bread scent of embarrassment rising from my skin. I want to grab his hand and go home, but we haven't got his shoes. I need to get him to sit down to do a blood glucose check. I call out again, ratching through the contents of my overstuffed bag to find his testing kit, stooping to collect the Hansel and Gretel trail of trinkets he has left behind.

Then he appears by my side, waving a pair of red patent-leather stilettos with six-inch, dagger-sharp heels.

'Buy these shoes, Mummy. They are beautiful. Buy them, Mummy, buy them for yourself,' he insists. He is so certain that these are the shoes for me. I thank him, wondering who he sees when he looks at me. Who is this woman who wears six-inch red patent heels? He has never seen me in anything but walking boots. My feet are wide from years of sensible footwear. Even when I was a child, Cinderella's shoes were always the wrong fit. Reaching deep into my mother's tall mahogany cupboard, I would pull out silver-buckled evening shoes, lacy garden-party sandals, kitten-heeled boots with copper hooks and eyes. Imagining myself a princess, I would slip them on but, unlike the Little Ash Girl, these shoes were never mine to fit. When I tried to walk, I'd always fall. Frustrated by my lack of grace, I would push them back into the dark, and pretend I did not care. 'Who wants to be a girl, anyway?' I said, although in time I would try, like the wicked sisters, to change my shape to fit.

I look down at the red shoes. They will never fit my life. They are meant for a dame in a gritty noir film. Even though he begs me to buy them, we cannot afford this waste. Yet, I love that he sees me as someone who could wear these impractical scarlet shoes 'just because'.

I put them back on the shelf, but I don't forget.

Honeysuckle

LONICERA PERICLYMENUM
Goat's-leaf, woodbine

A honeysuckle growing outside the door
will keep love alive and bring good fortune

Honeysuckle is said to sharpen intuition, encourage psychic dreams, and stimulate a positive outlook. Medicinally, the flowers have been used to treat inflammation and infection, from coughs and other respiratory complaints to sore throats, colds, flu, fever and urinary tract problems. While the nectar can be sucked from the flowers, its berries and leaves are highly toxic and should not be consumed.

Honeysuckle grows in hedgerows, scrub and shady places.

There are over five hundred competition classes in the local agricultural show. They range from 'Flower Arrangement in a Candlestick' to 'Best Mule Gimmer Lamb', and everything in between. My son has chosen forty-three entries including, in no particular order of value, a miniature garden on a biscuit-tin lid (specific measurements adhered to), an animal made from vegetables, a painted egg, a model made from recycled materials, a Victoria sponge cake (jam-filled, no decoration allowed) and a jar of home-made blackcurrant jam. Three months ago, when he made his selection, I envisaged an organised timetable of preparation, diligently achieved over a period of some weeks. The reality is a frenetic week of baking, cutting, glueing, picking, painting and arranging. Today is Show Day, and we are running out of time.

The 'Rules of Entry' booklet states that all entries must be displayed, with the appropriate classification cards, no later than 9 a.m. My husband and I have been awake most of the night, after an insulin cannula fail, and my patience is running short. It is 8.25 a.m.

'Come on! We're going to be late!' I shout, forgetting that this is meant to be fun. I am hungry and tired, and it is beginning to rain. I don't want to go and spend the day getting wet in a field. I want to stay home, read a book, and maybe even have a nap. My husband sits on the sofa, checking messages on his phone. He refuses to hurry.

'Relax. It's only the parish show,' he says, laughing. I stop, and look at him. He gets up without saying a word.

His entry is four chocolate brownies, submitted into the 'Men's Baking' class. His gender identification has little to do

Honeysuckle

with his culinary skills but, evidently, it warrants a special prize. He fetches the small brownie box. I add a much larger box to his load. This one is heavy, and filled to the top.

'Careful!' I shout as he takes it out to the car.

My son is hopping up and down, wanting to be gone.

'Hurry, Mummy, hurry!' he shouts. I lock the back door, carrying a vase of wildflowers in one hand, keys in the other, and an interpretative painting of the gardens at Giverny shoved under my arm. I try to work out how we are going to get up the road and across a bumpy field without the water spilling out of the vase. I will learn the answer to this too late: a more seasoned show competitor would take a bottle of water to fill the vases once there. They would also leave more time.

My son has now strapped himself into his seat and is ready to go. I remind myself that all I do, I do for him. I also promise myself that I will never do this again.

'Showtime, Mummy!' he calls.

This is his first show. He loves the ceremony of it all, the polished silver-plate cups, the anticipation of what the competition might hold. I am trying to resist the reflex reaction of preparing him to fail. Disappointment was a given when I was a child. There was no point getting hopes up; better to be prepared for the let-down, so it doesn't catch you off guard. Every time I set my sights on success, I was offered the same advice: *you can only do your best*. I was also warned this would not be enough.

These things were said to make me feel better, but they didn't. I was always preparing myself to fail. I told myself it didn't matter if I didn't win, but it did. Underneath my stoic acceptance of this fate was a quiet cry. 'Why not me?' the little girl said. I wanted to be the very best, just once, to know how that would feel. Though the lesson was supposed to be about taking part, the sense of disappointment was heavy and thick. I must not let it show, though. The double bind: to be upset about not winning was big-headed. After all, I should have known. The warnings told me so: *don't get caught out, pride comes before a fall*. Believing myself to be good enough was an invitation to fail.

Later, I will rewrite my own history. I will be the one who takes the leading role. I will be the one who shoots the winning goal. I will be the one who takes the prize. I will not be second. I will not be last. I will no longer be the one who is not good enough. Today is my son's chance to believe he can be the best. I still tell him that the fun is in the taking part but secretly, I make a quiet wish: let him win.

By the time we arrive, it is 8.55 a.m. We spill into the stuffy air, balancing bags and boxes, dripping raincoats, and the vase of flowers. I am given a stack of white cards and told to write his name, age and entry listing on each one. My son tries to help, running up and down the aisles to look for the correct numbers to each class. The marquee attendant waits at the side. Next to my dishevelled appearance, she is immaculate in her navy dress and neatly styled silver hair. I do not have a pen, and ask if I can borrow hers. She offers it without a smile, and checks her watch.

The flowers are wilting. The vegetable duck has lost a leg somewhere along the way. The edible jelly-sweet necklace is beginning to melt. The Victoria sponge has fallen into a black hole. My husband's brownies are holding strong. We still have a chance. We go to place them on the baking table. We have

Honeysuckle

presented them on a pink-flowered plate, and placed a small pink rose by their side. A voice comes from behind.

'Entries must be displayed on a paper doily,' the woman instructs. A different attendant; she appears to be in charge. We do not have a doily. I try to reason that the plates are pretty, not realising that this is a non-negotiable rule.

My son slides down my legs onto the matting and starts to cry. The excitement has chewed through his breakfast, leaving a large dose of insulin behind. He crashes into hypoglycaemia. I kneel down and reach inside his pocket for his insulin pump. It is warning low. The doily woman is standing by my side, clipboard in hand, tapping her pen.

'Do you have a doily, Mrs Bennett?' she asks. I look up at her, then back at my son, and decide this isn't the time to tell her that my title is Ms. I stay quiet and take the plate of brownies from the table to give to my son, who eats with both hands, forgetting everything but the need for sugar. Doily Woman leaves us alone.

I still have seventeen entries to put out. My husband is at the other end of the tent, balancing a biscuit-tin farmyard, a lunchbox with healthy snacks, a painted egg, and a Nerf-pistol with a poppy shoved in its end, representing the human cost of war. That one is my contribution. I look at the other entries in the 'Flower Display in an Interesting Receptacle' class. There is a silver thimble with a miniature posy of delicate violets, a wellington boot holding three sunflowers, a glass candelabra, each arm clasping a just-opened white rose, and a porcelain toilet cistern, spilling over in a riotous display of peonies. I don't think my floral political commentary will win.

We are over time. The only other people in the marquee are the attendant, and Doily Woman.

'Are we all done?' the woman in navy calls.

'Not quite yet. Just Mrs Bennett and her husband . . . or whatever he is,' Doily Woman replies. My husband and I look at each other from across the marquee, open-mouthed. I go to say something, but my son is up on his feet, pulling at my hand.

'Mummy, we have to be fast. Come on!' he instructs, and he is off again, his little sugar-sticky hands clasped around a three-inch flower arrangement and a slightly misshapen, home-grown courgette. I turn to Doily Woman, and explain that his blood glucose is low.

'Well, yes, we all know what it is like when our sugars get a bit low, especially when people insist on being late and we haven't had anything to eat since six o'clock. Perhaps you could come a little earlier next time?' she replies, punctuating her comment with a tight smile. Her words twist up my face like a sour sweet, but I stay quiet. I want my son to enjoy the show. Arguing with its stalwart matriarch won't help. Instead, we finish off our entries, pack my husband up with boxes to take home, and head out into the show.

We must wait until 4 p.m. for the results to be announced. It's now 10 a.m. and raining hard. My son doesn't mind. He has the whole day planned. He pulls at my hand, dragging me from stall to stall to look at wellington boots, shiny lawnmowers, fishing rods and bags of lurid candy floss. He has a go at milking a rubber-glove udder, but admits defeat when only a trickle appears. He urges me to have a go, but my attempt is not much better. It is harder than it looks, requiring strong hands and a good technique.

Honeysuckle

In the centre of the showground, grown men with white underpants pulled over their trousers wrestle each other to the grass.

'Why have they got their pants on the outside, Mummy?' my son asks.

'It's Cumberland Wrestling. It's traditional,' I answer, which is true but doesn't answer why. That, I do not know. The county of Cumbria only existed after 1974. Before that it was Cumberland to the west, Westmorland to the east, Carlisle to the north and Lancashire down south. My father came from Cumberland, home of competitive face gurning, and wrestling in pants.

After the wrestling, we visit the livestock marquee. The air is sweet and heavy, smelling of damp hay and wet waxed jackets. At the entrance, there is a display of eggs on a selection of white paper plates. Each plate, marked to a different cage, exhibits one whole and one cracked egg. There are rows of caged hens, cockerels, runner ducks, rabbits and three, incongruent guinea pigs. My son walks each row, congratulating every chicken, from the golden-brown Buff Orpington to the pompous, agitated Silkie with its glamorous crown.

'Hello, Mrs Hen. You have made a very good egg. Well done!' he tells each one. Then he goes quiet. I know what is coming next.

'I really miss Flora Ann and Rosalita, Mummy,' he says.

'I know, love, but we're not allowed to have chickens right now,' I reply, squashing down the residue of anger I feel inside.

'One day, when we have enough money to buy our own house, they can come home,' he says. I smile, though suspect the hens may be long gone by the time that happens.

'Come on, let's go see if we can win a prize, shall we?' I say, taking his hand and leading him back outside, away from the hens and regret.

I give him twenty pence to play the tombola. Each chance spin makes him squeal. He doesn't win, but the woman behind the stall smiles and hands him a packet of colourful sweets. He knows his blood glucose is high, and doesn't know if he should accept.

'Thank you, but I don't think I can have them right now,' he says, trying to be polite.

'I'm sure that Mummy won't mind,' the woman says, giving him a conspiratorial wink. It isn't as easy as just giving him the bag, but I don't want to make him feel left out and I know she means well.

'It's okay, you can have them if you like,' I say, mentally calculating the carbohydrates.

'Can I have one now?' he asks, holding the packet tightly. I hesitate. His rebound high is rising fast from the morning low and the overcompensation of my husband's brownie cake.

'Best wait until later,' I say. I put my hand out for the sweets, which he hands over. The woman looks at me, and then back at him.

'My son has diabetes,' I say, hoping this will be enough to prevent her from saying anything else. It doesn't.

'Oh, poor thing. I'm sure it will be okay, just this once?' she says, with a pitying frown. I count to five under my breath, then walk away. Sometimes, I get tired of trying to explain.

We spend the rest of the day walking in slow circles around a muddy field. We watch the sheep parade, take a look at the seven vintage cars parked in the mud, and have a go at the

HONEYSUCKLE

charity lucky dip. My son wins a decorated plate with a squirrel design, which he gives to me as a gift.

At 4 p.m. they open the craft marquee for public viewing. The space is crowded, bristling with competitive expectation. A young girl from the estate pushes past us, in tears. 'It isn't fair, mine was the best!' she wails. This is more serious than I thought.

We walk along the aisles, playing a game of spot the winning cards. Pink for first, blue for second, yellow for third. My son drags me through the crowd, gathering up slip after slip from under his entries, until he has thirty-six little rectangles in pink, yellow and blue.

'Look, Mummy, look,' he cries, holding them up. His smile is as wide as his face, and so bright.

'Woo hoo!' I shout, and we do a winning dance. Who cares who is looking?

The final class is for the Parish Garden Awards. At the top of the large noticeboard is a photo of our garden. Underneath, there is a pink card and a handwritten note from the judge. I read it out loud.

> First Prize: Most Creative New Garden, and Winner of the Environmental Cup. Judge's Note: I was very impressed by the knowledge and enthusiasm of this young gardener. This garden exhibited the very best in creativity, creating through the imagination a truly definite sense of place. Innovative permaculture, amazing creative use of space with eclectic, but thought-out, planning and a good knowledge of plants. It is a wonderful example of what horticultural education in action should look like. Tremendous potential!

Our little garden, dug out of rubble and rock in the rain, has won.

'Wow, Mummy! Wow!' my son shouts, throwing his arms around my waist, as we both jump up and down. We won, and even though it isn't about winning, even though I am a grown-up and I know this is small in the bigger picture of life, it is a win, and that feels good.

We collect his trophy, and exchange his slips for winnings at the judges' table. Doily Woman hands over thirty-seven little paper envelopes containing his prize money.

'We can buy more things for the garden now,' he says, holding tight to his hoard.

'I suppose you'll be taking part again next year, then, young man? Only, next time, maybe Mum can try to make it on time,' she says, looking directly at me. I smile, say thank you, and manage to resist the very strong temptation to stick out my tongue.

As my husband drives us home, our car filled with wilted flowers, sticky sweets and half-nibbled cake, my son lets out a loud, satisfied sigh.

'Thank you, Mummy. That was the very best day ever. Can we do it again next year?' he says.

'Of course we can,' I reply, my earlier exhaustion replaced with his joy. The little girl in me smiles. She didn't fail.

Goldenrod

SOLIDAGO VIRGAUREA
Wound weed, blue mountain tea, liberty tea, Aaron's rod

Where goldenrod grows, a hidden treasure will be found

Goldenrod is high in antioxidants and tannins. It is anti-inflammatory, astringent, antiseptic, decongestant, diuretic and diaphoretic. The whole plant is edible. It was frequently used in battle to reduce bleeding and treat injuries, and commonly used to improve cardiovascular health, flush out urinary tract infections, reduce inflammation and allergic reactions, relieve colds, lower fever, and treat fatigue and exhaustion. Folklore says that where the goldenrod grows, a hidden spring will be found. For this reason, goldenrod stems were often used as a divining rod for water-witching.

Goldenrod grows easily and prefers rocky ground.

All My Wild Mothers

At five-and-a-half-and-a-bit, my son has discovered the Romans. Today, we are the Roman Army. The Gauls are played by our unwitting neighbours. We march around the half-built estate, firewood bundles and provisions tied to our backs, our swords ready. In my pocket, I carry glucose, a testing kit and a bottle of water; time travel on medical grounds is allowed. My son laughs and shouts with gusto as we run over the rough ground, wooden weapons drawn, our battle cry echoing through the building site. He is still at the age when he is filled with delight at the simple act of play, and it is worth being cold and damp to see him so carried away.

I try to let go of the real world, and join him in this place. It doesn't always come easy. Some days, I crave silence. Other days, I long for conversation, or the chance to read a book in the sun, or just to drink a cup of tea before it goes cold. There are dark days too, when I am angry and brittle, when I try to marry the worlds of grief and motherhood, and feel crushed by both. On those days, there will be tears, and apologies, and promises whispered in the dark.

This is not one of those days. Today is a day for building a miniature version of Birdoswald Fort. We sift and sort through pieces of stone and as we do, he identifies them as marble, sandstone, slate, fossil limestone, river cobble. He stops searching and holds out a small, jagged stone from the pile.

'Look, Mummy, gold!' he shouts. The rock is a quartz of some kind, white with a band of copper, and delicately flecked with green. I turn it over in my hand, raise it closer to my eyes and then, as the sun breaks through the cloud, I see it: a small seam of gold running through its core, perfect and bright. My son has struck gold among the rocks.

'Is it really, really gold, Mummy?' he asks.

'It might be,' I tell him. A smile fills his five-year-old face.

'Keep that one safe,' he tells me, closing my hand around his precious find. Then we return to our building, his concentration back on the task at hand. I watch him decorate our fort with twisted nails and rusty scraps of metal, and think how wonderful it is that he has found gold where it appears there is only waste.

'I think I know what my work is going to be when I am older. I am going to build a museum, and I will learn archaeology and palaeontology, and you can live in the museum too,' he tells me. He smiles, satisfied with this discovery, and continues with his important work. Then he wobbles a little, and tells me he feels strange. We wipe his hand to do the check. He is low.

We go back to the house. I give him a biscuit and juice, and he wanders into the living room to watch a cartoon on the television, taking off his trousers and underpants as he goes.

I love that my son, who now watches a cartoon wearing no underpants and eating a biscuit, can discover a thin thread of gold in a pile of rubble. I love that he can discover something about himself that previously had not formed. I love that he understands work as being the thing he is passionate about, but not who he is.

His world is not easy. The lows drain his body of all energy, leaving him scared and confused. The highs flood his body with blood like thick maple syrup, making him tar-headed and angry. The needles hurt, and the constant control exhausts him. As he grows, he stumbles across truths, like the stones on the site where we play. Some of these are painful, too big for him to carry, bringing with them an awareness that makes his heart sad. I want to take this weight from him, even though he tells me that he can handle it; that he is strong. I do not like to see him struggle, do not want to see him fall.

Yet, there are also the small stones; those moments where he looks down, and finds gold. I turn the sharp rock around in my hand. There is something significant in this day. I have never allowed myself to think beyond the present that we have, but today he has named the possibility of his life to come. He has given me the first glimpse of a future with him in it. It is hard, but it holds gold.

Greater Plantain

PLANTAGO MAJOR
Soldier's herb, healing blade, waybrede, roadweed

Use to help bring hope and healing to those who feel wounded

Greater plantain has wide-ranging antimicrobial properties, as well as being anti-inflammatory and analgesic. It helps dry up excess secretions in the respiratory tract and the digestive system, and can be used as an expectorant for congested lungs. Shred and apply directly or as a poultice to relieve insect bites and other skin irritations. A tincture made from plantain is particularly good for colds and flu; or drink as a tea with honey to bring relief from stomach ulcers, IBS or other gastrointestinal inflammation. Rich in calcium and other minerals and vitamins, including vitamin K, it can act as a coagulant to stem bleeding from cuts and wounds. This made it a useful wound healer on the battlefield.

Greater plantain grows well on disturbed ground, roadsides, tracks and previously cultivated land.

My son and I explore the world outside our home. He carries a backpack with dinosaurs and jelly sweets for lows. I carry a blood glucose checker, and a bag for gathering seeds and autumn-foraged foods.

Today, our discovery is a bounty of fat, pear-shaped fruit, hanging heavy from the wall of an abandoned house. Creeping up its crumbling, lime-filled stone is a giant quince, higher than Jack's beanstalk. The sticky corpses of fallen fruit litter the ground but on the branch they are ripe and full, and ready to pick.

'Pears!' my son squeals with delight. Before I can stop him, he takes a huge bite and his face screws up.

'Not pears,' he says, sticking out his tongue, the sourness leaving his mouth dry.

'These are quince. They make good jelly,' I explain. He looks suspicious that something so harsh could make anything sweet but I reassure him, and we return home with our bag stuffed full.

I look up recipes to make with quince. Quince tart, roasted quince fool, quince jelly.

'Let's make membrillo,' I suggest. The sound of it makes my son giddy with excitement. We roll the word in our mouths – *membrillo*. I have no idea what it will taste like, but it conjures up Moorish sunsets, mint tea and gilded roofs.

Making it is less exotic. It involves several hours of boiling and thickening on the hob. Our cooker is cheap and difficult to regulate, so we must watch that the syrup doesn't burn. At first it seems benign but, as it thickens and heats, it begins to bubble and belch boiling, crimson glue.

Greater Plantain

'Stand back!' I shout, warning my son out of the way as a large lava flow rises up and out into the room. It burps itself across the wall, the floor, and up to the ceiling, until the room looks as though it has witnessed a slaughtering of quince. I read through the recipe again. It does not warn us of this potential risk. It promises that this is *'Easy Membrillo – Sweet Quince Cheese'*. Not only easy, but *'extremely easy'*. Simply peel and core the fruit, add it to a pan with water, vanilla and sugar, then stew, purée and set. The result will be *'a perfectly sliceable consistency'*, I am told.

Except, the syrup will not thicken beyond this gloop. Instead it explodes and stains the kitchen with splatters of sticky red goo. My son hides under the gap by the kitchen sink, as I cover my arm with a tea towel and pull the pan from the heat. The burps begin to slow and, finally, stop. I look up at the ceiling and start to laugh. My son laughs too, until we are both giggling so much it cramps our tummies and squeezes our chests.

'Membrillo is exciting, Mummy!' he says. I am not sure it is meant to be so exciting, but I am happy with this.

After it has cooled, we spoon it into lined, shallow pans and leave it to set. When the paste is ready, I slice off a piece and give it to my son, who eats it with delight, and then confusion.

'It does not taste like cheese at all, Mummy, but it is nice,' he decides. We cut it into blocks and wrap it in greaseproof paper and muslin, tying a green ribbon around each one, before storing them in a large, airtight box. These will be our gifts for Christmas this year.

When my husband returns from work, he opens the door to find the kitchen covered in red stains and the sink full of sticky, unwashed pans. Everywhere is coated in sugary paste.

My son and I are sat on the linoleum floor, with a pot of frozen peas and two metal bowls, playing pea football.

'Goal!' my son yells, before jumping up. My husband stares at the chaos, follows the splatters up the wall, across the ceiling, and back down. He opens his mouth to ask what has happened but my son interrupts, pulling at his hand.

'Look, Daddy. We made membrillo. It got a bit mad!' he says, and with that, we end up giggling again.

'I can see,' my husband says, raising an eyebrow. I shrug my shoulders, pop a piece of the quince paste in his mouth, and smile. Sometimes, it's good to go a bit mad.

Lesser Periwinkle

VINCA MINOR
Running-myrtle, blue buttons, joy-on-the-ground, sorcerer's violet

Gaze at a periwinkle flower to bring back lost memories

Lesser periwinkle is associated with the goddess Venus. It was used in love spells to increase a feeling of attractiveness, and to clear negative energies from the home. In Germany, it is an emblem of immortality, and was planted on the graves of children to help parents overcome their sorrow. Astringent, styptic, vasodilatory and diuretic, the dried plant can be used to treat sore throats, nosebleeds, heavy menstrual bleeding, gastritis, minor skin inflammations and various lung diseases. Used during medieval times as a remedy for headaches, dizziness and lapses of memory, studies have shown that it contains high levels of vincamine, more commonly used in medicines to protect against age-related memory loss. It has a tendency to smother out other plants.

Periwinkle thrives best in shade or semi-shade.

All My Wild Mothers

A long time ago, in a life far away, a woman asked a question. 'Name one thing that you love about yourself?' she asked. The rest of the therapy group stood in a circle, waiting for my response. I tried hard to find something, and that something opened wide like a sinkhole, into which I disappeared. Gathering my bag and coat, I ran from the room, and stumbled out into the cold, linoleum hall.

When I was a little girl, there was a mirror by the door. Not wide enough to fit in, but long enough to see myself from head to foot.

'There's no point looking in a mirror unless there's something worth seeing,' my mother said whenever she caught me taking a look, but I kept looking all the same. I wanted to see who I was, inside. I knew I would never be like her, although people told me that I had her face. She was tall, and slim, and wore her beauty with a natural ease that always seemed out of reach. I was proud of her that way. She never used make-up, and never shaved her legs. She told her daughters a woman didn't need to do these things to be beautiful, but she didn't see beauty as a right, or a gift. 'It's cruel to let a child think they are beautiful if they are not,' she said.

Like the mirror by the door, into which I kept looking, I tried to be worth seeing. The more I tried, the more I disappeared, until the eyes that stared back were not my own. If my reflection wasn't even worth seeing, then what worth had I?

By twenty-one, I had starved myself invisible, given up and started again. I fell in love, put myself through college and earned myself a degree. On the day of my graduation, I borrowed my mother's old lindy hop dress. With its tiny blue cornflowers and wire bodice, it was too tight around the waist, and too wide around the bust, but I didn't mind. My skin was brown from hiking in Spain, my hair was shaved short, and the man I loved was standing by my side. I felt good.

'I wore that dress when I was your age, and I could still fit into it even after you were born,' my mother said. When she looked at the dress, she saw the woman she once was looking back, but that was not what I heard. What I heard in that moment was: *you're fat*. I hid the dress under the shapeless ceremonial gown, stumbled my way up the graduation steps and, after it was done, I changed back into my jeans. I was meant to be moving home for a while, but I knew then it wouldn't work.

The next day, when I told my mother I had changed my mind, she began to cry.

'You never think of anyone but yourself. Look how sad you've made your mother,' my father shouted at me, as I packed my rucksack into my car.

'Oh for God's sake, I'm not the one who makes her sad!' I snapped back, furious at my father for holding me responsible again for the unhappiness in her heart. It was time to go.

As I drove away, my father stood with his fist raised in the air, like a punctuation mark. I waited until we had turned the corner before I cried, my not-yet-husband sitting silently by my side. All the years of squashing down my words and underneath this, a longing that could never be fulfilled: I will never be good enough.

But that was a long time ago. My son wakes, soft from sleep, and wraps his arms around my neck.

'Good morning, my beautiful mummy,' he sings.

'Good morning, my beautiful boy,' I reply. I tell him this every day, and I will keep telling him, because it is true. There is nothing more he needs to be, or do, in order to be beautiful, or loved.

Slowly, I am learning to see myself through his eyes, to see this world the way he sees it, with heart open wide. I stand naked in front of the mirror, my body rounded and lined.

Name one thing that you love about yourself?

What can I say?

This is my Praise Day. I am who I am: not perfect, but enough.

Motherwort

LEONURUS CARDIACA
Throw-wort, lion's ear, lion's tail, heartwort

Use a sachet of motherwort to
protect your child against evil spirits

Motherwort was considered an excellent tonic herb for new parents overwhelmed by self-doubt. Often referred to as the 'mother's herb', it is a uterine stimulant and can be used to encourage passing of the placenta. Good for stimulating the menstrual cycle, improving oestrogen, regulating hormones and detoxifying the lymphatic system, it can be used to alleviate premenstrual and menopausal symptoms, including mood swings, bloating and cramping, hot flashes, heart palpitations and anxiety. Antispasmodic, calmative, antidepressant and sedative, it is also used in treatments to lower blood pressure, and treat heart irregularities connected to stress.

Motherwort grows well on waste ground, rubbish dumps, roadsides and other disturbed areas.

The garden sags its way into winter, days blending into a quiet grey, the nights starless and hushed. Our little trees scatter the last of their ochre leaves, the fall not big enough to make a mound but enough to rake into a hide for wintering bugs and bees. Together, my son and I gather in the seeds, an echo of our last leaving, until our bag is full with black poppy, calendula, mallow, foxglove, corncockle, shiny columbine. In the bog garden, tall flag irises bend and brown. Mint stiffens and silvers between the stones. Nettles sway at the edge of the fence. We leave these be, as food for the birds when the days grow cold.

It is time to put the vegetable patch to sleep. It has given a good harvest of roots and greens. Where there has been surplus, we have pickled and preserved. It is not quite self-sufficiency, but is enough to feed. We leave the kale to overwinter, its taste made richer by the first frosts, but the rest we dig out. The skeleton peas and slimy stalks of slug-munched courgettes are pulled up for compost. The last potatoes are uprooted from the soil. Trailing beanstalks are wrestled off their canes; the woody beans are saved for next year's crop. We work to a steady rhythm, mizzle gathering on our clothes like spider threads. As we do, my son chatters, and I listen. His world is still one of *whats* and *whys*, and *ifs*.

'When they cloned Dolly the Sheep, did the clone begin in the same place, with the same memories, or did it have to start all over again? Do minnows run out of puff? Why do people go to war?' he asks, barely stopping between each one. He bends down to sniff a yellow nasturtium flower that has sheltered from the cold.

'Do bees sneeze?' he asks. It makes me smile, to imagine a sneezing bee.

'Those are great questions. Which one shall we find out the answer to first?' I say. He is curious to understand how things fit together, and I try not to close his world down with binary answers. Always stretching ahead of himself, his questions create places within me, where I must sit with the discomfort of not-knowing. I am learning to live with uncertainty, to ground myself within the limits of what I know right now: in this moment, I am with my son, and we are digging. Our fingers are cold, and our boots are heavy with mud. In this moment, I am happy, and all is well. I crouch down and put my arm around his small shoulders.

'I love you so much!' I tell him, kissing his cold-pinked cheek. He grins back at me.

'I love you too! You are the best mummy in the world!' he declares, planting his muddy hands onto my cheeks, and squishing me with a kiss.

Once the work is done, we go inside. As he drinks his cocoa I strip away the tough skins from the runner beans, to reveal shiny, purple seeds. I hold them out for him to see.

'Magic beans,' I tell him. He puts down his mug and offers his hand, reverently. To him, the magic is real. I place three beans into his opened palm, and curl his fingers round. He is silent, his eyes fixed on the fist that holds this gift.

'Make a wish,' I whisper, and he does, too quiet for my adult ears to hear. We blow on his hand, and send his wish into the wind. As we do, I add my own. It is always the same: let him stay.

All My Wild Mothers

'Thank you, Mummy,' he says, still clutching the beans. And there we sit, he and I, not saying a word, held in the hush of wonder, and the magic of small seeds.

SEED FIVE

Pellitory-of-the-wall

PARIETARIA OFFICINALIS
Lichwort, paritary, billy-beattie

Use to strengthen unions, aid reconciliation and calm the soul

Pellitory-of-the-wall was traditionally used to treat urinary complaints, digestive ailments, fever, coughs, rheumatic pain, gallbladder problems, metabolic dysfunction, poor circulation, migraines and toothache. Rich in vitamins A, B and C, iron, calcium, sulphur and phosphorus, the young shoots can be eaten raw or cooked as a green vegetable. The whole plant can also be used to clean windows and shine copper.

Pellitory-of-the-wall grows abundantly on walls and ruins, wastelands and neglected areas.

All My Wild Mothers

My mother was not like other mothers and in truth, I did not want her to be. I loved that she wore clothes patched from charity shops, sowed wildflowers in the lawn, and didn't quite fit in. She may not have cuddled me but I was always sure of her love, the way a root is sure of the ground. Growing up, I never stopped to consider that maybe other children didn't have to beg their mother to not jump out of the hotel window, or stop them walking into the cold North Sea. I never stopped to wonder about the tears and the times she would sleep, and sleep, and sleep. Though she would never see herself this way, I always saw her as brave, and funny, and kind, but in her own struggle to live in this world, she demanded everything from me. I wanted to rescue her but I couldn't and so, when I was sixteen, I left her behind.

There was no terrible argument. I quit school and told her I was moving to London, to live with some people I had met the week before. They were good people, I reassured, and luckily they were. My mother did not try to stop me leaving. Instead, she bargained. She would help me move, if I promised to ring home every week. I agreed. My father said nothing but, late that night, I heard him crying in the bathroom below my bedroom. It was a strange, unfamiliar sound that made my heart ache for him. I wanted to be small, and wrap myself inside his arms and tell him I would stay, but it was too late for that. I kept on packing, turning the stereo up loud so I would not hear.

Would I have stayed, if they had tried to stop me that night? I will never know. The next morning, they drove me to the station and did not stop to wave goodbye. As the rapeseed fields slipped away from view, Marianne Faithfull sang me out of my childhood towards the promise of freedom, 'The Ballad of Lucy Jordan' ringing like a fable in my ears.

When I unpacked my bag, I found a small, battered cookbook that my mother had slipped inside. On its cover pages, a handwritten list of basic groceries, and two failsafe recipes for my favourite meals. Each item was priced, categorised and calculated into weekly and monthly budget costs, just as she had done all her life. Scribbled into the last remaining corner of white space, four small words: *I love you, Mum*. I have kept it with me through twenty-four homes, and still have it now. In her practical way, she tried to equip me to survive in the world without her.

I did not want to leave. I wanted her to say, 'Don't go, I will look after you,' but I knew she couldn't, any more than I could stay. While her life had been cracking open, I had silenced my own pain. I knew it was me or her. Being young, I did what children are meant to do: I chose me. Being a mother, she did what mothers are supposed to do and she let me go but, as the house blew echoes through its empty rooms, she sat on the floor of my old room and cried herself into a small ball, wondering how was it that all those years of motherhood had suddenly stopped, finished without warning, so soon?

A hundred miles away, I put on my silver bangles, danced on tables and fell in love with a long-haired, golden-skinned man. My days were filled with mixtape soundtracks, sandalwood oil and sex. We walked hand in hand through Waterlow Park and listened to Dylan and Al Stewart, smoke hanging heavy in the hot, summer air. It was the great romance I had been waiting for, and the beginning of my new life.

Three months after leaving home, and six days short of my

seventeenth birthday, the love affair ended. I cried through the night and in the morning, I packed my cookbook and my bangles, and went home. I was not greeted with hugs. Instead, I was told that if I was old enough to leave, I was old enough to pay my way. If I'd had any illusion that I could run back to my childhood, I was quick to realise that it had gone.

Jobs in rural Oxfordshire were sparse, particularly for a seventeen-year-old school-leaver who couldn't drive. I worked underage in the local pub pulling pints, and got an apprenticeship on the nearby motorway construction site. I applied to be a trainee engineer, mostly because I remembered my sister singing the Peggy Seeger song, and partly because I thought it might run in the blood. When I got to the interview, they told me that the engineering apprenticeship was not right for a girl and gave me a secretarial job instead. I wasn't very good at it, and I couldn't type, but it paid.

At eighteen, I met and married a labourer who worked with the crew. Older than me, he offered me a stability that I thought I wanted to find. My parents said it would never work, and they were right. On the night of our wedding, he told me to stop behaving like a child and start behaving like a wife, but when I called home in tears the next day, my mother told me I had to make the best of the bed I'd chosen to lie in. I tried but things got worse and, after a year, I ran.

By twenty, I was divorced. I realised then that if I wanted rescuing, I was going to have to do it myself. I went back to school, and started the next chapter in my life, and even though I kept my promise and called home every week, it would be a long time before my mother could forgive my leaving, and years more before I could forgive her for letting me go.

Burdock

ARCTIUM LAPPA
Fox's clote, cockle buttons, happy major, love leaves

Drink burdock tea to release what is keeping you stuck

Burdock was commonly used to treat skin disorders and as a liver tonic. The root, leaf and fruit can be used medicinally as a diuretic and digestive. Antioxidant and anti-inflammatory, it can be used as a blood detox and to treat minor burns and reduce skin and joint inflammation. The root is well known as an ingredient in dandelion and burdock cordial, and the fleshy centre of the young flower stems can be boiled and eaten as an alternative to artichoke.

Burdock grows well in hedgerows and waste places.

All My Wild Mothers

When I was twenty-three, my parents decided to go travelling again. Their marriage had survived and all that stretched ahead was the wide, open space of time. My father had taken early retirement; the children had all flown. It would be different now, they said. They sold their home. It was a forward motion, underpinned by loss.

They only got as far as France before my father collapsed, his kidney rotting from inside. It was an unexpected twist that would return him to Cumbria, the county of his birth. Before that fate could play out, they had to let go of the past.

'Take it now, or let it go,' my mother said.

The rooms of my childhood home were like pirate chests, waiting to be discovered. As a little girl, I would lose myself in make-believe worlds, playing with polished fertility dolls, hand-blown glass birds and miniature cities carved out of ivory and bone. To me, these objects were tales to be told. I did not know that they were not my own. When I went to pick up my past, I found it had been claimed by someone else.

'Those are mine,' I said, as I watched my eldest sister bag up the books I had treasured as a child.

'They were mine first,' she replied. She packed her claim into a grey duffel bag, taking the books, the film projector and the 16mm family reels. She didn't have them long. On her way north, her bag was snatched, and the stories that we fought over were never found again.

I gathered up what was left, to take into my future life: a box of photographs, a one-eyed teddy bear, a wooden horse with a raggedy mane, and a collection of over eight hundred

BURDOCK

hotel soaps, one for each time my father went away for work. It was a peculiar dowry to own.

Thirteen years later, my sister drowned. In the absence of her life, I searched for something of hers to keep her anchored in this world. A keepsake. /ˈkiːpseɪk/ noun: *a small item kept in memory of the person who gave it or originally owned it.*

I wondered then about those things that were not mine to keep, the childhood that I thought I owned, but discovered was only on loan.

Forsythia

FORSYTHIA SUSPENSA
Golden bells, weeping forsythia, sunshine bush

Associated with anticipation

Forsythia is antimicrobial, anti-inflammatory and antioxidant. It has been used as an infusion to treat skin infections, acne, boils, vomiting, diarrhoea and sore throat, and to improve overall heart health. It can be propagated easily by bending the new branches down and sticking them into the soil. Once rooted, cut free from the parent tree and plant out.

Forsythia is adaptable to most soils but grows best in full sun.

FORSYTHIA

'Just a few weeds for the garden,' my mother says, as she arrives at our back door carrying a large willow shopping basket and a wooden trug filled with cuttings and muddy plants. She is short of breath, and starts to cough.

'Are you okay, Mum?' I ask. I am worried for her. She has had the cough for a while now, but the doctor has told her not to worry, and given her the all-clear.

'Oh, just getting old at last, I suppose,' she replies.

From inside the basket she brings out half a lemon drizzle cake, wrapped in tinfoil, and a small bunch of wildflowers. She shoves both these gifts into my hands.

'It's nothing much,' she says. Her gifts are always wrapped in an apology that borders on aggression, masking her insecurity at getting it wrong.

'They are beautiful. Thank you,' I reply, putting the flowers into water and the cake onto a plate. I call up to my son, who is busy playing in his room.

'Nana's here. She's brought cake!' I shout. I hear him bump on his bottom down the stairs. He slides, stocking-footed, around the door.

'Nana!' he yells, opening his arms wide for a hug.

'Slow down!' I say, worried he will hurt himself, but he is not listening. My son loves his nana, especially when she brings his favourite cake. She smiles, and pulls him in towards her for a cuddle. Physical affection comes easier to her with her grandchildren, though it is still a little awkward and stiff. He doesn't notice though. She is just Nana, and perfect in his eyes.

'I have some plants for your garden. Would you like to see?' she asks him, and off they go, hand in hand, to inspect her offerings. I listen as she tells him the names of each one: pulmonaria, red campion, mountain bluet, alkanet. They sound like the incantation of a spell.

'Just weeds, really,' she says again, apologetically.

'Weeds are treasures too,' my son tells her, as if divulging a pirate's secret code.

I put the tea on hold and go out to join them. My son digs the holes, and my mother and I plant in. We make a good team and, one by one, these new residents are bedded in with a pat, and a water, and a welcome wish from my son.

After it is done, I set down an upturned plastic grocery box and four salvaged garden chairs. There is a slight chill in the air today, but the sun is bright, and it will be nice to sit outside.

'Who wants tea and cake, then?' I ask, bringing out a tray.

'Nana's lemon drizzle is the best!' my son exclaims, and pats his belly. I check his blood glucose, and deliver insulin before he takes a slice, which he eats with lip-smacking approval. It makes my mother laugh. When he has finished, he wanders off, rooting out a T-rex and stegosaurus in the bog garden for his play. He straddles our worlds with ease. We listen on, eavesdropping from adulthood, remembering what it was to be a mother, and a child.

'You are a really good mum, you know?' she says, as she watches her grandson play.

'I learnt it from you,' I tell her, and it is true, for though the soil in that garden was full of stones, it is the love that pushes through. As I watch her, watching my son, this love makes my throat ache and catches my words. I want to tell her, but I know that there is a delicacy around these things.

Forsythia

My mother's love is quiet. I give her a small hug. She makes a harrumphing sound, but smiles.

We sit a while in silence. My son continues his game. The robin scratches in the disturbed ground. Bees land for a while on the poppy flowers. Nothing much happens, and that is good. I am thankful for these quiet days.

When the tea is done, she pulls the last plant from the trug. It is a forsythia cutting.

'It's probably the wrong time to plant it really, but it takes well,' she tells me. We sit without speaking for a short while, my hand resting on hers. I know the story of this plant. When my parents moved to Cumbria, my sister planted a cutting from her own forsythia tree in the field at the back of their new house. It was the first plant to go in, and the start of my mother's garden. Seventeen years later, what began as a field is full of flowers. In its corner, the forsythia blooms its blousy, yellow flowers each spring. Now, my mother brings a cutting for our garden here.

'It won't plant itself,' she says, brushing my hand away. She kneels back on the earth, with a stiffness that is hard to see. I unwrap the cutting, and kneel beside her. Together, we dig a hole and settle the cutting in.

'Welcome,' I whisper. The cycle moves another round, and the roots that connect us stretch out to gather us and carry us home.

Blackcurrant

RIBES NIGRUM
Quinsy berries, bugberry, stinkshrub, stallberry

Wrap blackcurrant leaves around
a silver coin to attract abundance

Blackcurrants contain vitamins A, B and C, magnesium, potassium, glycosides, essential oils, enzymes, calcium and iron. They have twice the amount of potassium found in bananas, twice the amount of antioxidant as blueberries, and four times the vitamin C of oranges. The leaves, fruit and seeds are edible. Anti-fungal, anti-inflammatory and antibacterial, they can help boost the immune system, stimulate the adrenal glands and inhibit blood clotting. It is commonly used to treat menopausal symptoms, painful menstruation, breast tenderness, joint inflammation, eye strain, muscle fatigue, bruising, minor wounds, insect bites, bladder complaints, diarrhoea, gum disease, and to relieve and protect against colds, flu, respiratory inflammation, sore throats and tonsillitis.

Blackcurrants are hardier than most other fruit bushes and can tolerate poorly drained sites.

Blackcurrant

'The Wild Women are here,' my son calls out. He has grown up with these women in his life, and considers them family too. They arrive with arms full, bringing a feast to eat, and plants to grow: rosemary, thyme and an apothecary rose. They busy themselves in the kitchen, an ease to our companionship grown through the years. There is an African proverb that says, '*it takes a village to raise a child*', but it also takes a clan to raise a woman wild. At twenty-eight, I did not know where I could belong. In that lonely space, I dared to ask the question: what if the thing that makes us a weed in someone else's perfect garden is the very gift that makes us shine? I set my question to the world, and these women heard the call to come celebrate our wild. Since then, we have conjured poems from the dark, laughed so hard we've peed, and cried our salt tears into the wounds of time. This world can feel hard, made of loss and sorrow, and I am thankful for the friendships we have sown.

As I get plates sorted for a garden picnic, my son invites his wild aunties into the garden to explore. He is proud of what we have created. As he leads them along the little paths, they name the plants that grow: selfheal, knitbone, eyebright, heartsease. In a different age, these women were healers and witches, their wisdom not written but told. The weeds we seek to spray and kill can be the medicine we need. Each plant and seed, each soil and root, even the broken ground that lies beneath, can heal. It is a knowledge that seems much-needed now.

My son takes them to his blackcurrant bushes. He has cared for these with the tenderness of a parent, planting their roots deep into compost, wrapping them in straw over winter to keep out the frosts, and cuddling them each day.

'These are my blackcurrant bushes. Love helps them grow,' he says, in a whisper of secrets known. I watch him, as he shines bright with the gift that his kindness brings. As I do, I recognise the truth. All life is interconnected. To grow one thing, it takes another.

Our garden is planted with the gifts of many. We are not doing this alone. There has been so much breaking, it can become easy to lose sight of the love that grows, as easy as the dandelion, through the cracks of our lives.

Wild Daffodil

NARCISSUS PSEUDONARCISSUS
Lent lily, chalice flower, daffy-down-dilly, bell rose

To see the first daffodil of the year brings good fortune

The daffodil is the flower of the dead and the Underworld and symbolises rebirth, resurrection, renewal and new beginnings. Ruled by the element of water, it helps bring about inner peace, hope and self-love. Extracts of narcissus have shown some success in pharmaceutical studies into the treatment of Alzheimer's disease, but it is highly toxic in its natural plant form.

Narcissus grows in grasslands, forests, along riverbanks and in rocky areas.

I am trying to teach my son multiplication. This is a struggle for us both. He wants to understand but doesn't know how the sums work. I want to help but keep getting the answers wrong, and a familiar shame rises up again. I have always found maths difficult. I can't see numbers, in the same way that my dyslexic husband cannot see words. Even though I tried hard, the sums would never stay fixed. I now know it is called dyscalculia but at a young age, I was labelled a dunce. The teachers placed me at the back of the class and told me to be quiet. When I was ten, long after everyone else was in bed, my practical sister, never afraid to reach into the fire, sat up with me and tried to explain algebra. But no matter how many times she tried to make it clear, I still could not understand why x and y would equal z. She refused to give up. Although she and I often fought as children, all my life she has appeared when I needed help the most, always willing to stay up all night, and keep trying.

Before long, my son and I are both crying on the floor. This is not the day I wanted to have, for him, or for me. I am trying to be a good mother. I am trying to be a good daughter, and sister, and wife, but I am drawn so thin by care, some days I feel like I am failing them all.

Which is how we find ourselves here, crying on the floor, surrounded by brightly coloured, laminated learning cards strewn out across the floor. I look at my son, his face crumpled up with confusion. Maths is not the cure for how we feel. I need to find a way to help us both. I get up, and leave the room.

'Where are you going, Mummy? Come back, Mummy, please,' he calls, worried that I am cross.

Wild Daffodil

I return, carrying a plastic box stuffed with brightly coloured acrylic paints and several large brushes.

'Come on,' I say, taking the box outside to the little shed by our back gate. After two years of use and weather, the door hangs off, the roof is peeling back and the flimsy, plastic windows are blown out. I squeeze and tip the paints out onto a slate. My son watches from the kitchen door. I take a brush, dip it into the primrose yellow and push the paintbrush all the way across the shed door. It leaves a fat, buttery mark. Then, I take another brush and dip it into the Windsor Red. This time, I flick the brush, firing it across the roof. My son comes a little closer, looking from the paints to the shed, and back to me.

'We will get into trouble, Mummy,' he says, concerned. I give him a paintbrush.

'If anyone asks us, we will tell them it is your art class,' I say, and dip my brush into another pot.

He chooses cerulean blue, and swirls the brush around until it is thick and shiny with paint, before sliding it across the yellow to create a streaky green. He picks up the red brush and daubs thick, vertical stripes. Then, he mixes them up to see what other colours he can make. Sometimes, he throws whole pots, roaring as he does. Other times, he sits in quiet concentration, carefully shaping a heart, a daisy, a creeping clematis flower.

A neighbour walks by and casts a side-eye at our mess. I smile, then turn conspiratorially to my son, grinning. The shed, the path and both of us are transformed into a riot of colour. We are no longer crying. I feel myself relax. Sometimes, it is good just to be a child.

*

All My Wild Mothers

When I was six, a friend and I found a large pot of blue enamel paint, buried among the tools in the shed. We worked all day, painting the furniture in the barn. My mother had a little antique business that she ran from home. This was her stock but to me, it was my treasure haul, and I made a playhouse of it all. We decorated drawers and wardrobes with blue stripes, coloured in the woven wicker seats of chairs, and redecorated the porcelain rose-covered washbowls with gaudy new flowers. The paint was sticky, and the smell made my nose sting, but 'no job is worth half doing', that much I knew.

After we had run out of things to paint, we stripped down to bare skin and painted ourselves, shaping ourselves fancy knickers and bras. Unaware of our Emperor's clothes, we walked through the village to her farm to play in the hay. Her mother took one look at us and drew a scalding bath. She scrubbed us with a green scouring pad and Ajax powder, until our skin bled and every last stitch of blue was gone.

'You should be ashamed, letting your child run wild,' the woman said when she returned me to my mother, washed and clothed. My mother took one look at me, with my bloodied skin and my tears, and pulled me inside.

'How dare you do that to my daughter! She was only being a child!' she shouted at the woman, then slammed the door. And that was that. She never told me off for the furniture that I had ruined, and the girl never invited me back to her farm.

'Why weren't you angry at me?' I asked, later in life when I was grown.

'Well, sometimes, you just have to let a child be a child,' she said.

*

Wild Daffodil

My son wraps his painted hand into mine, looks up at me, and smiles a big, gap-toothed smile.

'That was fun, Mummy,' he says.

And that is more than enough.

Wild Pansy

VIOLA TRICOLOR

Love-lies-bleeding, Johnny-jump-up, love-in-idleness, heartsease

To pick a pansy with dew still on will bring about a death

Wild pansy was frequently used in love potions and balms for heartache. It is associated with death and rebirth. Common medicinal uses include the treatment of inflammatory lung conditions, lymphatic impairment, liver complaints, cystitis, rheumatic pain, eczema, chronic fatigue, heart palpitations and other cardiovascular problems. Rich in vitamins A and C, both the leaves and flowers are edible, and the flowers can be used to flavour honey, custard, syrups and vinegars.

Wild pansy is a very hardy plant and grows abundantly in wastelands and grasslands.

Wild Pansy

After growing, the harvest comes. My son and I kneel in the damp grass, absorbed in the rhythm of the work as we pick soft bundles of blackcurrants from the stems and drop them into the bowl. Occasionally, we lift up our hands to brush away the curious wasps that land, attracted by the sticky juice. It is a long and quiet task and takes all morning. When our bowls are full and the bushes bare, we stand up and stretch out our limbs. My son grins.

'Wow! Well done,' he says, giving the bushes a congratulatory hug.

In the afternoon we sit around the table with my parents, topping and tailing to make ready for jam. My mother and I catch up on family news. My siblings and I joke that she is the Mother-Central Operator Exchange, through which our lives are joined, but there is some truth in that name. She is the root, and we are the fruit.

I notice a shadow of pain on her face as we talk. The last few months have been hard, and we have sat together in waiting rooms and doctors' surgeries, afraid of the answers they will give.

'Is it getting worse?' I ask, but she brushes my question away like a wasp; it has landed too close to home.

'Just a bit tired,' she says. We both know that it is likely to be more, but we all want good news.

My father does not speak. When I was younger, we both shared a love of words, but we struggled to find a common language as I grew. Now, as we both age, our words are lost to his deafness and my own left-over mistrust. As time pulls us on, I am aware that I will never know this man, nor the boy he was. What did he hide within himself, what did he give up, to have the life he did? Does he feel it was worth it, now that the years can never be regained?

I see him sneak my son a handful of pennies under the table, with a wink. I see my son hug his grandfather with uncomplicated affection; this grandfather that he sees at least once every week. Perhaps this is enough, then: to be here now, together, preparing fruit.

After my parents return home, my son and I add blackcurrants, water and lemon slices to the large pan, then simmer it down into dark, glistening jam, which we decant into sterilised jars. Our harvest gives us twelve pots.

While it cools, we walk the garden, taking in the courage of colours as they glow in the deepening dusk. We pick sprigs of viper's bugloss and mayweed, and place them gently in between the fading pages of my flower press, next to the lace-thin flowers from my own summer days. I take each one out, and hold them up to the light: violet, flowering currant, laburnum, bluebell, primrose, narcissus; each one leaves its echo on the paper, a mark to show the life it once held.

'These are our memory-flowers, so we will always know the gardens we have grown,' I tell my son, as we screw the wood slats down.

At bedtime, I make mugs of cocoa and slices of toast, which we slather in butter and hot blackcurrant jam. My son's face lights up, and he holds his finger out for a blood glucose check. Snuggled together in our big family bed, we share our feast. He closes his eyes, rolls the taste around his mouth, then eats.

'Thank you, Garden,' he says.

Nasturtium

TROPAEOLUM MAJUS
Nose twister, Indian cress

Plant nasturtium in your garden to help you stay on your path

Nasturtium is used to help overcome resistance to change, and to help ground. Rich in iron, vitamin C and minerals, it was taken on long sea voyages to protect sailors against scurvy. Antibiotic and antibacterial, it can help to boost the immune system, treat infections, cleanse and tone the skin, hair and scalp, and reduce fatigue from anaemia. The leaves and flowers are edible and can be used raw in salads, and the seeds can be eaten fresh or pickled like capers. It is an excellent companion for potatoes and cucumbers, and an infusion can be brewed from the whole plant to treat an aphid attack.

Nasturtiums are very adaptable and can grow in poor soils.

I have wanted a lemon tree for seventeen years. When I see one in the supermarket, reduced to half price, I pause, checking my purse to see if I can afford this treat. I count out the thirteen pounds, then put it back again. I cannot justify the expense. My son watches, then takes the little tree from the stand.

'You can have it for your birthday. It can be your wish tree,' he says, handing it to me. To him, it is a simple thing. He doesn't ask for proof that I deserve this gift, but sees in me the joy it gives. The simplicity of this self-love is something I am slow to learn. I buy the tree, and take it home.

I place it on my bedroom windowsill, where the sun shines brightest. Its scent conjures up hot evenings beside the lemon groves in Andalucía, where my husband and I once sat, dreaming of horizons before our future was set. We were on an adventure.

'Let's run away,' I'd begged. Things were falling in on me, and I was afraid. To escape was my reflex. At the end of my final year at college, we handed back the keys to our seafront flat, shaved our heads and abandoned the road laid out. For three months, we walked, our feet dusty and brown. On days too hot, we sat in street-side cafés, drinking cheap beer and staving off hunger with hand-rolled cigarettes. At night, we camped beside the lemon groves, the sharp, citrus sunset clinging to the air. I knew, even then, that I could not walk far enough to escape what was unravelling inside, but those lemons made what followed a little brighter for a time. When the walls closed in on our return, when I paced the room like a caged

Nasturtium

animal, longing to escape but terrified of what might be outside, I kept that scent of citrus buried safe within.

I hold the lemon between my finger and thumb, scratch its skin, and inhale. It is the first harvest from the little tree. The fruit is green. Citrus fruit will not ripen off the vine, and the northern summer isn't long enough for this Mediterranean tree, but it does not matter to me. It does not matter that this lemon will never ripen. It may give us inedible fruit, but on a sunny day, the memory of those two lovers sat beside the citrus groves fills the room with hope. I scratch the skin, breathe in the sweet, sharp sting of joy that it brings.

Make a wish.

Today, I am forty-three years old, and this is my life.

Bugleweed

AJUGA REPTANS
Carpenter's herb, sicklewort, carpetweed, green-wolf's-foot

Stuff a poppet with bugleweed to protect from hexes

Bugleweed was widely used in the fourteenth century to treat exhaustive consumption. Analgesic and narcotic, it can aid sleep, promote relaxation, reduce stress, regulate the menstrual cycle, and treat premenstrual disorders, palpitations, respiratory complaints, stomach disorders and the effects of alcohol withdrawal. The whole plant is edible and has a strong, bitter taste. The roots can be boiled as an alternative to artichoke, while leaves and shoots can be used in salads, casseroles, and to brew a tea. It is a rich source of nectar for bees, butterflies and moths.

Bugleweed grows well in dark places and scrubland.

BUGLEWEED

As a child, I swam in the wide, open lakes of America, each stroke leading me further into the silence; and yet, I am afraid now of what the water holds. When my son ran towards the stream, eager to paddle, I held his hand tight. When he wanted to follow his friends into the spring-fed pool that swells, ice-sharp, in the beck, I pulled him back, warning him about the cold. I have taught him that water is beautiful, but never benign; that nature can heal, but it can also kill.

I do not want him to be dry-docked by my fear. Which is why I am here, at the side of a pool, watching my son learn to swim. He looks over at me, pleading in hand signs for me to take him home. I get up to comfort him.

'Stay where you are!' the instructor shouts, pointing for me to sit back down. I obey, shocked into submission, and watch as she guides him into the water. She speaks calmly, maintaining eye contact with him all the time, as he takes his first unsupported strokes. After each spluttered width, he begs me to take him out. I sign to him with our 'love each other' code, but do not move. He looks to me, confused by my inability to understand his needs. It takes every measure of my self-control just to stay still.

My wish to comfort and protect him is at odds with my wish for him to move beyond his fears. I cannot tell him that, if he lets them, those unnamed fears will stop him again, and again. I cannot tell him how far that fear can drag you down. He does not have the luxury of a carefree life. He must be as strong as he feels with me beside him, even when he is most alone. So here we are, beside the pool, learning once more how much courage his small heart can hold.

He keeps swimming, and crying, until it is time to get out. I open my arms to him, ready to comfort. He runs towards me, wrapping his wet arms around my body, an unexpected smile on his face.

'I did it, Mummy! I did it!' he says. I bend down, and kiss his chlorine-soaked hair.

'You did, poppet. Well done,' I reply, my throat aching with love.

Later, as we cuddle in bed, he asks me why I did not come to him and when I try to explain, he tells me I could have told him that at the time. He is right. We are both learning how to do this, and these moments make us face the fears we hide.

'I love you to the edge of the universe, and beyond,' I whisper to him, as he falls into sleep.

'I love you more,' he replies, his voice drifting into dreams.

His love has given me the world to walk in. I hope that I can give him the same.

Calendula

CALENDULA OFFICINALIS
Merrybud, marygold, summer's bride

Hang a wreath of marigolds over your
door to stop evil from entering your home

Calendula has been popular as a medicinal, culinary and magical plant throughout the ages. It was used by ancient Egyptians, Greeks, Romans and Aztecs for culinary and healing purposes. Its Latin name *calends* refers to its habit of flowering at the beginning of each month and it has a long association as a woman's herb, used to ease menstrual problems. Anti-fungal, anti-inflammatory, antibacterial and antiseptic, it is used in healing salves, washes and creams to treat minor wounds, insect bites, burns and skin irritation. The petals create a light golden dye, similar to saffron, for cosmetic or culinary use. Leaves and flowers are edible and rich in fibre and vitamins. Planted alongside vegetables, they protect against a variety of pests, above and below soil. Often planted at the door to welcome good luck and prosperity, and on graves to protect and guide the dead.

Calendula grows well on roadsides, rubbish tips
and wastelands.

As autumn turns, my son and I search the local hedgerows for sour sloes. Grave foods, dry-mouth; nothing sweet to be found in this bitter fruit and yet, we gather them for gin. In spring, the roadside hedges are shorn back by huge, mechanical scythes that rip the blossom from the trees and strip the shelter from the nesting birds. Without blossom, there is no later fruit. We must look deeper into the fields to find our harvest.

Goddess of the waning moon, keeper of secrets; blackthorn wood was once offered to the fire, to banish the winter dark. I worry that my son carries his burdens too close to his heart. I see them whispering just behind his eyes as he tries to stop his tears, his body undoing him again and again. He gets scared. He has learnt to bury it inside.

'When you have a secret sadness that is too hard to carry, you can give it to the blackthorn,' I tell him. I know tying your sorrow to the blackthorn won't make the burden disappear, but sometimes, there is wisdom in what is said.

He thinks about it, then looks up at me, and smiles.

'I don't have any secrets, Mummy,' he tells me. I give him a hug, and wonder how long it will be before he does. There are secrets that I keep from my son; the way the world is harsh and full of thorns. When will the right time come to tell him of these things? Do I protect him, or myself, by keeping the darkness hid?

He knows of dying. My milk was curdled by grief. When I nursed him, I cried over his soft-crowned head. Every day, his body reminds me of how fragile we are, how close we walk to the precipice; how thin the thread is that ties us. Is it wrong,

Calendula

then, that I want his world to stay as soft as it can, to shield him from the truth of sorrow that this being human brings? There will be time enough for him to know the monsters can be real. For now, he greets the world open-hearted, throws his arms wide to embrace it, and finds sweetness where my fear finds thorns.

As we twist the fruit from the prickly branch, my son chatters about dinosaurs, and whether diplodocus would have eaten sloes. I tell him about Ötzi the Iceman, found on the mountain border between Austria and Italy, perfectly preserved over five thousand years. I tell him about the birch and sloes found in the medicine pouch buried by his side. As we talk, I remember a poem I once heard read, in a lifetime I no longer know, about Ötzi and the sloe, and viaticum given for the dead. Do those who die without warning travel hungry to the other side?

Back home, we wash each fruit and prick them with pins before putting them in the freezer; our false frost to speed up the season. The sloes look enticing, the colour and shape of black grapes.

'My tummy is empty, Mummy,' my son tells me, pointing to his stomach. Before I can warn him of the taste, he pops one in his mouth. His face puckers.

'Yuck!' he splutters, sticking his tongue out, trying to wipe the bitterness away with his hand.

'You have to wait until the first frost bites to make it sweet,' I tell him. He does not try to taste again.

The next day, they are ready. We drop them in a large glass jar, adding in sugar, cloves, star anise, orange peel and gin. Then, we hide it in the dark, and wait for the magic to begin.

'The jar must be turned three times each day, to help the

fruit release,' I tell my son, who listens with the intentness of an apprentice. He wants to be trusted with this important act. Each day, he sits down on the linoleum floor and sets to work, tipping the jar first this way, then that, counting out twelve times. We watch the liquid darken to the colour of arterial blood, the bitterness of the sloes now turned sweet. This strange fruit that needs the kiss of winter to break down its sour skin. Without the frost, the fruit would not yield its flavour. Without the thorn, the seed would not ripen, and survive.

The year is closing now, and the shadows whisper once again. As the gin steeps in the dark, I drive my mother to hospital, where we spend our days waiting in dull, beige corridors. Strangers scan my mother's body in windowless rooms, interpret the unseen landscape of her lungs. We wait. I learn a new language with which to understand this world we travel through. My father wants to believe in miracles. I tie red thread to the blackthorn tree, and brace myself for what is to come.

When midwinter turns, and the sloe-berries deepen to their darkest point, my son and I decant the gin. Though he cannot drink it, we pour a glass onto the soil to toast the waning year. Blood spell, viaticum, I whisper a prayer. *Let us make it through.* Not quite throwing the branch onto the fire, but an act to mark the darkness, and the light that I must believe will return.

Blackberry

RUBUS FRUTICOSUS
Bumble-kite, cloudberry, thimbleberry, blackbutters, gatterberry

To dream of blackberry foretells loss and sorrow

The blackberry is associated with protection, prosperity and healing, and is sacred to the ancient Celtic goddess Brigid, goddess of healing, poetry and blacksmiths. They were used in ancient Britain as a barrier, similar to modern-day barbed wire. Astringent, antiseptic and high in tannins, antioxidants, potassium, calcium, omega 3, fibre and vitamins A, C and K, the whole plant can be used for food, medicine and dye. The fruit can protect against skin ageing and improve memory. The juice can be used to ease labour pains, encourage clotting and regulate menstrual cycles. Young roots can be steeped as a tea or tincture to treat bowel upsets, and the leaves and berries can be used to treat thrush and promote mouth hygiene.

Blackberry brambles can be planted to prevent soil erosion, and grow well on scrubland, cliffs, roadside verges and wastelands.

The good news that we wait for doesn't come, and the cough that will not shift turns out to be tiny asbestos fibres, taken root inside my mother's lungs; breaking and scattering like malignant seeds, to bloom slowly in the dark. She is dying. The consultant confirms the diagnosis: pleural malignant mesothelioma. She is the fourth member of her family to die this way, exposed through her father's work cutting asbestos board.

'Oh, bugger. That's bad luck,' my mother says. The cancer nurse tries to reassure but she cuts her short.

'Look, I've seen my sister and my brother die of this already. I know what's what,' she says. I begin to cry. She offers me a pressed floral handkerchief from the pocket of her cardigan.

'Come on, now. Don't cry,' she tells me. I wipe the tears away, and suck up the sobs. I am here to look after her today.

When the appointment is done, and the leaflets are taken, we sit in the hospital café and drink coffee from cardboard cups. Tinsel glitters from the ceiling, and a volunteer plays 'Silent Night' on the out-of-tune piano by the door. It is Christmas Eve. I look at my mother, and wonder how it can be that she is dying, this moment determined seven decades before by a tiny thread of dust. I take hold of her hand.

'You don't have to do this alone,' I tell her. It is time to meet death face on.

'I do,' she says, and laughs. I suppose she is right. The last part, she must do on her own.

'Let's wait until after Christmas to tell the others. I don't want to ruin it for everyone,' she says.

'Are you sure about that?' I ask, knowing that secrets never make the truth any easier to hear.

Blackberry

In the end, she changes her mind. It is done quietly and without fuss, as she hands out home-made mince pies. There is no wailing, no beating of breast, no cries of '*why?*' I burn my tongue on the hot fruit. Pastry crumbles onto my lap. I brush it away. There is a pause from which we all try to escape what is coming.

'We need to decorate the tree,' my mother says, breaking through the silence to rescue us all. We are grateful for the release.

Growing up, there was an order to Christmas that my mother insisted we keep. In the days leading up, she would transform the kitchen into a witch's cottage, stirring up sugar and colouring to make coconut ice, peppermint creams, marzipan mice. On Christmas Eve, the tree would be picked and my father would carry it into the house, wedged into a bucket of water and sand. My mother, always the conductor of good taste, would oversee the decorating. As the youngest, I was allowed to place the angel on the top of the tree, but for the rest, it was best not to interfere.

After the mince pies and sherry had been left by the fire, and we had gone to bed, our presents would be wrapped and placed under the tree, ready to surprise. The unwrapping of presents was directed with care: one present at a time, and an appropriate pause given for appreciation, and thanks. One Christmas Eve, when my sisters were old enough to go to the pub, and I was still young enough to be left behind, they came home late and drunk, to find the presents already waiting. Carefully, they unwrapped each one, then wrapped them up again. In the morning, every time I opened a gift, they pre-empted the surprise to tell me what was hidden inside. I cried. My mother was furious. This was not the order of things.

The regimented unwrapping ritual was also the only time my mother had during the day to sit down with us and see our joy. The rest was spent in the kitchen, cooking the meal. How many moments were missed, with us racing on to the next bright thing in our lives? Now, it is Christmas Eve, and we are grown, and all I can think about is how little time there is for us just to sit, and celebrate the gifts of our lives.

My mother takes the decorations from the box. Fewer each year, yet they survive; this little box of broken baubles, made beautiful every time. The delicate, hand-blown glass spheres that refract the light, like oil on water; the threadbare tinsel she refuses to replace, because 'the new stuff is too garish'; the little garland of sugar-coated lanterns, bashed and bent, whose broken windows glow green and red in the dark; and the pointy-hatted elves, their pipe-cleaner limbs stretched and wriggled out of shape. Underneath it all, a squashed cardboard dodecahedron that I made when I was seven. It is ugly, but she insists it must go on. Sometimes, the order of things can be broken.

For fifty-eight years she has carried out these rituals for her children. Years of wrapping presents late into the night, her eyes prickled with sleep. Nights of stuffing the hand-stitched stockings with clementines and sherbet dib-dabs, and little wind-up ducks; my father creeping into our rooms to lay them on our beds, even long after we knew the truth. This year, we have told her not to worry about it all, but my son is still only six, and believes in the magic. She doesn't want to let him down. This is her gift to him, and to us all. She hangs the cranberry and orange garlands above the hearth, and lays the hand-stitched stockings by its side. As the log fire burns, I show my son how to twine ivy binds and holly leaves around a hoop to make a wreath. The house fills with memories, caught in fairy lights and gingerbread twists, and little, twinkling stars.

SEED SIX

Germander Speedwell

VERONICA CHAMAEDRYS
Fare-well, mammy-die, angel's eyes

If a young child picks speedwell,
the mother will die within a year

Germander speedwell is associated with vision, and is a traditional remedy for afflictions of the eyes. It is used for spells to bring about clarity, focus and purpose. Diuretic, astringent and expectorant, the leaves can be brewed into a tea, or made into an infusion to cleanse sore eyes, reduce fevers, soothe stomach irritations, alleviate bronchial congestion and detox the kidneys.

Germander speedwell grows widely in meadows, lawns, roadsides, railway banks and wastelands.

All My Wild Mothers

The calendar has turned, each pencilled mark another annotation in the final chapter of my mother's life. Today's heading is '*chemotherapy*'. My mother does not want it. She is tired of hospitals, and wants to live out what life is left away from their disinfected rooms, but the language of battle that surrounds cancer makes her feel like she is a coward if she does not try.

'I've got to give it a go, for Dad,' she says, even though we know that, at best, it will only give a few months of extra time. I tell her we would understand if she wants to stop, but she just smiles. It is something she must do.

We sit in the back of the hospital transport. My mother is worried that she will have to speak to the driver, and pretends to be asleep. He stays silent, and I am thankful for this quiet. I stare out of the window, watching the fields slip by. There is a certain shade of grey that falls across the Eden Valley in January; an old, washed-out-linen light that makes it hard to believe it will ever be green again. Hope feels very distant today.

We sit on hard, plastic chairs, in a windowless waiting room. My mother thumbs through *Hello!* magazines, trying to name the celebrities without looking at the captions. She is proud when she gets 'Brad and Angelina' right, and her satisfaction makes me laugh. The two women opposite us wear beige tweed skirts and brown jumpers that echo the brown and beige decor of the room. My mother does not blend in. She wears a long velvet patchwork skirt, pink top, and an oversized purple cardigan with deep pockets at its sides. 'A woman needs pockets,' she always said. I grew up with extra pockets sewn into all my clothes, and a hanky for each one.

On her studio wall is a faded copy of the Jenny Joseph poem,

'Warning'. She put it there to remind herself. 'That will be me one day,' she said. It feels unfair that this is her end. These later years were meant to be hers, a chit cashed in as her reward for all those lunchboxes and darned socks; a time when she would wear purple, and spit.

'What do you think those old ladies are in for? Do you think they're dying too?' my mother says, nudging me. She has no filter, and forgets to whisper, but she means no offence. She also forgets she is eighty-two.

The women in brown chat about the Christmas holidays just gone. The one on the left has had her extended family to stay.

'Well, you just don't know if it will be your last, do you?' she says. The one on the right has spent it alone.

'The grandkids were all full of colds, so what could I do? Can't take any risks now, not this far along,' she replies. I listen to their conversation, and wonder which woman I will be when I am old – the one who lives her last days full, or the one who won't take risks? I wonder which woman I am now.

The nurse comes and takes us into the chemotherapy suite. My mother sits in an oversized blue vinyl recliner and a large cannula is inserted into her arm. She looks so small as she sits there.

'I suppose I might lose my hair,' she says, then is quiet. I have bought her a magenta cap, just in case. It curls in my pocket like a mouse, unsure of when to make itself known. I take it out.

'I suppose you might,' I say, handing her the hat. She puts it on.

A different nurse wheels over a sealed metal trolley, marked with a radioactive sign. She connects the cannula to a colour-coded plastic pouch, and hangs it onto a metal hook. At precise

All My Wild Mothers

times, she reappears to silently disconnect and reconnect the bags. Clear liquids drip through the plastic tube into my mother's blood, violent and invisible. This will not cure her, we know that. There is no cure for mesothelioma yet.

As we wait, the nurse brings us scalding tea in plastic cups, the tannin so strong it dries my mouth. My mother sips hers and pulls a face, then smiles.

'Cheers!' she says. I take a photo of her holding up her cup, a magenta cap on her head, and grinning a big smile.

'Send it to Dad, so he knows I am okay. He'll be worried,' she tells me. I send it out to everyone in the family, and to her closest friends. I am not allowed the privilege of not worrying. As we walk into this strange new world, I must keep myself wide open. It hurts, but it is a gift too; a memory of hot tea, and laughter, and time.

Fairy-tale snowflakes start to settle outside the window. There was no forecast of snow. I begin to worry about the journey back, but try not to show it. As the drugs drip-drip into my mother's veins, I mentally process disaster scenarios. I have been given a leaflet, with an easy-to-understand colour-coded system, to help me understand more about chemotherapy and assess when I need to call for emergency help. It tells me that the worst post-treatment sickness often occurs on the journey home, and warns me that there is a heightened risk of sepsis in the first seventy-two hours. What if she starts to vomit in the car? What if the roads close? What if no help can get through? My internal traffic light switches to amber, the red warning signs pulsing urgently behind my eyes.

A quiet hush falls over the city. It is only January. Our last year begins.

Honesty

LUNARIA ANNUA
Moonwort, silverbloom, penny-flower, money-in-both-pockets

Gather moonwort at midnight to reveal what is hidden

Honesty was an important plant to sorcerers and witches during the Middle Ages, used to ward off demons, attract prosperity, unpick locks and reveal what is hidden from sight. Its energy is helpful in recalling what has been forgotten or repressed. The seed oil contains fatty acids that have been shown in some studies to have benefits in treating multiple sclerosis. It is used more commonly in the treatment of wounds. The young root can be roasted and eaten, the leaves can be used as a green vegetable or salad, and the seeds can be crushed and mixed into a paste as a substitute for mustard.

Honesty grows along paths, field edges, hedgerows and wastelands.

All My Wild Mothers

Our village sits at the bottom of the valley. It gives us shelter from the worst of the weather but sometimes, I long for the openness of sky. If we walk up the hill at the back of the estate, we can make out our house, and the route of the beck as it winds through the bracken fields and hawthorn trees behind. In spring, we watch the skylarks rise up from the fell, their song loud and full. In winter, starlings gather, the soft beating wings a murmured breath. Sometimes, we just sit and watch the wind spin clouds into shapes. I try to learn the meteorological names: cirrocumulus, stratocumulus, lenticular. My son picks out dinosaurs, spaceships, flying cows.

But today is special. Today, we have come here to watch the solar eclipse. We huddle on the rocks, coats zipped up tight against the wind, our hands warming around tin mugs full of tea. The sky is dense: stratus, the kind of cloud that looks like fog, blanketing everything beneath in a uniform grey. It is not ideal weather for sun-gazing, but we have made our cardboard pinhole camera, and we are undeterred.

As we wait, I try to explain the mechanics of the eclipse to my son. The sun is four hundred times wider than the moon, but lies four hundred times further away. A solar eclipse occurs when the moon comes directly between the sun and the Earth, so that the Earth lies in the shadow of the moon. Because the moon is much smaller than the Earth, its shadow only covers a small part of the Earth's surface, which means a solar eclipse can only be seen from one area at any given time. When the convergence happens, if you are in exactly the right place on Earth, you will witness a complete eclipse. It is the perfect dance of mathematics and chance.

Honesty

'Have you seen an eclipse before, Mummy?' my son asks.

'Yes, I have. Daddy and I saw one, a long time before you were here,' I reply. August 1999, the last year of the last century, when the future felt possible to reset. We sat on the hillside, and waited for the darkness to fall. It was the temperature change we noticed first, the summer heat dropping into a damp chill. Then the light, turbulent, refracting into sharpness and shadows, shimmering. When the silence came, we knew it was here. The birds drew in their song, and all the sounds of the fields ceased. We held our breath, and it was as if that single breath held the whole of the world. For two minutes and twenty seconds, the Earth and all upon it stopped its forward turn. Make a wish. Exhale.

Sixteen years on, and now my son and I wait on a hillside, and my husband is far from home.

'I wish Daddy was here to see it with us,' he says. Our world is dislocated right now, and he is leaning towards what is secure.

'Daddy will be able to see it with us from where he is,' I say, giving him a cuddle. I wish my husband was here as well. We never intended to be apart but as my life is drawn deeper into the shrinking days of care, my husband's is pulled outwards into the world of work. At night, his pixelated face lights up the dark, as we talk about our days, but it is not the same. I point up to the sky.

'The next time you will be able to see the solar eclipse in this country, you will be eighty-two, the same age as Nana,' I tell him. It is strange to imagine him an old man. I wonder what his life will have held by then, if the light will have measured out against the dark.

'Will you watch it with me?' he asks, and even though I

know the truth of it, I still feel the pain of that parting like a stone in my throat.

'No, sweetheart. By then, I would be over a hundred years old. I don't think I will live for that long,' I reply. He doesn't say anything then, but his hand wraps around mine and he holds on. This is the pain of love: to find it, and to know that you must let it go. Until then, we hold on, we hold on.

The sky cuts open the clouds, just above where we sit. The edges of the world shimmer, and the silence comes.

'This is it!' I say. We watch, enthralled, as the sun, and moon, and Earth, fall into line to give us a moment of pure dark. Around its perfect void, a golden halo forms. Darkness. Light. Life stands witness to it all.

And then, it is over. The light returns and, like a wind-up toy, the world begins again into its noise. We hold our stillness a breath longer, our hands held together in a quiet prayer: let this moment last.

When it is done, we build a small bonfire in our garden, to mark the equinox and the lengthening of days. Together, we watch the flames, and toast marshmallows that get stuck in our hair, and we laugh, our moment shimmering in joy.

We are all still cloud-watchers, in the end, waiting with one north eye on the signs, the other toward the ground; measuring the balance between the darkness and the light. I know the signs. What now? Everything, and nothing. Time to let go. Time to hold on. Into the dark, I let the light pour in.

When the evening folds away the day, we pack our bag once more, and head back to the world of medicines, cancer and care. Darkness and light; this day, a quiet pause.

Bluebell

HYACINTHOIDES NON-SCRIPTA
Fairy flower, ring-o'-bells, crowtoes, cuckoo-boots

If a child picks a bluebell from the wood,
he will never be seen again

Bluebell has a dual energy. Associated with grief and mourning, as well as being one of the first flowers of spring, they were often planted on grave sites to represent the rebirth of the dead. Folklore warns that to bring a bluebell indoors will bring sorrow into the home. Used to bring truth to the surface, it is said that those who wear a wreath of bluebells are compelled to speak the truth, to themselves and others. While not widely used in medicinal form, due to its toxicity, the bulb is styptic and diuretic, and can be used sparingly under guidance when powdered and dried. The whole plant is high in mucilage and was a common fabric starch in Tudor times, and used in bookbinders' gum.

The native bluebell is vulnerable to localised habitat destruction by cultivated varieties, and grows in shady woodland, hedgerows and damp areas.

All My Wild Mothers

I sit with my mother in her garden, watching my son as he builds a den at the foot of the big ash tree. Beside us, her spade stands upright in the soil, resting next to a clump of shy-headed bluebells and pale narcissi. The sun rings around the rainclouds, breaking through the dark to offer us early warmth. We turn our faces towards its heat, and let it soothe.

My father walks slowly down the garden path, balancing a cup of tea on his walking frame. He pauses to look at his wife, maybe remembering the girl with raven hair who dreamt of a world where the rooftops were golden and not smothered in smog.

'It will be a life of adventure,' he said.

'Yes,' she replied.

These are their love stories, scattered in their passing like seed-heads, to gather after they have gone. I watch these two people who gave me life: my father, who reads poetry but cannot find the words to tell us how he feels; and my mother, who loves us fiercely, but does not understand the ways it is shown. Together, they have raised six children, from the belly to the grave. Now, it is our turn to care.

'Your father gave me daffodils, the day he proposed. It was April Fool's. I suppose he might have been joking. Backfired a bit if he was,' she says, remembering that day, all those years before, when he offered her the world.

My father falls asleep beside us, his head resting on his chest, as he sits on the wooden bench. I think about how we grow old, and younger at the same time; how the years refuse to stick to time. Our different selves condensed into the single moment: my mother, the young woman who said 'yes' to the boy with the yellow flowers; my mother, holding her firstborn daughter among the March daffodils; my mother, walking by the coffin on a bright October day; my mother, watching her grandson build a den beside the old ash tree; my mother, preparing to die. I wonder how many of these women I have known over this lifetime. It feels as though I am only just getting to meet her, and now, I have to let her go.

Common Mallow

MALVA SYLVESTRIS
Cheese weed, billy-buttons, dwarf mallow, buttonweed

Use mallow to protect against demons
when travelling into the astral realm

Common mallow is high in protein, fatty acids, potassium, magnesium, zinc, selenium, calcium, fibre, and vitamins C and A. Antioxidant, antimicrobial, antibacterial and anti-inflammatory, it can be used to treat inflammation in the urinary, respiratory and digestive systems, soothe sore throats, and as a tonic for acne and dandruff. The whole plant is edible. Its leaves can be eaten as an alternative to spinach, and used as a thickener for soups and sauces. The seed pods can be boiled and used as an egg substitute. The roots are rich in inulin and can be stewed to make a healing broth, and the flowers and buds can be picked and pickled in vinegar or brine.

Common mallow grows well on roadsides, waste areas and cropland.

Common Mallow

It has been seven years, seven months and seventeen days since my sister died. As my mother's own end rolls in like fog, it is important for her to know where her daughter's ashes will be left. My sister's family have not been ready to scatter them yet, but have agreed to do it now, and we gather at Derwentwater to lay her to rest.

'We used to come here to canoe,' her daughter says.

I stand beside my mother at the shorefront, one hand supporting her arm, the other holding on to my son. She stays quiet, carrying a small bunch of narcissi in her hands. It is time.

We do not know how to do this. We are worried about the current, about whether it will carry the ashes back to the bank, and decide we must scatter them further out. I leave my parents and son on the shore, roll up my trousers and wade into the cold, my sister's family by my side. When we guess the distance is far enough away, we open the lid. I feel the weight of the urn, the functionality of this municipal, green plastic box.

Human ashes do not fly like dust. This surprises me. They are coarse and heavy, like chicken grit. They land on the water, and bloom into a white flower on the still surface of the lake, lingering as an iridescent sheen before sinking down. Her eldest son takes off his shirt, dives in and swims through the ash-lily out into the cold deep of the lake; an act of intimacy to mark this end. From the shore, my parents watch but do not speak. We have no prayers, no blessings for this time. There is nothing to say. Even now, seven years on, it is still too hard.

As we watch my sister sink below, another family arrives on the shore. They launch their kayaks into the lake, the paddles cutting through the ripples, and the ash. I want to shout at them to stop, but I keep quiet. They do not know.

We watch the water a little longer. When there is nothing more to see, and the lake closes over what remains, we return to the shore. My mother throws in the flowers and starts to cry.

'How can that be all that's left of my beautiful daughter?' she asks, as the flowers float away. I have no answer. I want to believe that my sister is now at peace, at one with the wild she loved so much, but that isn't how it feels. All the love, all the sorrow, all the bright and beautiful sadness that her life held; it comes back to this: her ashes sinking in the cold, green water, the pale spring sunlight like silverfish on the surface of the lake, and a handful of wild narcissi, carried away on the lightest of waves.

In time, I will return here with my son. We will fish on the water in a small, wooden boat, owned by a man my sister once knew, though we do not know this yet. A cardboard casket will float out beside us, a bunch of plastic flowers stuck into its top. The man will reach for it with his oar, remove the flowers, and push the casket down.

'So many of them here. They wash up on the bank, but it's the plastic that's the worst. It kills the birds,' he says.

I tell him about my sister then, about her ashes, and the bloom. He looks at my face, sees her traces in its lines, and smiles.

'I knew your sister well. She changed the world,' he says, and with that, he rows on. The quiet of the lake surrounds us, as the silent pike swim in the deep below.

Hedge Bindweed

CALYSTEGIA SEPIUM
Hooded bindweed, old man's nightcap, wedlock, granny-pop-out-of-bed

Carry an amulet of dried flowers to counteract negativity

Hedge bindweed is associated with thresholds and liminal spaces, and used in rituals to bind souls to the earthly realm and provide a thread to cross safely between worlds. The roots were said to encourage strength of will. It can be made into twine, and the leaves and stems can be used to make dye. It was traditionally used as a purgative remedy to cure blockages of the bowel, stimulate bile and increase menstrual flow. In Ayurvedic medicine it is used to treat confusion and neurological blockages but, due to its toxicity, it is not commonly found in contemporary herbal remedies and should not be used without guidance.

Hedge bindweed grows well on roadsides, in moist thickets, and around waste areas.

How do I release the hand that I have always held? '*Keep hold of my hand, and don't let go,*' the mother says to her child and yet, here she is, letting go. When my son was very small, I told him if he ever lost me, the safest thing for him to do was stay still until I found him again. Is that true?

I stay put. I do not run away. I wait. I am not the only one who is waiting. My father waits in his silent world, hoping for a miracle that will not come. My son waits for me to have time for him, follows me around the rooms, afraid I will disappear. My mother waits in a hospital room, for radiotherapy that she hopes will ease the pain. My sisters and brothers wait for news at the end of the phone. We are all unsteady, and exposed. Our houses are being blown by the wolf of cancer, but we do not know yet which one is made of straw, and which of stone.

Unable to reassure either myself or them, I suggest a distraction. It is my son who comes up with the plan. He wants to build a den in the garden. We haven't had much time to spend there in recent months, our days taken up with care. I think it will do us good to be in its wilderness now.

'We can build the strongest, mightiest fort, so it will never fall down!' he says. He draws out the plans and, together, we scavenge all the wood we can find. By the end of the day, we have collected four building pallets, an old cot, ten thick wooden fence posts, a broom handle, two shields, a broken sword and several assorted offcuts of laminate floor. It is a good haul.

The next day, we pick up my father and drive him, and his toolkit, to our house. He takes his magnifying glass and looks over his grandson's plans, takes out a stubby pencil from his

Hedge Bindweed

trouser pocket, and draws in some amendments to increase the strength and durability of the design. Although his eyesight is almost gone, his years as a mechanical engineer have not left him yet.

We work all day, stopping for tea and cheese sandwiches, which we eat in the long grass. Grandfather and grandson check building progress against the plans. I do as instructed, a hod-carrier to their master plans. Despite needing two sticks to walk, my father tries to help lift the heavy posts into place. He forgets that every day I lift and move my mother, whose swollen body weighs much more than a wooden plank.

My palms blister against the hammer as I hit in the six-inch nails.

'You're doing it wrong. Hold it like this,' my father tells me, taking the hammer away.

'I know how to hammer a nail in,' I reply. He looks at my son and pulls a face. The familiar static of shame rises up. Behind closed lips, I bite down on my replies. He cannot hear them anyway.

'You are doing really well, Mummy. You are good at this,' my son says, resting his hand on my arm. He is a good teacher. I smile, and pick up the hammer again.

My father watches with an engineer's eye. Because of this, the fort will not fall down, no matter how hard the storms. I carry out the tasks to get the job done, and my son brings the magic to transform. Together, we build. By the end of the day, the fort has a window, a lookout tower, a secret hatch, three shelves for weaponry and a swing door made from the bars of a cot. We step back to admire our work.

'Not quite finished yet,' my son tells us. He searches through the woodpile again, finding a broken broom pole. We find a scrap of upholstery fabric and cut out a large triangle. It isn't stitched or embroidered, but my son is satisfied. Together, we hammer it onto the post, then nail the pole high to the fort, flying our flag for all to see.

'It is the best fort ever,' he says. We stand and look at what we have built, together, on this day.

'That will keep you safe for a long, long time,' my father replies, patting my son on the head.

The light is fading on the day. We have waited, and we have worked, and now we must rest. I take my father home, then I feed my son, and sing his world to sleep. As I watch him breathing softly in the dark, I hold on to his hand. We can't stop the wolf from blowing, but, perhaps together, we can make our fort strong.

Woodland Sunflower

HELIANTHUS STRUMOSUS
St Bartholomew's star, comb-flower, golden-flower-of-Peru

Plant sunflowers around your home
to help the deceased pass over

Sunflowers are used to clear soil of toxic, industrial waste, including arsenic, lead and uranium. The stems contain phosphorous and potassium, used to fertilise poor soil. The leaves and flowers are astringent, diuretic and expectorant, and were used to treat fever, malaria, lung ailments, skin sores, swellings, and poison from venomous spiders and snakes. The seeds are high in vitamin E, magnesium, selenium, phytosterols and iron, and have a long medicinal history of being used to lower cholesterol, relieve migraines, reduce joint pain, ease muscle cramps, repair damaged cells and alleviate fatigue. All types of sunflowers are highly attractive to birds and butterflies.

Woodland sunflowers tolerate a wide range of conditions and soils.

All My Wild Mothers

I try to give my mother the space to live in these short days, gathering up the bureaucracy of life and death. When she can no longer care for my father or herself, we move into my parents' spare room to care for them both.

We stretch to fit this new role of care into the rhythms of our days. Into our routine, I add extra cooking, bed-changing, pharmacy trips, shopping, cleaning, doctor's calls, hospital visits and the rigorous alarms of our medicated hours. Six times a day, I crush different-coloured pills in the pestle and mortar, mixing them with crème caramel to try to disguise the taste. I wash, and change, and lift, taking her weight into my own, her feet on top of my feet, like a child at a dance. Every morning, I pick flowers from her garden, and place them in a vase beside her bed. When she can eat, I make her favourite puddings: lemon tart, strawberry flan, tiramisu. Each night, I oil her swollen skin with rose, and brush her fading hair, letting the silver curls rest in my hands. Where once she was the hub through which we shared our family news, I take up the role. I send out evening email updates about the difficult, dull and beautiful parts of our days.

My days are minuted by a list of things to do, that run like ticker tape through my head. My head vibrates with pharmaceutical names, dosing times, medical terms. I move through the tasks without pause, so that the transition points between become a fog. Exhaustion wraps around my brain like a drug, and renders me vague. Journeys between hospital, home, doctors, pass by without my noticing. I forget what it was that I was doing, or even if I was doing anything at all. I put the milk in the washing machine, and the washing-up liquid in the fridge. I stop mid-sentence, forgetting what was being said. I enter rooms, then leave again, not knowing why I am there. The leaflets from the cancer support charity tell me about self-care. My husband is so concerned about these lapses in memory, he suggests I speak to the doctor, but there is no cure for this tiredness, other than the one that I don't have: time. Caught between the needs of those I love, at either ends of their lives, I know the precious days we trade.

At seven, my son is patient, but afraid.

'I don't know where I fit in your heart any more,' he cries, when it all gets too much for him to carry. It breaks me, and I hold him close.

'I love you more than anything in the whole wide world. You are the centre of my heart, but right now, Nana is very sick and Grandad can't look after her, so we need to look after them both,' I tell him.

'I know, Mummy, but I miss us,' he replies, holding my hand.

My husband, who has worked so hard to keep us safe, is finally seeing reward but it comes with a price. Right now, he is in America, promoting a children's educational show he has helped to create. He calls from a taxi, somewhere in Los Angeles.

'It's crazy,' he tells me, at once excited and baffled by the change that has come. I try to balance the phone under my chin as I help my mother to the commode. I hear a glass smash in the other room. My father has dropped a tumbler and is trying to sweep it up, balancing one hand on his walking frame, and bending over to pick up the shards. I am worried he will cut himself, or fall, but he can't hear me shout. My son runs barefooted into the room, his diabetes sensor alarm warning low.

'I can't talk right now,' I say to my husband, and hang up. Later, when I call him back, I apologise. He asks me how my day has been, and listens as I tell him about the commode, and the glass, and the sensor alarms.

'I am just so tired,' I say. He tells me about the conference, and the swimming pool, and the fancy desserts. I know he is telling me this to share his day but all I keep thinking is, *what is this parallel life he is living now?* I do not want to be anywhere else. I do not want to be in Los Angeles, talking to a room full of people about my art, and yet, I feel angry. What I do here, this counts too. What of these invisible lives of care? These matter too.

As night wraps around the house, my son and I curl up, warm under the covers, to whisper stories in the dark. He sings me homespun lullabies, his small body nestled into mine, as sleep takes hold. It is a seed of softness, planted between the rocks of life.

I close my eyes but sleep is brief, and shallow. Before long, another alarm sounds for help. I kiss my dreaming son goodnight, and begin again the balancing act of care. I watch over them all. I do what I can. It is never enough.

When no one is watching, I put on old songs, and cry. This is the Last Chance Saloon that does not close. Death makes whisky sours in our kitchen while Life, in all its red and gold, plays show tunes on the honky-tonk, and sings of love. I want to stop. I want to change this. I want to not feel so damn lonely. I want my husband to not be so far away, following the scent of work. I want my father to not be frail, to be the strong one in the house. I want the ones who have died to be alive again. I want to find the laughter we once had. I want to mother

Woodland Sunflower

my son, without the needles and the nights of never-sleeping. I want to get drunk in a pub with the beautiful man I once knew, talk utopias, and make love, and not care, not care, not care.

And then, I put the record away. There will be a day when no one needs me to hold their hand against the dark, and I will grieve a different grief, but that is not today. Today, I must do what needs to be done.

I get up, and begin again.

Yarrow

ACHILLEA MILLEFOLIUM
Staunchweed, Devil's nettle, woundwort, Venus tree

Hold the feathered leaves to communicate with spirits

Yarrow was named after the Greek hero Achilles. It is the herb of the warrior and has a long reputation as a wound healer. Antibacterial and antibiotic, it is excellent for cleansing infections from the blood, and treating extensive blood loss from injury, childbirth or menstruation. It can be used topically to aid muscle strains, sprains and bruising to the bone, as well as in an infusion or wash to treat the acute stages of colds, influenza, fevers, respiratory complaints, digestive upset and urinary tract infections. It is used to help those who are always there for everyone else, and overwhelmed by the responsibility of caring for others, and is a useful remedy for when feeling worn down to the bone.

Yarrow is found on wasteland, waysides, coastal dunes and stable shingle.

Yarrow

As I learn to carry the cradles of care, some things are let go. Even so, we try to keep a grounding in the year's growth. Once a week, another daughter comes to take my place, tending our mother's needs so I can take my son home. It is hard to walk away, but I must.

Last week, we spent our respite planting seedling vegetables for the summer to come. I am not sure if we will be here to harvest but it feels important to keep ourselves anchored in the garden. Seven days later, we return to find every little plug plant, salad, cabbage and bean stripped down to skeletons and stalks. There is nothing left. All our work has been undone.

I look at the barren vegetable plot, and drop down to my knees. My chest heaves, wrenching out hot, heavy tears. The sound is ugly and strange in my mouth, but I can't stop. Somehow, suddenly it all seems so unfair, even though I know that fairness has no place in it at all. I rock back and forth, trying to comfort myself, a wounded child huddled on the ground.

My son watches me, unsure. He looks at the garden, at the spaces where there should be plants. I feel his arm around my shoulder, as he stands beside my keening body.

'It's okay, Mummy. Don't cry. It doesn't really matter who eats the garden. The slugs must have been very hungry, and they left us some silver to pay,' he says, pointing at the silver trails glistening across the soil.

I lean into his warm body. My wise and patient gardener; he is right. Sometimes, it is about what grows; sometimes, it is about the seeds; and sometimes, it is about the shimmering traces of the magic that happens, unseen.

Wood Avens

GEUM URBANUM
Herb Bennet, clove root, colewort, star of December

Wear as an amulet to ward off the demons

Wood avens is named after the twelfth-century German Benedictine abbess, writer, composer and philosopher Hildegard of Bingen, who nicknamed the plant 'benedicta', or 'blessed'. Astringent and high in tannins, it is useful for treating sore throats, bad breath, toothache, chronic bronchitis, nausea, vomiting, dysentery and other inflammatory bowel disorders. Used as an alternative to quinine and valerian, it can reduce fever and offer a mild sedative. The young leaves can be added to salads, soups and stews, and the dried root can be used as a moth repellant, or used as an alternative to cloves in soups, cakes, liqueurs and beer.

Wood avens grows well in landfills and other disturbed ground.

Wood Avens

My mother accounts her life in measures, not months, rounding up instead of down. With each count, she declares the same. 'I will stay alive long enough to . . .' she says, and sets her sights.

Today, she is eighty-three, and another measure is weighed out. As the house sleeps, I stir in butter, flour, eggs and cocoa to bake a cake. On the counter, a monitor keeps watch over my son upstairs, my eyes and ears alert to change. His small snuffles mix with the beeps and hisses of the oxygen machine that breathes beside my mother's bed. These are the sounds of night care that tell me that my charges are safe.

When the dawn breaks light enough to see outside, I go into her garden, my feet bare in the cool, wet grass. The old ash tree by the riverbank ripples with early birdsong. This is my between-time, where night falls away, and the day is yet to start. I take it slow, allowing myself the morning ritual of gathering flowers. I pick the powdery heads of Queen Anne's lace, still gilded in the Cinderella-dew of night, and a clutch of pale-pink roses from the climber that creeps up the back of the house. They match the flowers on her new nightdress that sits wrapped in pink tissue, a gift for the day.

I put these morning offerings in a chipped china jug and place them beside her bed. She will see them when she wakes.

'Happy birthday, my beautiful Mummy,' I say, as she opens her eyes. I haven't called my mother *Mummy* since I was a small girl but now, it seems to fit the mouth of the daughter who doesn't want to let go.

'I made it to another day,' she says, when she sees the light.

The house begins to wake and her children spill from its

rooms. Now grown with children of our own, we have gathered for her birthday. Death has walked too often with us these last years. It is easy to forget the joy, but not today. This day, my mother sits like a queen in her wheelchair throne, with her family at her feet. We eat cake, and drink tea from flower-patterned porcelain cups that don't hold enough to quench our thirst. The saucer shakes in her hand, and my son reaches up to place his small hand beneath her own to steady it. When there are toasts to be made, she taps on her cup and apologises for not having the right words.

'There's one good thing about dying this way. I always thought I was a rubbish mum, but maybe I wasn't so crap after all, because you are all so lovely,' she says.

I feel sad when she says this, because I realise I have forgotten to tell her how much I love her, how much I am grateful for. The brain is stimulated to remember unexpected events, but what of those that slip by in the quiet background of our lives; the little acts of love that go unnoticed at the time? The truth of it is that I never even really noticed, let alone thanked her, for the many things she did to show us that she cared, and the many ways she showed me to be strong.

As the day lengthens, there is laughter, and ice cream, and we sing 'Happy Birthday', out of tune, to this woman who cycled with the man she would marry through post-war Europe at seventeen, a wide-brimmed hat tied to the front of her bike just so she could wear it in Paris; this woman who painted wild Scottish coasts, and packed our lunchboxes every day, for thirty years; this woman who often cried, and sometimes tried to die, but, when she thought no one was looking, flapped her arms to see if she could fly. I want to tell her that I can see her, the beautiful, wild woman who the years have tried to tame, and the mother she became.

I do not know how long we will keep hold of this thread that ties us together. It stretches with loss but in the end, all we have is life, and death, and all the mundane miracles we almost miss between. Even though we weep, we must still give thanks for the moments that we have, and sing.

And when the singing is done, we wash the pans, and tidy the plates. My father sleeps in the recliner chair, dreaming of a love story we will never know. My son plays with his cousins in the upstairs room, his laughter filling the silent spaces of the house, as I measure out medicines, and remake the sheets.

'Goodnight, my beautiful Mummy,' I whisper, before shutting out the summer light and soothing her to sleep. My mother only ever sang one song. 'Silent Night', which she sang in German, though I never knew why. She didn't like singing. When my father sang his hand-me-down, wartime songs, she stiffened as if in pain. Still, she sang this one lullaby, and it was beautiful, and sad. As the dark comes closing, it is her voice that I remember, singing soft and low. I rest my hand upon her cheek and sing to her, as she once did for me.

Stille nacht, heilige nacht, alles schläft; einsam wacht . . .

Hawthorn

CRATAEGUS SPP.

May-tree, hagthorn, quickset, hawberry, bread-and-cheese

Take hawthorn into the home, and a death will soon follow

Hawthorn has a long association with death and rebirth and is a traditional remedy for soothing heartbreak and grief. Antioxidant, anti-inflammatory and astringent, it can be used to treat coronary artery disease, reduce cholesterol, dilate blood vessels, strengthen and regulate the heartbeat, treat nervous energy, improve mood and soothe sore throats. Because of its ability to suppress appetite, it was commonly eaten as a meal supplement when food was scarce, earning itself the name of 'bread-and-cheese'.

Hawthorn is a hardy hedge tree, and adaptable to most soils.

Hawthorn

I push my mother's wheelchair through shabby, beige corridors, and up in the lift to the third floor of the hospital. We wait in a small room, where posters tell us we are not alone. The room is full. Everyone is alone. An elderly porter offers tea, and custard creams wrapped in cellophane, from a metal cart. We pay a pound into the charity pot, and take the tea. My mother isn't able to swallow solids now but she insists on taking a handful of biscuits, furtively putting them in her handbag for later need.

'You might get hungry on the way home,' she says. It is a habit I have inherited from her, and now passed on to my son. In any hotel, the first thing he does at breakfast is fill his backpack with the miniature pots of honey and jam. Pocketable condiments, and the hotel gets his five stars. For my son, this is a measure of its worth.

She puts the little biscuits into her bag, and sips on her too-hot hospital tea. A man dressed in a perfectly tailored, navy twill suit strides through the waiting-room door. As he passes us, there is a soft squeak on the linoleum floor; not the harsh squeak of plastic, but the smooth pad of well-crafted leather shoes.

'Italian,' my mother says. I go to ask her how she knows this man is Italian, but realise she is not talking about him. She is talking about the shoes. She approves. They speak of quality and craft, not cash. It seems the years at *Vogue* haven't left her.

He ushers us into his room, smiling at us with two rows of perfect white teeth. When we are seated, he turns the computer screen around, so we can see the grainy black-and-white scans of my mother's lungs, the telltale white intrusion pushing out all the black. The end of summer has brought a dark surprise.

He folds his long, manicured fingers together, rests his hands on the desk, and begins to explain what all the other doctors have avoided saying thus far.

'I am afraid there is no good news,' he tells us.

'How long do I have left?' my mother asks. Doctors are reluctant to answer this, even though it is nearly always what people want to know; but this time, the oncologist replies.

'The rate it has spread, possibly two weeks, maybe six,' he says. There is a pause. We are not expecting this. How can a life be measured out in weeks and days?

I try not to cry, knowing it will embarrass my mother, but I fail. She reaches to comfort me, awkwardly patting my arm and frowning, unsure of what she is meant to do next.

'Oh dear. Come on now, love. It will be all right,' she soothes, a mother to a child, even now. She turns to the consultant.

'My daughter is sad because I'm going to die,' she says, feeling the need to explain my sudden tears to this man. Then she smiles, and nudges me.

'I guess if I'm going to be told bad news, I'd rather be told by a man with nice hands, and good shoes,' she says. I look at my mother and laugh. She looks confused.

'I wasn't trying to be funny,' she says. It makes me laugh even more. The consultant looks on, bemused at the woman and her daughter, laughing and talking about shoes.

'I am very sorry. I think there is no point making you come here again. My advice is to go and live what is left of your life,' he says, before rising to his well-heeled feet, and showing us the door.

Hawthorn

As we sit in the hospital taxi, I pour out a measure of liquid morphine to help with my mother's pain.

'You look like you need it more than me,' she says, pushing the bottle towards me. My mother, who doesn't even drink, is offering me morphine in the back of a car. Again, she makes me laugh, despite it all.

We are silent for a while, the tarmac roads pouring us onwards towards home.

'The worst thing to do with life is waste it wishing it was something else. It's the sum of the parts: some bad, some good. You need to live it,' she says, taking my hand. I don't know what to say, and so I stay quiet.

As the road slips away, she drifts in and out of sleep. I watch the traffic slide by, and send a message home.

'Not good,' I say, when my husband asks for the news.

She startles me when she speaks again.

'I think they should be white, with flowers on. That would look nice,' she says, without opening her eyes. Conversation is often this way, as we wander the morphine trail.

'What should be?' I ask, confused.

'The stairs. I'm going to paint them before I die,' she says. She can barely stand now. I admire her determination, but the tired part of me is annoyed. Taking extra risks means giving extra care, and I am already worn thin by it all.

'How are you going to paint the stairs when you can't even walk?' I ask, irritation snapping at the edges of my voice.

'I'll find a way,' she replies.

Pineapple Weed

MATRICARIA DISCOIDEA
Rayless chamomile, disc mayweed

Burn with human hair to stop a loved one from leaving

Pineapple weed derives its botanical name from the word *matrix*, meaning 'of the womb'. It was commonly used as a remedy to assist post-partum delivery of the placenta, alleviate morning sickness and encourage milk flow in nursing mothers. Sedative, anti-inflammatory, antimicrobial and antispasmodic, it can be used to ease nervous exhaustion, relieve insomnia, counter stomach upset, cleanse infected skin, reduce eye irritations, soothe sunburn, lower fevers, and as an insect repellant. It is frequently used as an essential oil in the perfume industry. The dried and preserved flowers were a traditional sweet treat for children. A common chamomile, the fresh flowers can be used in salads and jellies, and made into syrup, cordial or aromatic infusion to aid sleep.

Pineapple weed grows best in pavements, poor soil and wastelands.

Pineapple Weed

My mother's people came from the land of mudlarkers, the ones who saw value in what was thrown away. She encouraged me to do the same. My husband cannot see the reason for filling pots with coloured glass and broken plates, but my son and I know: these are our talismans of time.

When we find a piece of pottery in the soil, my son is excited. No bigger than a thumbnail, it reveals the smallest fragment of soft, blue willow plate.

'Let's take it in to Nana, she knows about old things,' he says, going indoors to show her his find.

Her world reduces in small breaths, becoming first a country, then a county, then a village, a garden, a room, a bed. My son notices this, but does not hide. Instead, he finds a world where they can both adventure, and our evenings are spent watching reruns of antique shows. They try to guess what will be the best find, and he is impressed by her knowledge every time. As I busy myself with the routines of care, he takes hold of her hand, and explores the past.

'This is blue willow-pattern china. See, you can just make out the tree,' she tells him, pointing to the catkins.

'How old is it?' my son asks, standing by her side, attentive to her word.

'You see where all these little lines are? The earlier the pottery, the more cracked the glaze. I would say that maybe, it is even older than me,' she says, as she turns the pottery over in the palm of her hand.

There is a story behind the blue willow design. My mother used to tell it to me, and now she tells it to him. As he settles down to listen, on the rug at her feet, I am reminded of an earlier time: my mother and me, sitting on the red rug beside the radio, waiting for the familiar chime of bells before the opening line. 'Are you sitting comfortably? Then I'll begin . . .'

Once upon a time, there was a young woman who fell in love with a good, but poor man. Her father was rich and powerful. He did not approve of her choice and banished the young man. Then, he ordered a high wall to be built around the garden, so high that the young man could never see in, and the daughter would never see out. It was a beautiful garden, but the daughter was sad. Each day, she walked the gardens, and sat beneath the willows, and wept, but the young man, determined to be with her again, found a way to rescue his love. The father saw, and chased them over the bridge, shouting and screaming for them to stop, but they escaped, sailing away on a little boat. The father was so angry by then, and chased them on and on, until one day, he caught up with them and killed the young man. The daughter, broken-hearted, wept and died, and on their deaths, they turned into doves and flew away, free at last . . .

'What do you think about that? It's all here, in the design,' my mother says, after finishing the tale.

'That is a big story for a little piece of plate,' my son replies.

'Well, you only have part of the picture here. The rest of the story will be out there somewhere, for you to find, and I've got a perfect place for you to keep it too. There's a tin box on my dressing table. You can have that, if you like,' she tells my son.

My son goes and fetches the sweet tin from her old bedroom, and brings it down to her. It is decorated with roses, and rattles when he gives it a shake. He gives it to my mother, who opens it. Inside are several pieces of cullet, worn smooth and opaque by the tide.

'Grandad collected these for me when we were young. I don't think he'd mind me giving them to you. You can put your other treasures in here too,' she says, handing it to my son.

'Thank you, Nana!' he exclaims, hugging her gently. He takes the tin, and adds his small piece of pottery to the glass; another fragment of the story for it to hold.

Red Clover

TRIFOLIUM PRATENSE
Bee-bread, honeystalks, suck-bottles
Carry clover for protection when walking between worlds

Red clover was used as an anti-cancer remedy until the 1930s. Rich in vitamin C, potassium, phosphorus, chromium, niacin, thiamine, calcium and magnesium, it can be helpful in reducing free radicals in the body, and to boost the immune system. As a remedy, it has been used to treat lung congestion, bronchitis, whooping cough and similar respiratory illnesses. It may also be used to alleviate symptoms of the menopause and premenstrual syndrome, assist healing in skin complaints, and slow down the appearance of wrinkles.

Red clover increases soil fertility, and grows well on wastelands.

Red Clover

September comes to its end, and the days are shrinking faster now. When I go into my mother's room, I find her already awake.

'I told you I would make it to your birthday,' she says, handing me an envelope. I open it to find a small card, no bigger than a cigarette box, with one of her paintings on the front. A Scottish coastline, with a little, white house nestled into the rocks. All those wild, open spaces, but it was always the little house I wanted to reach. 'The trick is to have a point of focus, to make the viewer want to step in,' she once told me, when I asked why she always painted one into the landscape. Home.

Inside, there is a short message. She has crossed it out and rewritten it three times, trying to make it neat. Her hands, which once could stitch the most delicate flowers, now struggle to write.

'*Thank you. Love, Mum*,' it says.

'Get me my bag,' she says, pointing to the grey leather bag that hangs on the door. Popping open the brass clasp on her purse, she takes out five ten-pound notes, pressing them into my hand.

'Buy yourself something special, just for you,' she says, with a smile, before resting back onto the pillow to sleep. As I adjust the padding under the nasal oxygen tube, I wonder how it is that, even now, she has managed to make this day a treat.

After the hospice nurse arrives, I take my son into town. It feels luxurious to have the whole day for ourselves. We wander through displays of Roman artefacts in the museum, drink frothy hot chocolate in the bookshop café, and look for hidden treasure in the charity shops.

All My Wild Mothers

I find it in among the £1 bargain box books: a first-edition, hardback copy of *Lemonade Serenade; or The THING in the Garden* by Don Madden, its dustjacket starting to yellow and crack. Inside, I find the previous owner's name. 'L. A. Bowden, 1976'. The year I turned five.

I start to read aloud, stepping in through the portal of the page.

'... *Every morning as soon as the sun woke up, Emalina Twig stepped lightly into her garden ...*'

*

'Time for elevenses,' my mother calls, bringing out a tray. There is black coffee for her, sour lemonade for me, and two slices of sweet fruit cake. We sit on the grass. It is newly cut, and smells of hay and soil. A white chicken scratches in the mint bush. Everything is hot, and slow. Across the field, I can hear the low drone of a tractor. We are alone. She opens a book, and together we read, our voices sing-songing over the familiar words. My mother is teaching me to read. I lean against her shoulder, breathe in the scent of coconut and rose. Her skin is warm and brown, weathered by sun. This story makes her smile. I watch a small, white cloud bubble across the blue sky. The wood pigeon calls its five-beat song from the tall pear tree, claiming its roost. I drink my lemonade, the tang of citrus against the sweet.

*

'... *It was such a happy place that it didn't seem possible anything frightening could happen there ...*'

I loved Miss Twig, with her impossible hat, ostrich feathers and long, purple gloves. I loved her insistence on biscuits and lemonade, and her garden, with its exuberant ferns, hidden

Red Clover

bathtub lilies and preposterous Boombamaphone. I loved her, but I had forgotten her. After all this time, I had forgotten her, but here she is; hiding between these brittle pages, waiting to be found.

'Is this your special thing?' my son asks.

'Yes,' I say, taking it to the counter to pay. The volunteer smiles down at my son.

'A new book? Who's a lucky girl?' she says.

'Thank you. I'm a boy. It's Mummy's Special Thing for her birthday. She is forty-four,' he replies. The woman looks at me, and I smile. It is difficult to explain. We leave, the book carefully stowed away in my bag.

With my birthday money, I buy lemons, sugar, flour, raisins and eggs to make lemonade and fruit cake, and after this is done, I sit in our garden, under the last of the September warmth, and read the story to my son. He fidgets, but tries to listen. He prefers stories of dinosaurs, and cat detectives. When he drinks the lemonade, its sourness makes his nose wrinkle. The cake has too much tea, and not enough heat, and is soggy to eat. Our day is nearly done. The book is closed. This is not his memory. It is mine.

But when all are asleep, and the night has come, I open it back up, and slip softly between the pages. There, hidden in that garden of vines and roses, I find Miss Twig waiting, in her impossible hat and long purple gloves; a jug of lemonade on the table, and the day stretching out like a cat, undisturbed by time.

Lavender

LAVANDULA ANGUSTIFOLIA
Elf leaf, nard, nardus, spike

Carry lavender to see ghosts

Lavender was traditionally given to women during childbirth to encourage strength and aid courage. Antibacterial, carminative, nervine and antidepressive, it was used in both World Wars as a field medicine. It is a helpful remedy for stimulating tissue repair, disinfecting wounds and treating minor burns, sores, cuts and ulcers. Frequently used to alleviate anxiety and insomnia, and relieve tension headaches and migraines, it can be dried, infused in oil, water or balm, made into a tea, or used directly in food as a floral flavouring.

Lavender attracts pollinators, and thrives in sandy, rocky and poor soils.

Lavender

Three years ago, when we moved to the estate, we bought two small lavender plants from the bargain-price store, to plant at our front door. In that time, these little plants have grown into blousy bloomers that spill out over the tarmac path. As the estate children make their way to school each morning, they absent-mindedly run their hands through the flowers, scattering lavender behind them as they go. A memory rises up, one in which I am a young girl, strewing lavender between the layers of tissue paper in my mother's linen trunk. It is caught briefly, then lost with the scent.

Today, the bushes thrum with the business of bees. It is always the same each year. The best time to harvest is right before the summer turns, but I don't want to deprive them of this late-autumn food, and so the flowers are left unpicked. This year, we are even later to the task. September has slipped into October, and the best of the lavender has gone. The flowers are damp with rain and there is no time to wait until a drier day.

My son and I set about gathering what we can. We snip the long stalks, and lay them in a cardboard box. We have an hour before we must return to my mother's care.

'I want to make Nana a lavender pillow. It will help her feel better,' my son says. Our house is filled with hand-stitched cotton hearts my mother made from scraps of skirts and worn-thin shirts. They hang from curtain poles, hide below pillows, and are tucked between clothes, each one stuffed with dried lavender and rose petals, picked from the flowers in her garden.

My mother is a talented stitcher. When I was seven, the same age as my son is now, she stitched a wedding gown for my doll. The doll was three inches tall and yet, my mother created a dress as fine as any real wedding gown, made out of an old handkerchief. She sewed on tiny mother-of-pearl buttons, and a bustle and train made from antique lace. The doll married a three-inch groom, who dressed in a shabby brown suit. They went on to have three children called Lucy, Paul and John. Their marriage didn't end well, and the wedding dress became grubby and torn.

A stitch in time saves nine. I never understood this saying. Maybe it is because I have never sewed. Spool the thread forward, and I reach eighteen. My mother kneels in front of the open fire, stitching my wedding dress from a white cotton sheet, a doily for the décolletage, and a cream satin sash made from a curtain pell. She opens the catch on her old jewellery box, takes out a necklace, and breaks the thread, the glass-studded clasp dangling from its broken string in her hand. Little river pearls scatter on the floor. She picks up each one, and stitches them on. She buries tight, pink rosebuds from her garden between layers of silver sand, and waits patiently for them to dry, threading each perfect, preserved flower with wire and coils of cream ribbon for my headdress. For three months, she stitches and picks, dries and wires, until the house spills over with soft pink roses, and clouds of baby's-breath flowers.

When my wedding day comes, she weeps. I want to tell her I have changed my mind, that I don't want to grow up, but I look at the dress, with its hundreds of tiny pearl flowers, and I don't say a word.

The wedding dress survived; the marriage did not. The year after my son was born, I took the dress out of the drawer, and unfolded it from the yellowing, tissue-paper cocoon. Crumbled roses scattered like confetti on the floor. What place did this dress have in the stories I might leave behind? Better to put it to use than keep it hanging around.

'Are you sure you want to sell it?' the woman in the dress agency asked, her fingers following the delicate pearls. I hesitated, remembering my mother's patient needlework, but I needed the cash for bills.

'Yes,' I said, handing over the dress and walking away.

Despite my mother's skill, and my teacher's insistence that 'girls should always know how to sew', I never learnt beyond a tacking stitch. My fingers were always too fumbling, and the patience and talent of my mother did not pass down the line. I fill our scrap box with offcuts, buttons and broken beads, imagining I might grow into her one day, but I am not that woman.

'Can we, Mummy? Can we make a lavender heart?' my son asks again and, even though I know it will never be like hers, I say yes to his request, hoping my mother's morphine haze will soften out my mistakes under her critical eye.

When we are done harvesting the lavender, we drive back to my mother's house. The respite nurse is readying to leave when we arrive. I see her out, as my son unloads the bundles onto the kitchen floor. Before we can use the flowers, we must bake out the damp.

My mother is asleep in the recliner. I want to leave her there, at peace in whatever world she is dreaming, but she is due her medication. Polypharmacy, in end-of-life care, is delicately measured out. If I don't wake her now, the pain will rise and we will be left chasing it into the night. I grind and empty the different pills into a powder, and mix it into a pot of crème caramel. It is disgusting, but she can't swallow solids, and it helps the medicine go down.

'Time to wake up,' I call, echoing her own sing-song call from my childhood, when my day would begin with her greeting, and a cup of tea. This simple, sure-start way into the day she gave would be a touchstone in later years. Time to wake up.

She pulls herself out of sleep, looks up, and finds focus. I hold out the china cup and saucer. She nods. I put them on the table, and replace them with the pudding pot. She grimaces.

'Yuck!' she says, sticking out her tongue. My son laughs, and takes hold of her hand.

'You have to do it, Nana. If you do, you can have the tea,' he tells her. He knows what it takes to bargain for the better thing, that sometimes the bitter has to be swallowed on the way. She understands, and complies.

We sit there a while, me holding the cup to her mouth for her to sip, and my son busily telling her about the bees, the rain, and the lavender that is baking slowly in her oven. When the palliative nurse comes to discuss hospice care, my son and I go back into the kitchen, returning with the warmed flowers and two large bowls. We sit on the stone floor, tucked away in the corner of the room, and quietly strip the stalks from their flowers.

As we strip and sift, the scent swallows the room, creeping under the doorframe and up the stairs until the whole house is heavy with the perfume of long, hot summers, linen trunks and laundered sheets. This soft enveloping of childhood, which stands at odds with my memory and yet, here it is, so clear:

Lavender

white sheets, bergamot tea, lavender flowers, silver sand, rosebuds, beeswax, dust; the quiet hush of ash, and her fingers, stitching those little river pearls. I long to claw them all back again.

Cowslip

PRIMULA VERIS
Key of Heaven, fairy cups, plumrocks, freckled-face, golden-drops

Place under your pillow to induce
contact with departed loved ones

Cowslip is listed in Hildegard of Bingen's twelfth-century
Physica as a treatment for melancholy. The plant is diuretic,
laxative, anti-inflammatory, antispasmodic, decongestant and
sedative. Its flowers and leaves are very high in vitamin C,
beta-carotene, potassium, calcium and sodium. An infusion
from the flowers can be used to treat insomnia, anxiety,
nervous tension, headaches, exhaustion, chronic bronchitis,
bladder infections, kidney stones, rheumatism and arthritis
pain, and alleviate allergic reactions. It can be applied
as a hot compress to relieve facial neuralgia and sunburn.
Edible, it can be eaten raw in salads, or used as a
flavouring in vinegars.

Cowslip grows well in disturbed areas.

Cowslip

There is not much left in my mother's garden, this late into November, but I can usually find one or two offerings to bring inside. Today, I have found wild marjoram and a late-blooming marigold. I place them on the table beside the bed. My father sits where he sits every day, in a chair next to her side, her hand in his. I move around them quietly as I dust and polish the wood, wash the tiled floors with soap and French lavender, and air out fresh sheets to put on. At the beginning of the cancer, she told me she was afraid of the smell of death.

'When I was a girl, there was a woman and her house smelled of death. No one ever said, but I remember the smell. Don't let me smell like that,' she'd begged. My daily ritual; I repeat these acts of care in every room, even those she will never see. At the end of each clean, I spray her perfume into the air: 'Diorissimo' by Dior. Lily-of-the-valley, emblem of the Dior fashion house; this flower of purity masks an undertone of metal, and yeast, and something darker, like syrup of figs; the sweetness of death.

My father speaks.

'Let's go for a walk,' he says. I wonder what he means. My mother's legs are too weak to hold her, and she can no longer get out of bed. I am irritated by his thoughtlessness. She will get confused.

Then, he surprises me. This man, who has become so rigid in my mind, starts to walk in words. He takes her hand and leads her along the chalk pits, through the meadow grass, under the trees. They stop to listen to the skylarks above, even though it has been years since he could hear birdsong in his ears. The sun is hot on their young skin, and their limbs are strong. On and on they walk, under that ripe, June sun.

I stop my cleaning, and stand behind the doorway, listening in. It feels voyeuristic to be eavesdropping on their private world. Whatever came next, whatever story they may have written along the way, this world has always been there. I ache with a longing to know these two lovers, who walk with nowhere to go, their whole lives rolling out in front of them, unknown. Would they have kept walking, had they glimpsed what was to come?

She looks peaceful as he speaks. My father, the teller of stories, who sat at the end of my bed when I was a child, spinning ghost-tales in the dark. This man, who gave me gilt-edged books, and cupboards full of poems; how many journeys has he taken me on? How many mountains, and deserts, and seas? All the beauty they have seen, and he picks this place; these rewilded industrial pits. Of all the places they have been, why here, where they began?

Sixty-six years between that walk and this moment now, but it can still be found, pressed between the pages of the past like a primrose, ready to tell its tale. It doesn't matter whether it is true, not now, and who am I to question this? I watch through this spyglass into the past, catching echoes of who they once were, before they imagined us into being. All my life, it has always been us, our strange and sprawling family, but here, at the heart of it, is them. As it has always been.

When he finishes, she smiles and opens her eyes. She sees me listening, and holds out her hand. I step forward, and kneel beside the bed.

'I liked that walk. Let's go on another one, only this time, let's all go,' she says, closing her eyes.

My father begins along the path. The gentian are beginning

Cowslip

to flower, deep blue in the grass, and the stream is bright with melted snow. His hands are strong, and he lifts me up with ease onto his shoulders. I am two, and wearing my new red shoes, my white-blonde curls catching the alpine light. I rest my head beside my mother's side. She strokes my head.

'There now, all better,' she says, drifting out into the morphine clouds. I close my eyes as tears fall silent onto the soft, white sheet. We continue to walk. My father takes my mother's hand as we approach the rocks to climb. I am not afraid. I know I will not fall.

Tufted Vetch

VICIA CRACCA
Cat-peas, fingers-and-thumbs, cow vetch

Use vetch to bind a spirit to this realm

Tufted vetch was traditionally used to increase milk production for lactating mothers. Edible for humans, it was a common feed for cattle as well. The seeds can be boiled or roasted, and young leaves and flowers can be eaten as a herb, or in salads. Able to create its own nitrogen, it provides a good cover crop for green manure, and can be used to slow soil erosion.

Tufted vetch grows well in disturbed habitats, waste ground and roadside ditches.

Tufted Vetch

It takes four days for my mother to die, slipping between the hours of sleep and waking dreams. As her body swells, and her heart begins to fail, the doctor cuts the wedding band from her hand. It is easy to do. Over the years, the gold has worn thin. She is cut adrift, between the worlds, loosening her hold. We do not have much time now.

I try not to ramble, knowing she would not like it, but I need to reassure her that she is not alone. As I sit the first night out, I find a recording of The Benny Goodman Orchestra. As they play 'On a Slow Boat to China', something wakes in my mother's memory, and she opens her eyes.

'He'd sing it to me on the way home, only he wasn't singing about boats, was he?' she says. I wait for her to say more. It comes as a rush, the song pulling her out of the dark. 'He called me his Calico Girl. It was the petticoats. I always sewed in extra. The bigger the petticoat, the bigger the twirl. He was always a good dancer.' Her eyes close again.

'Do you mean Dad?' I ask, trying to coax her to stay with me a bit longer. It works.

'No, Dad had two left feet. I did love to dance, though,' she says, before she slips away. As I watch her in the dark, I smile at the thought of her in her big, calico petticoats, dancing swing to the big bands on the Strand.

The second day, they put the syringe driver in. After that, she is lost. My father insists on silent vigil, though the visiting hospice nurse tells me the dying often seem comforted by hearing loved ones close by. It makes no difference to him; his world is silent all the time, but we sit mute, our arms folded in our laps, listening to her breathing slow. I don't know how to let her know we are here, except by holding her hand. When I take it, she stirs but does not open her eyes.

'Don't touch,' she says, then slips back into unconsciousness again.

Three more times, she wakes, screaming from the pain. Each time, I ask the nurse to increase the drugs, knowing with each rise my mother falls further away. She calls out our names one by one, counting us home. When she calls my sister's name, it makes me cry.

'You'll see her soon,' I tell her. What else can I say? My mother did not believe in life after death, but maybe this could be true.

On the last morning, she opens her eyes.

'I don't recommend this to anyone,' she says, and laughs. A little later, she wakes again.

'No, I got it all wrong. I got it all wrong,' she cries out, and I do not know if she means life, or death, or just this moment. I place my hand upon her head, and try to hold her gaze.

'No, Mum. You did everything right. It's all okay. All you have to do now is let go,' I say, trying to reassure. There is nothing more I can give. She seems to hear, or maybe not. She does not speak again.

When it finally comes, death is quiet, creeping in as the midnight clock turns. There is no parting promise, or declaration of love. Three small breaths and then, a slight brown bubble rising from her mouth, an outward sigh, and she is gone. I go outside, watch the stars shine. A cold wind picks up the night and I feel her leaving, light at last. I cut the final, budded rose from the climber on the wall, and place it in a small vase beside her bed.

Tufted Vetch

'Goodbye, my beautiful Mummy,' I whisper, part woman, part girl.

In the morning, I wake my son to tell him that his nana has died.

'I am sad Nana has died, Mummy, but I'm happy too because I can have you back,' he says. We snuggle down under the covers; my husband, my son and me. It is the first day of Advent. We open his calendar. The year moves on.

There is one final duty to do. As mesothelioma is an industrial disease, registering my mother's death is not straightforward. Forms must be filled in, and an autopsy done. Before this, because she has died at home, I must formally identify her body to the police. A young officer stands awkwardly beside the bed, and asks me to confirm the identity of the deceased. I wonder how much of who we are remains, after that last breath.

And so, it is done. The man from the funeral home cuts my mother from her clothes, folds them neatly and leaves them on the end of the bed. Then, he wraps her in the body bag and wheels her on the gurney past the breakfast table, where my son is eating his toast, and takes her away.

When the van drives away, I wave like a child, not looking away until it is out of sight. She will not come home.

I go back inside and pack my bags. It starts to rain, and does not stop.

SEED SEVEN

St John's Wort

HYPERICUM PERFORATUM
Grace of God, St Peterwort, Bethlehem star, John's grass

St John's wort is a powerful talisman
to ward off the demons and the dark

St John's wort is associated with midsummer. Believed to repel bad spirits, it was commonly used in funerary rites and exorcisms to scare off the devil and demons. Worn in battle as an amulet, it was considered to give the wearer invincibility. Used energetically to bring courage, and strengthen endurance when confronted with bad situations, it is clinically proven to be efficient in treating mild to moderate depression, as well as some other neurological conditions such as anxiety, OCD and insomnia. Used topically as a salve or wash, it is a common herbal medicine for minor burns, cuts and bruises, and joint pain.

St John's wort grows well in hedgerows, roadside verges and on wastelands.

All My Wild Mothers

It rains for seven days and seven nights, a storm that turns the roads into rivers, and the rivers into lakes. The flood defences fail. Trains are derailed. High winds take down pylons, leaving hundreds of houses without power. Cities, towns and villages are claimed. Drone images show acre upon acre of land covered by water. Livestock are pulled bloated from the fields. In our local town, the river gulps down the houses, spitting out plastic Christmas decorations, children's toys, sagging settees. We watch the news, see grown men and women crying outside what were once their homes. People send their thoughts and prayers. 'I can't believe it's happening again,' the old man says, as he clings to a dinghy in the rising water. Scientists tell us that floods like these are called 'one-in-one-hundred-years' weather events, and yet this one arrives after only three. We are living in exceptional times.

Meanwhile, my mother's body lies trapped in the mortuary, the hospital an island, stranded in a new sea. We wait for her to return.

'You can stop now, Mum,' we joke, but the storm carries on. It is unrelenting, and wild. There is something very fitting to this end.

Across the valley, in my father's house, my red-headed sister remains. Living up to her name as 'the practical one', she knows about water, understands how the river works; understands that the banks are bursting not because of the water, but because of the dredging and the loss of trees. She places a flood marker in the garden.

'When the river reaches it, we have three minutes to get upstairs,' she writes down, in large letters, so he understands.

St John's Wort

She tells him to choose what to keep. She cannot carry it all upstairs, but she will save what she can.

What do you choose to keep at the end of a life? The walls are filled with my mother's paintings. Does she save these? What about the wooden figures, or the little cobbler shoes, or the photographs on the shelf? And what of my father's books, whose pages have passed through more lives than our own? Are these the things we keep, when all else is gone?

The floodwaters keep rising, swallowing my mother's garden. Dormant bulbs float up to the surface. Trees stretch out to save themselves, grabbing hold of thin strands of grass that knot like hair around the black fingers of branch. Everything drowns.

My sister updates me on the telephone. She has moved what she can to the highest point of the house. She is not sure how she will move our father up there. I listen, unable to help. The floods have trapped us in our houses. We place sandbags at our doors. Our home was built on stone, but the river needs a way out, and cannot flood where it should. It forces itself along the lanes, tearing down ancient bridges and walls. We watch from our windows, alone.

Then, after seven days, the storm subsides and the waters ebb away, leaving the wreckage of what has been. Everything is turned inside out. Plastic-bag birds flutter in the breeze, caught on high branches. Cars land like turtles, stranded on their backs. Clothes hang limp from railings, like moles strung up along barbed wire. The streets fill with broken televisions, bedding, rolled-up carpets, all reeking of waste. People come out of doorways, blinking at the sun, wary of the calm. We sift through what remains.

Viper's Bugloss

ECHIUM VULGARE
Ironweed, bluebottle, Our Saviour's flannel, adderwort, cat's tail

Drink a tincture to protect the heart
against grief and melancholy

Viper's bugloss was thought to protect against snakes due to its resemblance to the viper's skin. It is attractive to a wide range of pollinators. The leaves and root of the plant are diuretic, anti-inflammatory, pectoral and high in allantoin. It can be used in treatments to alleviate fevers and headaches, soothe skin complaints, and increase breast milk in nursing mothers. It can be used as a tonic to treat melancholy and grief.

Viper's bugloss thrives in dry dunes, waste areas, and on roadsides.

Viper's Bugloss

Our garden, left untended through these months of care, has grown wild. Bramble leaves, bruised black and gold, mulch the wintered ground. Tendrils of nasturtiums trail their way through the disused fort. Mildewed stalks of marigolds stand, like headless sentries, between the slug-eaten skeletons of cabbage and kale. Everything is coated in a skein of mud. So much seems destroyed.

Normally I would let the old year sit as shelter until the spring, but right now, I need to clear away these vestiges of what has been. I drag out handfuls of die-back growth from the beds, my hands clenched with cold. My feet are sodden with soil. I stamp them, trying to relieve the numbness that takes hold. A furious grief bubbles up from within me, crashing out into a wave of rage.

'Am I supposed to do it all myself?' I shout up at the closed window. No reply. I keep hauling out fistfuls of nettles, withered stems of feverfew, ghost-wisps of willowherb. My body aches. It feels impossible. Nothing I do will make a difference. *Nothing I do will make a difference.*

'What am I supposed to do now, Mum?' I sob, my question hovering, unanswered, in the air. I kneel down onto the damp ground. I tried so hard, but nothing changed what came. She still suffered. She still died. She would always die, just like my sister would always die, and there was nothing I could do to make a difference to that.

And now the days, no longer defined by my mother's needs, stretch out before me, unclaimed, and I move with a quiet caution into the new shape of this life.

I look again at the garden. Despite my absence, and the

floods, it has survived. It tells a story in everything that remains. See here, the bare branch of forsythia? Or there, the clutch of yellow flag iris that clings to the edge of the bog garden? These plants that once grew in my mother's garden now make their home here. The leaves that bury over the cold ground come from the trees we planted. The nettles that sting my skin were placed here by my son. I watch a blackbird as it pecks out a fat pink worm. Even the soil that clings to my trowel was made by our hands.

Small green shoots push through the earth; the first early snowdrops daring to be found. Tiny flecks of golden blossom open up on the witch hazel branch. Fat red berries cluster on the firethorn bush. Here, where it seems all life has ended, there are flowers to be found.

My son comes out of the house and stands by my side. He places his hand gently on my shoulder. He is no longer the little boy who followed me, with his green wheelbarrow and Roman shield. As he stretches out into his life, learning to let go of my hand, I give thanks for the days we have had.

'Why are you crying, Mummy?' he asks, and I try to explain about the dead plants, the overwhelm; about the strange, motherless shape I feel inside. He stands a while, looking at the garden we have grown.

'Everything living must die, Mummy. Come inside,' he says, taking my hand. And I follow him, because he is right: everything living must die, and from it, something new will grow.

Grape Hyacinth

MUSCARI NEGLECTUM
Grape flower, starch lilies

Carry in an amulet to help ease grief when a loved one dies

Grape hyacinth is linked to Demeter and associated with death and remembrance. The essential oil has long been prized as a component of expensive perfumes. It was used in ancient times as a potpourri or in 'reeking bundles' to help the dead cross into the Otherworld. It has mild stimulant properties when inhaled, and the scent was commonly used to rid the home of negative energies.

Grape hyacinth grows well in verges, ditches, rubbish tips and grasslands.

A few weeks before my mother died, and long after she had lost the ability to use a pen, she said she had something to confess.

'I'm sorry. I haven't written any letters. I know I am supposed to, for after, but I don't know the right words,' she said, crying. I told her it didn't matter, but after she has gone, it feels important to have this trace. I go in search of anything written in her spindly hand. Tidied into drawers and boxes around the house, I find doodled telephone books, grease-spattered recipes, and notebooks of lists that catalogue her married life in pounds, shillings and pence. This mundane archive of a life now spent is precious to me. I touch the curled letters, trying to conjure her back.

Among these things, hidden at the back of the bureau drawer, I find a collection of covers from my school exercise books, each one covered with wallpaper offcuts, the edges tucked in tight. 'It keeps them safe,' she used to say.

Onto her neat covers, between the doodled love hearts and feminist slogans from my sisters' copies of *Spare Rib*, I wrote out anonymous poems. One day, the literature teacher, who wore a black leather jacket and rode a Triumph motorbike, held me back after class.

'You write very well,' she said, as she handed back my book. Inside the pages, she had slipped a note. 'Don't give up. I am here, if any of this is true,' she said. I never spoke to her, but I kept the note.

Through those years, I scattered words like breadcrumbs in the woods, hoping to be found. My mother never mentioned those lost poems, but here they are, carefully preserved, the changing patterns of wallpaper marking the rings of time. She heard.

Now, it is my turn to pick up her trail. In another notebook, her familiar, looping hand.

... My epitaph will say she made lovely meals, and always had cake ready at tea. I would like to be remembered for other things ...

For my eighteenth birthday, she gave me a book that she had made when she was sixteen. Inside its red, leather-bound sleeves, were poems by Blake, Yeats, Byron, Frost, written out in perfect, calligraphic script. Each one was illustrated in pen and ink, and signed with her maiden name. I did not recognise it as her own at first.

'I thought you could finish it with your poems,' she said, but I never did. Its pages are yellowing now, the neatly pencilled lines still waiting for words. I leave them unwritten. Their silence tells me so much about the woman I have known all my life, but will never know. This book, which her hands once shaped from leather and wood, was a baton from her unlived life. Those empty pages left unmarked; the dreams she hid.

People are surprised when they learn that my mother was an artist at *Vogue*. They cannot imagine a past in which this white-haired woman drank Hurricanes at the Colony Club, and danced in calico petticoats on the Strand. 'Do you regret giving up your life?' they ask, negating all the years of motherhood in between, and, even though I called myself a feminist, when I was thirteen I did the same. I was studying the suffragette movement at school, and returned home angry. She greeted me as she always did, with cake and a 'how was school?' I looked at the cake, and her apron, and her waiting smile, and hated her for being complicit in her domestic oppression.

'God Mum, don't you want to do something meaningful with your life?' I shouted. She waited a while for me to calm down, then replied.

'I am doing something. I am a mother. Now, do you want this cake, or not?' she said.

What is the life of a mother measured by? The unseen acts of love go unrecorded, the worth not recognised until the weight of what is lost is felt, like a sea rock in the hand. I wrap the notebook, and the receipts, and the little journal scraps into the remnants of an old patchwork skirt, to be kept safe. These are the letters that she lived.

My pen taps impatiently from the past, seeks to write onto the sleeve notes of our lives, before the words have gone for good. I want to tell her that I see, and I remember. All those small acts of love that make a life, they were the gifts she gave of herself, every day, and in each one she scattered the seeds of her dreams. What a garden she made for our own.

Dog Violet

VIOLA RIVINIANA

Gypsy violets, cuckoo's stockings, butter-pats, blue mice

Carry violets to ward off evil spirits

Dog violet thrives in darkness. High in flavonoids, alkaloids, beta-carotene, salicylic acid and vitamin C, the plant can help to lower blood pressure, strengthen capillaries, relieve joint pain, headaches, dizziness, nervous exhaustion and insomnia, relieve colds and bronchial congestion and treat skin complaints. It has a particular affinity with women and girls. Its leaves are included in treatments to soften hardness in body tissue, especially cysts, lumps, fibroids and tumours. Working on blocked emotional energy, it can help to soften the edges of traumatic loss, and assist in opening up hardened energies. Representing the long path of grief, it offers nourishment and gentle strength at the darkest of times.

Dog violet grows best in woodland and shady places.

I gave my son a bag of decayed wood and coffee grounds, some soil and a box. Together, we mixed, watered and placed it in the cupboard. That was four weeks ago. Since then, the box has sat in the dark, holding a mystery within.

Today, the secret is revealed. He takes off the lid to find a five-inch-wide, four-inch-high brown-cap mushroom, waiting to be picked.

'Wow! Look, Mummy, look, a mushroom!' he exclaims, in awe of what has come into being. There were meant to be more, but it doesn't matter to him, so it doesn't matter to me. One single mushroom is enough.

Twisting it off with care, he brings it to the table. He examines its pale-cream flesh, the pink fronds of its underbelly, sniffs deeply into its scent. Every part of his attention is devoted to this act of discovery. It is his mushroom and he has grown it in the dark, in secret, away from all that is busy, and loud, and light.

'I bet no one has ever tasted a mushroom so delicious as this one,' he declares, as he takes a bite, eyes closed to receive.

I love this mushroom. I love the rotting earth and deep wood smell of it; the way it evokes bluebells, and lovemaking, and days of childhood exploring. I love that my son is in love with this mushroom, that it holds him in rapture. We forget too easily about rapture, lose too quickly the ability to stop and be amazed by the miracle of small things. We interfere, we control, we predict, where maybe we need to leave things in the dark a little more.

I am not very good at living with the dark. I tend to see dark and write it with monsters. If there is something unknown,

Dog Violet

I want to unravel it, understand and pin it down, like a lepidopterist, eager to name. My son is not like me. He wants to keep the magic. He does not need to know its name.

He believes with the peculiar practicality of a child. When it freezes at Easter, I say that the Easter Bunny might get cold, and we might need to dig the eggs from the snow. He tells me, with patience, that the Easter Bunny is a bunny; it has fur, it will not get cold, and will hide the eggs on the compost heap because that is the warmest place in the garden. I cannot argue with this. The rationality of his logic places the myth in the reality of the world. Later, when he finds the little wooden toy that the Easter Bunny has left behind, he asks without cynicism how the Easter Bunny managed to get hold of it. He thinks about this for a while, and then finds the answer himself.

'The Easter Bunny obviously ordered it online, but they must have a computer,' he says. I ask how he knows this and I am told, as if it is the most obvious thing in the world, that the Easter Bunny would not be able to use an iPad because they have paws. Myth meets modernity. He has no trouble combining the two.

He knows magic cannot perform miracles. He never asks if magic can fix his body. He never asks me to kiss his sore and blistered fingers better. His illness has taught him that magic cannot step in and save him. It is science that keeps him alive. He is aware of this, aware that his life is held in the drip of a drug, yet it does not stop him from believing that the magic exists. It does not stop him from feeling rapture at the taste of a mushroom he has grown in the dark, in secret from the world. Can I achieve this same dichotomy? Can I allow myself to believe in the mystery, alongside the weight of truth, and learn to trust the beauty I find growing in the dark?

I have felt my life touched by the magic of the unseen. It was not found in the coldness of a church, or the heat of an ashram. Instead, it was found in the blood and tears of love, in the exhausted grief of endless nights, awake with a crying child. It was not a blinding light, nor a loudly proclaimed vision, but a little boy, who smiled and said, 'Oh my, so beautiful!' at the world he discovered outside his door.

'I love you, Mummy,' he tells me, resting his head against my side, unaware of the gift he brings; unaware of the love that he has grown within my heart, as if by magic, in the darkness of these days.

Common Tansy

TANACETUM VULGARE
Bitter-buttons, golden-buttons, cow-bitter

Use to contact the spirits of ancestral loved ones

Common tansy derives its name from the Greek word *anthanasia*. It was believed to promote longevity, lost youth and immortality. Although not found in many contemporary remedies due to its toxicity, it has a long medicinal history for inducing miscarriage, promoting delayed menstruation, and treating hysteria, fevers, flatulence, rashes, sprains, joint pain, intestinal worms and kidney complaints. A popular strewing herb and insect repellant due to its strong camphor scent, it was also used in the curing of meat. In Yorkshire, it was baked with caraway seeds into funeral biscuits. Traditionally packed into coffins, and wrapped into the winding sheets of the dead, it was used to preserve the deceased to guide them on to the afterlife.

Common tansy grows well in field borders, on riverbanks and along roadsides.

It takes six years for a horse chestnut to flower, and another to fruit. Last year, my son's conker produced conkers of its own.

'My tree is a mummy now, like you,' my son tells me, as he prises open a prickly case to reveal the glossy, rosewood-coloured seed.

'What shall we do with it?' I ask.

'We can plant it for Nana. She can have a special tree like mine,' he replies. One tree for birth, and one for death. We find a flowerpot and fill it with soil, to tuck the shiny seed in tight. Together, we stand beside this invisible tree, imagining it grown.

'How old will I be when this tree is as tall as Nana?' he asks.

'About eighteen, I think,' I reply. My mother will never see her tree grow. She will never get to see her grandson age into his adult world. If I am alive, I will be sixty-three; sixteen years older than my sister when she died. I look back at his tree that now outgrows its pot. The years fall away like leaves.

'Nana can have a whole forest one day,' he says. I remind him that we are not supposed to plant trees here. He stands firm, roots his dream into being.

'I know that, Mummy, but we can start it a little now,' he replies.

And so we do. We find out about the work of Japanese botanist Akira Miyawaki, and the benefits of micro-forests. By growing small areas of fast-growing, localised and native trees, Miyawaki was able to create resilient woodland habitats in waste urban areas. Even the smallest backyard forest can help improve soil biodiversity and air quality, and reduce noise

Common Tansy

pollution, carbon emissions and flood risk. A native woodland containing up to six hundred trees can be planted on a space smaller than a tennis court, and attract up to five hundred different species of animals and plants.

We begin by creating a study of trees growing within a one-mile radius of our house, using our daily walks to gather data. Then we select the weakest saplings, cramped into impossible places where they will never thrive, and carefully dig out single specimens of each, planting holly, yew, copper beech, wild cherry, rowan, hawthorn, sycamore and birch. We collect fallen acorns and let them germinate in a jar, before potting them on, writing labels onto broken slate to remember which bare pot contains a future oak, and what each stick will be when it is grown. Soon, we have a tiny arboretum growing in pots outside our back door.

When the hospital returns the cellular remains of my mother's autopsy samples, I break the rules to buy a single, flowering redcurrant, and plant them into its roots. I know it is not a local tree, but its scent is a memory key, unlocking childhood, and early spring days.

These little seeds and spindly twigs we plant are a promise of hope. She never got to live in her cabin in the woods but perhaps, one day, we can dream among her trees.

Mountain Cornflower

CENTAUREA MONTANA
*Perennial cornflower, bachelor's button,
montane knapweed, mountain bluet*

Representing positive hope for the
future and the fullness of life's cycles

Mountain cornflower derives its name *centaurea* from Chiron, the centaur in Greek mythology, who was cured by the plant after being wounded by an arrow tipped with the blood of Hydra. Traditionally believed to have the power to ward off snakes, the flowers are more commonly used now to treat conjunctivitis and as a wash for tired eyes. It is a frequent garden escapee, finding new homes in the wild.

Mountain cornflower grows well on disturbed ground, verges, scrub and wastelands.

Mountain Cornflower

My mother never liked other people getting too close. Knowing this about herself, she chose the spot furthest at the back of the cemetery for her grave. 'It's a good place to sit. Not that I will see much of the view,' she said.

I look out beyond the craggy hawthorn hedge, to the winter-stripped Pennines beyond. She was right.

It took time, but we have obtained permission from the parish council to plant wildflowers. There are conditions. If anyone complains, they will mow it back to grass. This place will be my mother's final garden, now her body has grown wild.

The almanac tells me I am too late, that bulbs are meant to be planted in autumn. The white-capped fells tell me I am too early, that *if you can still see snow, it's too early to sow*. I know these things, but sometimes, the planting must be done. Fifty-six years ago today, a mother held her newborn daughter, the narcissi watching silently in the early spring light. Now, both are gone. This garden grows for them.

The dense, clay soil is reluctant to give but I keep digging, my knuckles stiffening in the March cold. My son kneels beside me, hands dirty with digging. At eight, his body is changing, moving out of the soft folds of early childhood. As I watch him, I feel an ache at my centre; a quiet knowing that these days are all we have. We have given so much to loss, he and I, days that we will never get back. Yet, equal to this, I have found a love so great, it forces itself into light. I watch this boy of soil, and seed, and song, this child who came from the dark of me. Still his existence seems miraculous to behold.

Over the cold ground, we scatter wildflower seeds: white campion, cowslip, field poppy, columbine. Into newly dug holes, we place our bulbs, incanting the botanical names before burying over with clods of earth. *Anemone nemorosa*, *Ranunculus ficaria*, *Hyacinthoides non-scripta*. These are our votive offerings. With each one, we lay a hope. I know that for every bulb that flowers, another will rot; for every seed that germinates, another will be taken by the birds that wait in the elder tree. Perhaps, then, it is enough just to plant, and trust in what will grow?

I spent so long afraid of what the future might bring but now, I let it go. These days in which we live are made of one measure of joy, and one of sorrow. There is no pinnacle of happiness to be reached, no perfect life to be achieved. There is just this messy, terrible, beautiful life we live, and I am thankful for it.

My son reaches over, and takes hold of my hand.

'It will be okay, Mummy,' he says, and I know he is right.

Above us, the curlew calls, and the March clouds gather close to the fell. I stand here, all my wild mothers at my side, and I am not alone.

SEED EIGHT

Gorse

ULEX EUROPAEUS
Furze, thorny broom, whin, ruffet, frey

Use gorse to bring about completion

Gorse was one of the nine sacred woods and thought to guard entrances to the Otherworld. Traditionally used to start the Beltane bonfires, ash from the gorse is high in alkali and can be used as fertiliser to fix nitrogen in the soil, or mixed with fat to make soap. Both root and flowers were used for medicinal purposes to treat scarlet fever, relieve constipation, and as a remedy for mouth sores and kidney complaints. The flowers can be used to create a golden dye, similar to saffron, and to give a delicate almond flavour to wine and whisky. Associated with the sun, it was thought that wearing a sprig would protect against bad luck and encourage resilience and optimism.

Gorse can tolerate salt and grows well in poor, thin soil on rough hills, fells and wastelands.

All My Wild Mothers

I dug this ground to find my way out of grief but, in its breaking, found the way back to my wild, and the wonder of this world. A decade on, this small patch of earth we claimed as home continues to surprise. Each year, we find new life – cowslip and cranesbill, bird's-foot trefoil and field scabious – their seeds awoken from dormancy by our digging. The micro-meadow my son sowed now thrives with wildflowers – yellow rattle, yarrow, red campion, forget-me-not, vetch. Under the shelter of the greengage tree, hedgehogs root for bugs in fallen leaves, and honeycaps sprout from the decaying wood. The fort, once built to stave off fear, is now a compost heap, long outgrown by teenage limbs that stretch beyond its fit. In spring, the lemon-yellow forsythia signals my sister's birth. In summer, the sun-warmed evenings bring frog song from under the meadowsweet. The plum has gone, unable to thrive, but the apple survives and gives us fruit.

Fifteen springs have passed since my sister's death. Spiderwebs gather around my eyes, silver wefts through my hair. I move between maiden, mother, crone. It is at once an end, and a beginning; a quiet coming home. Into our vegetable beds, I seed phacelia and winter tares. Before summer, I will dig them back into the dark, a living manure that will feed the roots of what grows next.

Life, and death, continues. Last year, my son and I made a new pond. The rocks we dug were heavy, but he is strong. Around its edge, we planted loosestrife, water avens, marsh marigold. The day we finished, my husband called to say his father had died. He told me it was quiet, that they were able

Gorse

to sit with him at the end; that knowing how to sit with death helped him find strength to face what came, but could not take away the pain. After the call, my son and I sat under the lilac tree and listened to the bee-heat thrum on its purple blooms, and the water as it folded and fell over repurposed slate and stone. Grief had entered our garden again.

The years turn, and turn again. I dig the soil, and find long-lost dinosaurs, teacups, broken arrows; the archaeology of childhood unearthed. These precious things we thought he would never leave behind now lost, or packed, or put out for another life to hold. The days soon grow over childhood, these small moments quickly buried by time.

I know I cannot always hold my son's hand. His future is so close. I can feel it loitering by the door. He leans towards it, like a plant to light. In these uncertain times, it can feel hard to hold hope out to my child. Biodiversity is shrinking faster than at any other time before. Around a quarter of the world's animal and plant species are at risk of extinction. Everything feels fragile, and each day brings another loss. This world, that holds such beauty and such sorrow, is what I leave behind.

When the mother-plant comes under threat, it leaves a memory in its seed to help the future plant survive. In time, when outward circumstances change, the offspring plant must decide what it needs to remember, and what it needs to forget. As my son reaches outwards into his life, what can I give that will help him survive?

I can give him this: a seed, with all its defiant hope against the dark; and the memory that once, we grew a garden out of rock, and waste, and all things broken, and it thrived.

All My Wild Mothers

Onto the waiting soil, I scatter seeds, and remember what the garden taught me: when nothing else is certain, it is wise to return to the small things that grow.

Suggestions for an Apothecary Bookcase

Field Guide to the Wild Flowers of Britain and Northern Europe by David Sutton

A Modern Herbal by Mrs. M. Grieve

Wayside Medicine by Julie Bruton-Seal and Matthew Seal

Wild Apothecary: Reclaiming Plant Medicine for All by Amaia Dadachanji and Claudia Manchanda

Self-Sufficient Herbalism: A Guide to Growing, Gathering and Processing Herbs for Medicinal Use by Lucy Jones

Grow Your Own Physic Garden: Use the Power of Medicinal Plants Grounded in Science by Elaine Perry, Valerie Laws and Nicolette Perry

Holistic Herbal: A Safe and Practical Guide to Making and Using Herbal Remedies by David Hoffman

The Gift of Healing Herbs by Robin Rose Bennett

The Essential Book of Herbal Medicine by Simon Y. Mills

Folk Magic and Healing: An Unusual History of Everyday Plants by Fez Inkwright

Acknowledgements

*'I can no other answer make but thanks, and thanks,
and ever thanks'*

SHAKESPEARE, *TWELFTH NIGHT*

Just as the apothecary garden grew from the gifts of many, so did this story. It took a long time to get here, and there are a lot of thanks to give.

To my family. You are the soil in which my story grows. Thank you for being exactly who you are. A special thanks to my father, for the gift of poetry. And to my mother, and sisters – the wild mothers who raised me, guided me, and held my hand. The world is a better place because of you.

To Adam, my husband and best friend. Your love, support, and beautiful artwork is sown throughout this book. Thank you for the many times you have believed in me and kept me going, and for being the oak tree at the centre of my life. Our story is the best adventure.

To the dearest friends who have cheered me on, made me laugh, and let me cry as I have written this book. You know who you are, but it's still good to say thanks out loud. So here you are. Thank you to all the Wild Women. What can I say? We are clan. Special thanks to Ruth and Gill, for sharing your wisdom about plants and all things wise and wild. To Anna, my dearest friend of nearly five decades. Our story is forever joined. To Amy, my writing buddy and friend. Your insight and truthful heart are a precious gift. To Aimee, Renee and Debby, god-family to my son and the very best cheerleaders in this world. To Angela, for reminding me to see the lighter side. To Jason, my friend. Your keen eye and gentle encouragement have been such a help. To Simon, who knows how to make a garden grow. Thank you for always cheering me on.

To the writers, mentors, and early readers who have inspired, guided and supported me as I found my words. From the first teacher who told me to keep writing, all the way to the many poets and writers who have offered inspiration and instruction over the years – there are too many to list but I am thankful for each one. A special thanks to Catherine Simpson, Cal Flyn and Wendy Pratt. The wise and generous mentoring you gave, from first draft to final book, helped it (and me) grow immeasurably. To Alice Walker, for granting permission to include her wise words. To the Just Write Gang – thank you for reading all those early pages and cheering me going. And to all those who have read these words and helped them grow, from first thoughts to this book now, thank you for your support and the gift of your time.

To all the organisations, and the people working in them, who have championed my voice and the voices of other underrepresented writers. Without your hard work, so many stories would not be heard. Caro and all at the Nan Shepherd Prize, who first believed in this story and gave me the confidence to share it. New Writing North, for awarding me the Northern Debut Award, especially Will Mackie who has given such great

Acknowledgements

support. The Penguin WriteNow programme, for their early editorial feedback and encouragement. The Society of Authors, for awarding me an Authors' Foundation grant to help me write, and the Arvon Foundation, for providing access to their excellent online programme during the last two years.

To all those who have helped turn my words into a real-life book. There is something magical in what you do, though I know that behind the magic is a lot of hard work. Jenny Hewson, my agent and champion, and all at Lutyens & Rubinstein. Your belief in this story is more precious a gift than you may yet know. Kate Hewson, my editor, book midwife and probable superwoman. Thank you for nudging, guiding, and knowing when to water and when to weed. Rosie Gailer, Charlotte Robathan, Alice Graham, Kate Craigie, Jocasta Hamilton and all at Two Roads/John Murrays who have helped to bring this book into the world. It takes a village, and what a village you are. And to Lisa Highton, former Two Roads chief, who brought me into the Two Roads family and told me to believe in this book.

Finally, and always, my deepest thanks goes to my son, without whom there would be no garden, and no book. Being your Wild Mother is the greatest joy and privilege of my life. I love you.

About the Author

Victoria Bennett was born in Oxfordshire in 1971. A poet and author, her writing has previously received a Northern Debut Award, a Northern Promise Award, the Andrew Waterhouse Award, and has been longlisted for the Penguin WriteNow programme and the inaugural Nan Shepherd Prize for under-represented voices. She founded Wild Women Press in 1999 to support rural women writers in her community, and since 2018 has curated the global Wild Woman Web project, an inclusive online space focusing on nature, connection, and creativity. When not juggling writing, full-time care, and genetic illness, she can be found where the wild weeds grow. *All My Wild Mothers* is her debut memoir.